"This book is in a class by itself. It exudes honesty, compassion, and humor as it proffers the possibility of deep and embodied common-sense wisdom right here and right now. It is also a precious opportunity to be—at least metaphorically—in class with a truly great dharma teacher, investigating the most important question: What is this wild and precious life really about? Larry provides a supremely friendly and disarmingly honest glide path into the universe of mindfulness as both a formal meditation practice and a Way of being. He is speaking straight to you, the reader, out of his own lifelong search for an honest, unromanticized truth about what matters in life and the possibility of waking up into its unadorned fullness. Dive in and be carried along by his inimitable and disarming sense of humor and his intuitive resonance with your own aspiration to live the life that is actually and uniquely yours to live. His easygoing and humorous teaching style brings you face-to-face with your own experience, doubts, confusion, romantic spiritual aspirations—everything—and reflects it all back to you as if you were right there together in the very same room—which of course, in the deepest of ways, you are."

—JON KABAT-ZINN, author of *Wherever You Go, There You Are*

"With characteristic warmth, humor, and a grounded sense of immediacy, in *The World Exists to Set Us Free*, Larry Rosenberg distills decades of deep dharma practice into teachings that are as profound as they are accessible. Whether he's illuminating the subtleties of mindfulness or sharing stories from his own path, Rosenberg's clarity and compassion shine through, offering guidance that speaks directly to the heart, reminding us that freedom is possible."

—JOSEPH GOLDSTEIN, author of *Mindfulness: A Practical Guide to Awakening*

"In this profound collection, beloved meditation teacher Larry Rosenberg offers wisdom that feels like a conversation with a trusted friend. Drawing from over fifty years of Buddhist practice, Rosenberg illuminates how dharma naturally weaves through our everyday challenges and joys. With his trademark humor and directness, he strips away pretense to reveal Buddhism's practical heart—not as an exotic philosophy but as a clear path to living with authenticity in our complex, troubled world. A treasure for both beginners and seasoned practitioners seeking to deepen their understanding of meditation's transformative potential."

—DEVON HASE, coauthor of *How Not to Be a Hot Mess*

# THE WORLD EXISTS TO SET US FREE

*Straight-Up Dharma for Living a Life of Awareness*

LARRY ROSENBERG

*with Madeline Drexler*

SHAMBHALA

Shambhala Publications, Inc.
2129 13th Street
Boulder, Colorado 80302
www.shambhala.com

Li Po, "Zazen on Ching-t'ing Mountain" from *Crossing the Yellow River: Three Hundred Poems from the Chinese*, translated by Sam Hamill. Copyright © 2000 by Sam Hamill. Reprinted with the permission of The Permissions Company, LLC on behalf of Tiger Bark Press, tigerbarkpress.com. "*Anapanasati Sutta*: Mindfulness of Breathing" in Appendix C is excerpted from *Breath by Breath*, by Larry Rosenberg. All other excerpts that appear in Appendix C are translated by Thanissaro Bhikkhu © 1994 via the Access to Insight website, www.accesstoinsight.org/.

COVER ART: ALONG THE MARSH (detail) by Robert Roth
COVER DESIGN: Daniel Urban-Brown
INTERIOR DESIGN: Katrina Noble

9 8 7 6 5 4 3 2 1

First Edition
Printed in the United States of America

Shambhala Publications makes every effort to print on acid-free, recycled paper. Shambhala Publications is distributed worldwide by Penguin Random House, Inc., and its subsidiaries.

LIBRARY OF CONGRESS CATALOGING-IN-PUBLICATION DATA
Names: Rosenberg, Larry, author. | Drexler, Madeline, 1954– author.
Title: The world exists to set us free: straight-up dharma for living a
life of awareness / Larry Rosenberg with Madeline Drexler.
Description: First edition. | Boulder, Colorado: Shambhala, [2025] |
Identifiers: LCCN 2024044783 | ISBN 9781645473947 (trade paperback)
Subjects: LCSH: Dharma (Buddhism) | Meditation—Buddhism. | Mind and
body—Religious aspects—Buddhism.
Classification: LCC BQ4190 .R67 2025 | DDC 294.3/4435—dc23/eng/20250110
LC record available at https://lccn.loc.gov/2024044783

The authorized representative in the EU for product safety and compliance is eucomply
OÜ, Pärnu mnt 139b-14, 11317 Tallinn, Estonia, hello@eucompliancepartner.com.

*Dedicated to the memory of Thich Nhat Hanh, with immense gratitude for his brilliant teaching and warm friendship.*

—LARRY ROSENBERG


*Dedicated to the memory of my beloved mother, Barbara M. Drexler.*

—MADELINE DREXLER

# CONTENTS

# THE WORLD EXISTS TO SET US FREE

# THE WAY IT ACTUALLY IS

*A Portrait of Larry Rosenberg*

LARRY ROSENBERG DESCENDED from fourteen generations of rabbis, the fourteenth being his paternal grandfather, a Russian émigré who arrived in New York City at the turn of the last century. The rabbi's son—Rosenberg's father, Nathan, a disillusioned Communist—held all religion in contempt. Rosenberg, who was born in 1932, split the difference between piety and skepticism, sacred and secular, faith and doubt: he became a renowned teacher of the form of Buddhist meditation known as *vipassana*, which means to see things as they really are.

Now, this is just a story. It's factually true but still a story. Rosenberg has devoted his life and teaching to demolishing the convenience and comfort of self-narrative, the tales on which we hang our identities. In this way, he is out of step with our time, which values personal storytelling and the way it can level barriers between strangers, shine a light on hidden lives past and present, and make our own existence comprehensible to us. He is also out of step with the modern meditation milieu, with its mannered niceness. He doesn't teach people how to become good or find calm or lower their blood pressure. He teaches one thing only, his lifelong obsession: how to get free. His journey has been steadfast and surprising. He gave up a prestigious academic sinecure to become a wandering medicant. He studied with the foundational figures in twentieth-century Buddhism and translated their wisdom into Brooklyn wiseguy-ese. He wrote three small classics (on breath awareness, death awareness, and the method of total attention known as choiceless awareness). He established the first nonresidential vipassana meditation center for laypeople in the United States, in a busy urban setting. Today, at ninety-one, Rosenberg is physically frail but mentally sharp. As Buddhism has become popularized, secularized, and Americanized, he has doubled down on the basics.

Rosenberg's may not be a household name, but among leading dharma teachers and serious students of meditation, he is widely admired and beloved for a unique style of instruction: witty, spontaneous, unvarnished. In a cohort of Western dharma luminaries, he has kept a low profile, even turning down an appearance on *The Oprah Winfrey Show* at a time when his first book was a bestseller. "No two dharma teachers are the same. But in Larry's case, it is just so insanely beautiful. The whole arc of his life has been so Larry," said Rosenberg's best friend, Jon Kabat-Zinn, himself a major contributor to the mainstream mindfulness movement.

In the spring of 2023, after a half century of teaching, Rosenberg led his last class. Fittingly, it was titled "Learning How to Live: The Four Noble Truths in Action," capturing the main themes of his hard-won wisdom. Largely immobile, Rosenberg convened the group, comprising both longtime devotees and newcomers, via Zoom. His diminished body looked unanchored, floating incorporeally on the screen, but his face had a fierce, monkish aspect. Compared to earlier classes, these had fewer jokes, fewer digressions, but more urgency, more patience, and more kindness. He didn't waste a word. The sessions crystallized everything he had learned on a rich and idiosyncratic path; he was dispensing—and embodying—190-proof dharma. Longtime students, some having followed him for more than four decades, said his teaching had never been sharper. Then again, Rosenberg had always said that living and dying are the same thing.

—

Buddhism originally was an oral tradition, passed on from mouth to ear. Rosenberg's teaching style fits this form well because, although skeptical of narrative, he is a natural storyteller and a pithy wordsmith. His talks are woven through with indelible maxims, many of which come from his own teachers, stars in the firmament of modern Buddhism: "The clearer the mind, the fewer the choices." "A bad situation is a good situation." "Start with what is rather than what should be." "The world exists to set us free,"—the last borrowed from the yoga teacher T. K. V. Desikachar in his classic book *The Heart of Yoga*.

By now, for many readers, these may conjure up familiar concepts in Buddhism. But any -ism, including Buddhism, is a fabrication. During the time of the Buddha, Buddhism was not called Buddhism—it was just one particular dharma, a set of teachings and practices about the truth, the way things are, which included the nature of the mind. In ancient India, spiritual masters each taught their own dharma. So while the Buddha was not a Buddhist, he preached what we now term *Buddhadharma*.

Rosenberg, you might say, teaches Larrydharma. It comes from the same rootstock as Buddhadharma but mixes in other influences— notably, the bracing ideas of Jiddu Krishnamurti, the twentieth-century Indian philosopher and spiritual teacher who pushed the tenets of Buddhism to their ultimate, radical end point. Rosenberg has also mixed in dialogue from cowboy movies, a genre he loves. (When conveying the experience of profound understanding through direct perception, he would say, "I know it bone deep," a phrase he says he copped from a Robert Duvall western. When reflecting on his own death and his wish to stay aware right up to his last breath, he would say, "I want to go out in the saddle.") He is plainspoken, unsentimental in an era of saccharine posturing, irreverent in a time of self-cherishing. His emotional calibrations as a teacher haven't always been flawless—he could sting. But for thousands of people over the years, his words have been enlivening, often life-changing.

Rosenberg spurns the word *enlightenment,* preferring *awareness* or *awakening.* Meditation, in his view, is not a technique or method; it is a way of life. No English word quite captures this orientation in the world. Close, Rosenberg says, is the German word *gewahren,* which means "to become aware of "—or, as he intransitively tweaks it, "awaring."

His teachings carry the flavor of the classic South Indian tradition known as *Neti Neti,* which means "not this, not this"—a subtractive shortcut to the present moment. Put simply, one gets to know what is true by seeing what is not true—knowing patience by seeing impatience, compassion by seeing cruelty, sacred by seeing desecration. It's getting to the oomph, or to use Buddhist terms, the "suchness" or "thusness" of experience. When one is done with "not this, not this, not this," the stripping away of the inauthentic, what's left is "this"—and "this" is always now.

This *via negativa* approach, illuminating what is real by showing what is not, is the bedrock of Rosenberg's method. One does not acquire a quality by striving after it—that's just ego—but by seeing its absence. If you are someone who is, say, stingy or angry, the way out of your suffering is not to mimic generosity or tranquility but to really see your stinginess and anger. If you want to become humble, take note of your arrogance. If you aspire to bring peace to the world, be aware of your inner wars and turmoil. If you are someone who stakes your identity on being educated or wealthy or beautiful, try being a nobody; it's what you are anyway. Rosenberg shuns the approach of cultivating wholesome mind states, calling that "doing an impersonation of a good person." He also waves away the noble motive of self-improvement, because the self is the source of most of our suffering—as he says, "The story of me, starring me, produced by me, directed by me, written by me."

Although Rosenberg supports any methods that improve our quality of life and lead to inner freedom, he tends to prefer firsthand observation over cultivation techniques. In dharma circles today, for example, many people do *metta* meditation, reciting formal phrases of loving-kindness and sending compassion to oneself, a benefactor, a friend, a neutral person, and, most challengingly, a difficult individual in one's life: "May you be happy. May you be healthy. May you be free from suffering." Although this simple verbiage strikes some people as off-puttingly sentimental, the goal is to nurture a befriending feeling toward people and the world, which can lead to a transformative sense of ease and connection. Metta is one of the four divine states or "immeasurables" in Buddhism, and indeed much of the Buddha's teaching pertains to qualities such as goodwill, generosity, and nonviolence.

Rosenberg has found that, for people starting out on the path, metta practice is easy to apprehend and can be effective in letting go of self-importance and self-righteousness. But it should not be mistaken, he cautions, for wisdom. That can come only from directly seeing the ways that one is unkind, resentful, vindictive. Registering and apprehending, in an instant, the emotional states that trigger one's own suffering, he says, *is* the healing, the action, the change. When that fundamental change takes place, metta naturally emerges from the heart—it doesn't have to be mechanically intoned. Yet as he also reminds his students: wisdom without compassion is not wisdom, and compassion without wisdom is not compassion.

There is a human reflex against directly facing one's deepest flaws. Rosenberg cites a survey of Hollywood films, which found that the most common phrase uttered in modern cinema was "Let's get out of here." "We keep busy so that we don't have to face the pain that is kept down. We repress it. We drown in it. If you're intellectual and sensitive and read a lot of spiritual books, you have brilliant explanations of it," he said. "But what you're looking at isn't as important as the quality of your looking. That's what will help you get free."

The stakes, he added, have never been higher. "I'm an apocalyptician—I honestly think the human race is too ignorant to save itself," he said. "Right now, the planet is heading toward total destruction. From a dharma point of view, the human race is asleep. From a dharma point of view, the challenge is to wake up."

—

In early 2023, Nitin Patel, a biotech executive and a longtime student of Rosenberg's, launched a project to transcribe, through artificial intelligence, all of Rosenberg's talks recorded between 1983 and 2023. It resulted in 473 separate documents, totaling some 2.7 million words, a breathtaking archive. The endeavor was just one example of how cutting-edge technologies are being deployed to make accessible classic Buddhist ideas. In 2023 and 2024, I added a bit to the archive, recording thirteen new conversations with Rosenberg as well as interviews with his colleagues and friends. The goal was to produce a book that synthesized Rosenberg's life and wisdom.

At first Rosenberg was reluctant to take part: "I felt like, 'Oh, I need this like a *lokh in kop*'"—Yiddish for "a hole in the head." At this point in his life, he told me, he simply wanted to stay in the present moment, not rake over the past. At the time I thought it was a specious excuse; later I discovered he meant it. Fortunately, after a few weeks, he realized that the conversations were another means to share the tradition that he has found so inspiring. During our talks, I never got the impression that he was on an ego trip or taking a victory lap after decades of teaching. Even as his body was disintegrating, he remained on a mission to spread the word.

My talks with him followed a familiar format. I would arrive at his apartment in Cambridge, Massachusetts, in the early afternoon, always bearing homemade scones or breads. Rosenberg agreed to be interviewed only as long as I brought baked goods from my kitchen. It was a transaction not quite in the spirit of Buddhadharma but very much in the spirit of Larrydharma. For somebody following a renunciant tradition, he is an astonishingly avid eater.

Since 2000, I had studied vipassana, or insight meditation, with Rosenberg at Cambridge Insight Meditation Center (CIMC), which he founded in 1985. I took to his ideas and methods immediately. He was a wiser and notably freer version of my (equally funny) male Jewish forebears. After a few years, he and I struck up a friendship, at first based on our mutual love of fine tea, sourced from Asia. As our friendship deepened and his physical health declined, I would pick him up at his home and walk him to class, offering an arm to hold on to. Sometimes he would ask me to serve as his "bodyguard" after class, reminding the students who thronged him with urgent personal questions that he needed to go home and eat supper. Much as he might complain afterward and sink from fatigue, he seemed to bask in the role of dharma counselor, putting even the most awkward petitioners at ease.

Like all of his loyal "yogis," or dharma practitioners, I had witnessed his strong, supple body give way to age. In his sixties, he looked strong, fit, perfectly composed in the full lotus position. He was of middling height but solid and sturdy, with strong hands and a graceful stride. He had a wide face, a fringe of wavy silver hair, wire-rim glasses, a wry grin that conveyed warmth and a touch of arrogance. His metallic, slightly raspy voice was avuncular but infused with the deadpan rhythms of a stand-up comedian, minus the eagerness to please.

By the end of his in-person teaching, Rosenberg was stooped and slope-shouldered. No longer able to sit cross-legged, he resorted to a chair. When stairs became impossible, he took a little-used elevator, steadied by staff and student attendants. His balance grew shaky because his feet were numb from peripheral neuropathy. He suffered unremitting and often lacerating pain from sciatica and lumbar stenosis. In the last days of pre-COVID-19 classes, students would begin their forty-five-minute meditation without him. Ten or fifteen minutes into the session, he shuffled inside the meditation hall. Hearing him make his unsteady way, I would break the rules and open my eyes to make sure he didn't fall. Sometimes our glances would meet, and he would faintly smile. When the pandemic hit in 2020, Rosenberg switched to Zoom. Initially reluctant, he found that the medium somehow forced students to pare down their questions to the core. He did the same with his answers.

During our interviews, we would sit together in his living room—he in a big black recliner, with a heating pad draped around his neck and shoulders and chest, me leaning forward in a wooden kitchen chair, steno pad in hand, audio recorder perched on the seat of Rosenberg's rolling walker. As always, his sartorial palette consisted of dark earth tones: black or gray turtlenecks, sometimes a black Indian kurta vest, baggy gray or brown meditation pants woven in Korea, thick socks, Finn Comfort leather sandals—raiment of a bygone counterculture. The conversations were not always smooth. A tremor caused his hands to flap uncontrollably, particularly the left, which slapped the armrests. At times, he groaned from spinal pain and had to shift position. Though he tired easily, he insisted that the interviews keep going.

After one of our conversations, as I was packing up my gear, he held a hand level in front of his neck. "From here on down, I'm a ninety-year-old man. From here on up"—he paused to calculate—"there's no number."

—

Rosenberg belongs to the small cadre of seekers who brought Buddhism to the West in the 1970s. Among the leaders of this first generation of converts were Jack Kornfield, Joseph Goldstein, and Sharon Salzberg—Americans who spent considerable time in temples, monasteries, and meditation centers in Asia. This trio went on to found, in 1975, the Insight Meditation Society in rural Barre, Massachusetts, the first Theravada Buddhist organization in the US established by non-Asians. Their goal was to teach vipassana in a simple and approachable form palatable to Westerners. Keeping the spiritual kernel of the practice, they shucked the Eastern rituals and ceremonies—the "cultural baggage," as they saw it.

Many of these pioneers were secular Jews who discovered deep cultural resonances in Buddhism. Both traditions are steeped in the awareness of suffering. Both value inquiry and learning. In Judaism, "Questioning is just part of things—even to answer a question with another question. It's also part of the humor," Goldstein said. And as Kabat-Zinn pointed out, both traditions emphasize that there's a reality behind appearances and that if you are stuck in appearances, it is a prescription for delusion. Rosenberg was part of this group of early enthusiasts. But he was also something of an outsider—serious but self-deprecating, academically trained but nonsectarian, learned but drawn to simple methods, and also about a decade older than the others. "He was so lively and bright . . . playful and kind and just naturally wise," said Roshi Joan Halifax, the abbot at the Upaya Zen Center in Santa Fe, New Mexico, who met Rosenberg in the mid-1970s.

It was an open and innocent period in Western dharma. The newly minted teachers and their students read everything they could get their hands on, attempted to master an endless variety of techniques, and diligently compared various schools of thought. They had a wide range of motivations, "from genuine seekers of the real deal to some fantastic psychedelic experience," Goldstein recalled. Many harbored romantic notions of enlightenment. In her book *Heartwood: The First Generation of Theravada Buddhism in America*, the sociologist Wendy Cadge paints these seekers as "largely misfits, eccentrics, hippies, ex-psychedelics, ex-political radicals"—a characterization that she said came from Rosenberg. But the truth, Rosenberg also told her, is that "what brought us to it all along was just suffering."

The first generation of Western teachers was particularly enamored of Eastern meditation techniques. In Asia, they had embarked on what felt like a courageous and sometimes hellish journey to acquire methods—giving up secure jobs, traveling from place to place, living frugally, often falling ill. When they returned to the US, they were considered fools for preaching strange new ideas.

Rosenberg, however, loved every bit of it, deeming the obstacles part of the hero's journey.

In America, there was a shadow side to the newly transported wave of spirituality. Trained in a hierarchical, patriarchal, rule-bound, and effort-oriented system, the Asian monk-teachers could be punitive and humiliating, yelling at students or striking them with sticks. More disturbing was the open secret that a number of Zen and Tibetan masters who had set up shop in America—men who had trained in all-male communities—were sexually abusing their female students, leaving a trail of wounded women. One married Zen master had five simultaneous affairs with female students, and none of them knew about the others. To Rosenberg—whom one colleague described as having a "supergood sniffer" for spiritual posturing—this suggested that at a time when Westerners were ever on the hunt for meditation methods and other tools to shake up the mind and capsize assumptions, they skipped over the ethical dimensions of their newfound traditions.

Back then, many naïve Westerners "checked their intelligence at the door," Rosenberg said. As he sees it, no outside agency can certify a dharma teacher. Ultimately, only the teachers themselves know if they are cutting corners or deceiving students. The essence of spiritual discipline, he pointed out, is honesty.

Rosenberg angrily confronted one of the more notorious miscreants, with whom he was studying. The Japanese Zen priest had passed all of his formal koans, demonstrating a mastery of the form and allegedly an advanced level of insight.

"But there's one koan you missed," Rosenberg told him.

"Which one is that?" the roshi asked, incredulous.

"The woman koan." And with that, Rosenberg walked out the door and never returned.

Today, the drama has simmered down. The most popular offshoot of Buddhism in the West is mindfulness meditation, a practice shorn of historical or spiritual lineage. It can even be delivered via handy apps—with names like Headspace, Calm, and Buddhify—and bonus features such as music, bedtime stories, and intention-driven workout videos. "Today, 36 million Americans meditate, fueling a $1.86 billion industry comprised of meditation and yoga centers/studios, books, DVDs, workshops, online courses, websites, apps and supplies," noted a 2022 marketing report from the company Research and Markets. One popular aid, which relies on a headband that streams real-time biofeedback about the wearer's brain state, is trademarked "Meditation Made Easy."

On the one hand, like most teachers of his generation, Rosenberg approves of any contemporary method that brings people in the door, where they may later be exposed to the original Buddhist texts. But he worries that something may be lost in translation. Drifting on contemporary cultural currents, the practice has become consumer-oriented and monetized; yogis are customers, teachers are employees, boards of directors are bosses. "Are we watering it down," he asked, "to make people feel comfortable instead of free?"

—

As part of Rosenberg's unpresuming persona, he would often say in class, "I run a small shop." One obvious meaning was that he never sought celebrity, staying close to home both literally and figuratively. But when I asked, Rosenberg said he had a different meaning in mind. "It means I'm starting with the person in front of me." He would proceed intuitively. From the vipassana tradition, he borrowed the slow, painstaking exploration of a student's present moment. He would scrutinize their eyes, voice, and posture. He repeatedly asked, "How are you feeling right now?" sussing out a student's emotions and nonverbal energies. Vipassana is part of Theravada, the oldest school of thought in Buddhism. Among other things, it features breath awareness, inhabiting the whole body, calming the body, and achieving a mind that's fit and stable enough to see into itself.

From Theravada he absorbed the centrality of individual liberation and impermanence—seeing everything arise and pass away. He calls impermanence "the doorway into everything," because to be alive is to change, and to see that dynamic process, frame by frame, is "the art of pure observation." What one observes are the *kilesas*, the three poisons of the mind—greed, hatred, and delusion—that color our view of ourselves and others. As he often says, such watchfulness weakens the energy of everything it touches because it allows the kilesas to, in a sense, tell their own story and run their course. Today, most meditation students just want to get calm. But Rosenberg insists that vipassana is not a serenity how-to. Rather, it's a wisdom path. He calls this vigilant self-awareness a "quiet passion."

In his far-flung explorations, Rosenberg crossed many philosophical borders. From ten years of Zen practice he incorporated the Mahayana point of view that one frees oneself in order to liberate all beings, as well as the idea of nonduality or nonseparation from everything around oneself, just sitting and breathing with life. Seung Sahn Sunim was an early teacher and the first Korean Zen master to live and teach in the West. Though he had a tenuous grasp of English, Seung Sahn could read human character. "You're a freedom-style person," he once told Rosenberg, coaching him on how to give a dharma talk. "No notes. You're like a jazz musician. Get a theme and then just blow. Don't rehearse. The main thing is to be open."

What distinguished Rosenberg's teaching was "simplicity, clarity, and profundity," said Doug Phillips, a psychologist, vipassana and Zen teacher, and Rosenberg mentee. "In a culture that teaches avoidance at every opportunity, to look at how you're actually living is pretty tough stuff because it'll turn your life upside down. Who's going to want to sign on for that?"

Before launching into a dharma talk, Rosenberg would close his eyes and tilt his head down, tuning in to his mind and the moment.

After a minute or so, his head would tilt up again, his eyes would open, his face would brighten, and he would achieve verbal liftoff.

For somebody who railed against the tendency to make our lives into narratives and then attach to those stories, he drew on a deep well of witty set pieces, polished parables delivered with impeccable timing. Rosenberg's students would recognize these greatest hits from shorthand titles: The Yellow Cab, The Year without Books, The Week without Sleep, and so forth. Compared to the teaching style of traditional Asian monastics, Western teachers are far more likely to use their own life experience to illustrate dharma principles. By revealing their own flaws and the mistakes they made along the way, they convey, "I'm a person just like you. My mind was also wild. You don't have to be a monastic to follow this path."

Teaching is also the art of listening, an art he refined over the years. "The main way I've learned how to listen is by listening to how I don't listen." When someone would ask him the same question class after class, Rosenberg made the exchange fresh each time. He wanted to know about each student's world, how life was for them. He tried to find different ways of persuading people to talk about what they didn't want to talk about—their suffering. Sometimes he would answer a question with another question—a skillful tactic, because it uncovers the worldview of the questioner. With that, he would tease apart the student's constructed reality—Buddhism being, after all, a practice of deconstruction. He wouldn't end an interaction without making sure the student's question was satisfyingly addressed and there was a "click" of understanding.

"When he responds to a question, he's not merely responding to the question. He's responding to the heart of the person who's posing the question," Kabat-Zinn said. "He's reaching out to engage your humanity, saying, 'Look, is this working for you? Let's be real—forget about all the theory. Practically speaking, is this working for you? What is your actual experience?' He's constantly bringing you back to first principles."

For Malaika Tabors, an integrative medicine practitioner and Rosenberg's student since 2003, Rosenberg was a "freedom fighter, and he's fighting for us against any attachment." In her case, he watched for the ways in which she was holding her emotions too tightly. When Tabors's mother died after a long and difficult struggle with cancer, Tabors resolved to face the tragedy squarely. During a private dharma interview with Rosenberg, she studiously detailed her exemplary practice—what she was doing, seeing, and feeling moment by moment, as Rosenberg had always taught. "He just looked at me and said, 'Malaika, take a break. Watch some movies. I see that you're being a very good student of the dharma, but cut yourself some slack. This is unbelievably hard and painful. You do not have to be there for every second of it.'"

For Matthew Daniell, a teacher whom Rosenberg has mentored since 1990, the advice was almost diametrically opposite. Daniell had spent more than a decade shuttling between the US and Asia. He studied vipassana meditation in Burma and India, ordained as a Theravadin monk in Thailand, immersed himself in Soto Zen in Japan and Tibetan Buddhism in India. Rosenberg called him "a high-class dharma bum," an affectionate put-down. Daniell had the skills and experience to be a good teacher and practitioner, Rosenberg told him, but he needed to bring his dharma into the real world to fulfill the promise Rosenberg saw in him. "He said, 'You haven't committed to something bigger than you.'" So Rosenberg taught Daniell to be a dharma mensch. Daniell, for his part, married, helped raise a stepson, cofounded a meditation center, and has led classes here and abroad for more than two decades. "He taught me a connectedness of being in the world while also living spirituality moment by moment, really being devoted to living daily life."

Rosenberg has always been unusually bold and direct. In a 1999 interview for *The Insight Journal*, he explained why: "My feeling is that a number of people who are strongly committed to meditation are afraid of life, or afraid of relationship, or afraid of work on some level. But in my view, dharma practice is not to hide. It is not to become a hothouse plant—thriving only in a protected environment. It is to jump into life." At times, students interpreted his straightforwardness as aggressive or cold. "Larry had a direct style of teaching that could sometimes rub people the wrong way—especially if they were expecting to be coddled or thought Larry should fit their preconceived notions of what a meditation teacher should be. If the humor wasn't working or his direct approach didn't land, all of a sudden the room would get nervously quiet, like: uh-oh," Daniell said. Typically, after the first few days of a retreat, people relaxed and settled into Rosenberg's cheeky, matter-of-fact style.

Still, Rosenberg held students to account. He would throw questions back to them, demonstrating that they already had the answer if they were willing to look. "Mainly, what I value is helping the person to understand that I can't help them—which is a huge help, because all along they've been seeking help from the outside or blaming the outside. I'm trying to say, 'It's all in here,'" he told me. A good teacher, he once said, is like a midwife—encouraging and assisting students as they give birth to themselves. He also borrowed from the teaching style of the ninth-century Chinese master Lin-chi, who insisted that all he did was sit, listen to people, and snatch away their prized possessions—the notions that they clutch or identify with. (Lin-chi was also known to wield a stick on his disciples if those attachments proved too sticky.)

In his last decade of teaching, Rosenberg emphasized the Four Noble Truths, the first teaching given by the Buddha—there is suffering; there is a cause of suffering; there is cessation of suffering; that cessation comes from following the Eightfold Path, practices centered on ethical refinement, stability of mind, and wisdom. The schema comes out of the Ayurvedic medical model: disease, diagnosis, cure, and medicine. "It's Buddhist, but it isn't. It's so commonsensical. It's so practical and down to earth," he said.

Always, Rosenberg's throughline has been clear seeing. At the end of each class, he would put his palms together, close his eyes, and recite a spare blessing: "May we continue to look into ourselves. May we see things exactly as they are. And may such clear, direct seeing free us." The words surfaced unbidden in one of his sittings. After a while, it became a Pavlovian cue; his students couldn't stretch and yawn and stand up at the end of a class until they heard his benedictory send-off.

—

Rosenberg came to Buddhism "from the top down," as he puts it. His was not the desperate suffering of somebody whose life had come apart but the exquisite pain of a conventionally successful person in search of authenticity. "He was always inquiring: What is life really about?" Kabat-Zinn said.

A New Yorker born and bred, Rosenberg first lived on the Lower East Side of Manhattan, then moved with his family to Brighton Beach, Brooklyn, when he was five. He and his parents occupied one room, his grandparents another, three aunts and an uncle a third. No bathroom—just a communal toilet at the end of the hall. No privacy. And certainly no silence, dharmic or otherwise: a fire department on the corner, a streetcar that thundered by, a train overhead, restaurants and an ice cream parlor. Russian Jews and Italians and Irish lived discordantly cheek by jowl, the Coney Island waterfront a refuge both on- and off-season. "If you went to high school five minutes away from the world's most famous amusement park at the time, you had the Parachute Jump as your icon, not the synagogue or the Catholic church," he quipped. On summer evenings, neighbors cooled themselves on rooftops, reminiscing about the old country and discussing their doctors and afflictions. When he landed decades later in the leafy university hub of Cambridge, it felt like a "forest paradise."

Rosenberg's parents had fled the tyranny of czarist Russia, a sorrow wordlessly passed down in the family. They were a study in opposites.

"My mother was pure love. I never heard her say an unkind word about anyone." Once, when she listened in as Rosenberg and his dharma buddies talked about metta, she inquired in her thick Jewish accent, "Metta, metta. What is all this metta you're talking about?" Rosenberg explained that it was loving-kindness, sent to yourself and to other people. "Oh, I've been doing that all my life," she said dismissively. "What's the big deal?"

Rosenberg's father was smart, funny, well read, critical, cynical, and moody. Although his formal schooling ended at fourth grade, he harbored ambitions of becoming a lawyer, even a judge. He settled for being a cab driver and printer's proofreader. By turns a Marxist and a labor movement activist, he ultimately became an inward-looking man, discrediting as full of baloney political radicals, unions, and everything else. He was, in other words, a soured idealist. "He questioned everything," Rosenberg said, "to the point where he cut himself off a lot."

Born during the Depression (he has a sister nine years younger), Rosenberg completely identified with his father growing up, a filial worship. While Rosenberg's days were spent in study and sports, the usual boyhood fare, in the evenings his father read him fables by Ivan Krylov, Aesop-like wisdom tales that often subtly satirized Russian bureaucracy. He drew out Rosenberg about the stories' meaning. He also taught him how to fight, a vital skill when schoolyard skirmishes between ethnic groups flared.

While the older man detested religion, he made Rosenberg go to Hebrew school to please his mother and grandmother. His cynicism had a mischievous streak. He instructed his son to press the rabbi in class about exactly how Moses parted the Red Sea. At Rosenberg's bar mitzvah, his father handed the rabbi a substantial cash gift with a request *not* to give the usual speech at the end of the ritual—perhaps the first such bribe in Jewish history. (The rabbi gave the speech anyway, and Rosenberg's father was incensed, bellowing, "You people are hopeless!") "I got used to freedom of inquiry," Rosenberg said, "that it is natural to question, to challenge."

Growing up under the shadow of Adolf Hitler and World War II, Rosenberg closely followed battles and saw gruesome photos from concentration camps—too horrifying to publish—that his father came across in his proofreading job. Well before details of the Holocaust became public knowledge among most Americans, Jews knew what was going on through whispered conversations. That formative exposure to genocide would inform all of his life choices.

Brooklyn holds a mythic place in Rosenberg's life. He was the little Jewish guy who fought his way out, and that cocky sensibility coursed through his life and teaching. Rosenberg had the confidence and the chutzpah to live an unshackled and unconventional life, mixing ingredients he picked up from both parents: the skepticism from his discontented father, the kindness and self-assurance from his doting mother. When Rosenberg's parents visited Cambridge Insight Meditation Center a few years after it opened, they quietly sat at the back of the meditation hall. It was the only time they heard their son teach. At the end of Rosenberg's dharma talk, someone turned around and said, "Mr. and Mrs. Rosenberg, you've known Larry his whole life. Has meditation improved him?" His mother, normally shy, jumped up and exclaimed, "Improved? Improved? He didn't need improvement. He's always been perfect!"

———

At twenty, years after World War II had ended, Rosenberg pulled strings to join the American army of occupation in Germany. He could easily have secured a college exemption from military service, but he was obsessed by the question of how Germany, the center of European culture, could have taken such a barbarically murderous course. Back home, Rosenberg had kept a photo of Mahatma Gandhi above his bed. But in basic training he found that he enjoyed shooting rifles and especially machine guns, becoming a skilled marksman. He witnessed a soldier die during airborne maneuvers, another lose an eye, and men in uniform go psychotic. "I was very disappointed in myself. I actually could have been a decent soldier. I liked it," he said. "I thought I was Gandhi. It turns out I'm Adolf Hitler." Repulsed by his own aggression and the possibility that he could kill someone, he asked for a transfer to the medical corps, where he would not carry a gun. The Germans, he concluded, possessed immense knowledge but not wisdom—a distinction he would frequently hammer home in his teaching. Looking back, he believes his dharma path began with his Holocaust obsession.

"He didn't say from the start of basic training, 'I abhor machine guns on principle.' Instead, he admitted to loving to shoot the machine gun because it conferred so much power at a distance," Kabat-Zinn said. Rosenberg turned his back on the military at the height of the Cold War, though at the time he didn't have a pacifist bone in his body. His about-face came out of the most sought-after state of mind in Buddhism, the Holy Grail: direct perception.

Back in the United States after his service, Rosenberg felt at loose ends. After graduating from Brooklyn College, he enrolled in law school at the University of Chicago; he thought it would please his father. He lasted a year and a half, ultimately dissuaded by the celebrated legal scholar William Prosser's *Handbook of the Law of Torts*. He then entered the school's illustrious program in social psychology. It was a time when social scientists were trying to fathom humankind's ambivalent attitude toward freedom and how conformity could obliterate individual moral conscience. For Rosenberg, Chicago was an awakening. Surrounded by odd, brilliant, impassioned students, "It was like the French Foreign Legion. We were all thrown together, and I felt like I had never been so at home in my life."

Notebook and ballpoint pen in hand, old-school style, he earned his master's degree by studying race relations among schizophrenics in a locked psychiatric ward. His PhD on communication styles among educators was equally ambitious. But the anthropological participant-observer model that he loved—a way of being in the world comparable to a yogi's—was giving way to dry, computer-generated statistical analysis. A well-received doctoral thesis in hand, he landed a position as a social psychologist in Harvard Medical School's Department of Psychiatry. Before leaving Chicago for Cambridge, he tossed his dry, number-laden dissertation into Lake Michigan.

In Cambridge, Rosenberg wore a Harvard sweatshirt, wrote on Harvard stationery, and had money for the first time in his life. Women were interested in him. But he saw that his eminent colleagues were just people, with ambitions and vanity and bitterness. He returned to the University of Chicago, which soon felt just as stale. He concluded that the problem wasn't with Harvard or Chicago—he needed to look at himself, but he didn't know how. Social psychology had taught him about everyone else's mind, while his own was roiling. "I could tell you about the Trobriand Islanders but I couldn't tell you about the Coney Islanders."

A job offer in 1966 from Brandeis University, just outside Boston, changed the trajectory of his career—and his life. He led campus protests against the US war in Vietnam and the bombing of Cambodia. His classes in social psychology and social psychiatry were loose and unstructured. Partly that reflected the ethos of the 1960s. Like so many of his peers, Rosenberg was experimenting with drugs and often taught under the influence of marijuana and LSD. Summers were spent stoned with friends on a Mexican island. "I was part of a movement in the culture that was concerned with the liberation of almost everything," he told the filmmaker Marty Ostrow in the moving documentary *Long Path Home.*

In his classes, Rosenberg would read from a book by the influential Burmese Buddhist monk Mahasi Sayadaw. The aim was to get calm by following one's breath at the abdomen and mentally noting, "Rising. Falling. Rising. Falling." When students asked him questions about meditation, his answers were unaccountably comprehensive, yet at the time, he had virtually no acquaintance with Asian philosophy. He felt he knew more than he was entitled to. Looking back on this period, he uncharacteristically broaches the possibility of rebirth. "It is conceivable that, in a past lifetime, I'd already done this."

At Brandeis, Rosenberg taught a popular course with the camouflage title "New Directions in Social Psychology." It was an evening class—he didn't want school administrators around. He brought in celebrity spiritual figures such as the Tibetan Buddhist meditation master (and notorious drunk) Chögyam Trungpa, the American teacher Ram Dass, and Maharishi Mahesh Yogi, the Beatles' Indian guru. The Japanese scholar Michio Kushi discoursed on the macrobiotic diet. One night a Syrian mystic taught Sufi dancing, and a few ecstatic students took off their shirts. "It was a crazy house," Rosenberg said. When the administration got wind of his New Age pedagogy, it was the beginning of the end. Rosenberg and Brandeis parted ways in 1973. He was forty years old. The future was a question mark. His immigrant parents were crushed.

—

Though Rosenberg had been a college professor for ten years, "The gap between the actual experience of my life and my résumé was like the Grand Canyon." After leaving Brandeis, he became a homeless wanderer, bouncing between Asia and the US, staying in Buddhist monasteries, crashing on friends' couches. He gave away his clothes, his books, his furniture: everything. "I had tremendous conviction or faith that whatever it was that I had done, there was something lacking, and it wasn't minor. I wasn't a spiritual playboy," he said. His life in academia had felt like a prison. But he was also motivated by the real misery he had seen in childhood—immigrant men forced to earn any kind of living to put food on the table.

Rosenberg's academic colleagues mocked his decision. One admonished him for giving up the rare privilege to live a life of the mind, trading in a prestigious intellectual perch for "this Asian bullshit,

Ouija board, tarot cards." Back then, yoga, meditation, and any form of Eastern mysticism were considered the far side of the lunatic fringe. "He had all these highly accomplished sociologist professor friends. With one exception, they all thought he was out of his mind," Kabat-Zinn said. "But they also admired him, I felt, because he was free from the various constraints of the academy. They saw that Larry was intentionally taking a different path from theirs, leaving the comfort and security of the university, even if he didn't know exactly where it was leading. Larry was a combination of uranium—don't touch it because it's radioactive—and kryptonite—incredibly powerful, explosive stuff."

Unlike other countercultural converts to Asian philosophy, playing out a youthful adventure, "he actually gave something up. He was an established professor," noted the Insight Meditation Society's Joseph Goldstein. Rosenberg's about-turn, Goldstein surmised, sprang from seeing that things were not what they were cracked up to be—that is, from disillusionment. In Buddhism, the term has a positive connotation: to be dis-illusioned is to be free from illusion.

—

It would be misleading to paint this pivotal moment in Rosenberg's life without talking about Jon Kabat-Zinn. They met in the mid-1960s and have been best friends ever since. When Rosenberg set out on his quest, Kabat-Zinn was his only source of emotional support—finding places for him to live, storing his belongings, helping out with moving, even delivering his wife's chicken soup when Rosenberg came down with the flu. "We're true dharma brothers," Kabat-Zinn said. Or as Rosenberg put it, "We've been the two supports of each other in an ocean of doubt." Not long after Rosenberg left academia for points unknown, Kabat-Zinn, a longtime teacher of meditation and hatha yoga by that point, began mulling the foundation of what would become mindfulness-based stress reduction (MBSR), which has been adopted globally in a vast range of applications, from the corporate world to education to the armed forces. Like Rosenberg, Kabat-Zinn also faced ridicule—in his case, for apparently throwing away a PhD in molecular biology from the Massachusetts Institute of Technology, where he worked in the laboratory of a Nobel laureate. Fittingly, Rosenberg and Kabat-Zinn were in adjacent rooms at a meditation retreat in 1979 when Kabat-Zinn hatched the revolutionary idea of MBSR. "Who else could I talk about it with but Larry?"

Outwardly the two men were opposites. While Rosenberg was a convivial hermit, solid and earthbound, with a low center of gravity, Kabat-Zinn, twelve years younger, was outgoing and effusive, lean and kinetic. While Rosenberg became a vagabond for many years, Kabat-Zinn chose the Buddhist "householder" route—marrying, having children, holding a regular job. "Our paths took very different directions, but beneath all appearances, they're exactly the same," Kabat-Zinn said. "We were always looking for ways to live our lives committed to embodied wakefulness and wisdom." He sometimes referred to Rosenberg as his "windshield" because Rosenberg was often the first to make contact and check out Asian teachers passing through the spiritual bazaar of Cambridge, giving Kabat-Zinn the green light only if the itinerant masters were up to snuff. Unlike today, when a book search on Amazon for "Buddhism" turns up tens of thousands of results, dharma literature back then was scarce; the two friends spent hours scouring underground bookstores specializing in esoterica of all sorts. Among other things, Rosenberg came across a series of thin pamphlets called *The Wheel*, published in Sri Lanka, written by practicing monastics, and chock-full of what felt like dharma gold.

For a time in the early 1970s, they led classes together on Tuesday nights at various churches around Harvard Square—Rosenberg teaching meditation, and Kabat-Zinn, yoga. (During one, while Rosenberg and his students were deep in meditation, a thief sneaked in and stole wallets and purses that the yogis had casually piled on a stage.) After teaching, the dharma bros went out to dinner and talked for hours. "It was like we were in love. Two minds, two hearts, delighting in inquiry, sharing, humor—a lot of humor," Kabat-Zinn recalled. "Most people, understandably, come to the dharma because they are hurting, often badly. They are seeking relief. They want healing. They want transformation. Larry and I came to the dharma mostly out of wonder, out of love, out of a sense of exploration and inquiry into the nature of reality beyond the conventional explorations within the academy. We were deep into the koans Who am I? and What am I?"

I asked Kabat-Zinn how the two maintained such an intense friendship for so long: "I listened to him. He listened to me. It's very easy to talk, but to be heard—that is a whole different story. When you feel met and heard, and you're talking about only the most important thing in the universe—your love for dharma and what you're going to do with your life, which is the only thing we ever really talked about—you only need one friend like that. You're way ahead of the curve to have even one friend with whom you can connect around a common love of practice and have a conversation like that every week." To this day, on the less frequent occasions when they can meet in person, they rarely reminisce, preferring to have lunch, drink matcha tea, and share the increasingly precious moments together that they have left.

—

In retrospect, Rosenberg's unsentimental education looks fatedly directional and coherent. Part of that coherence stems from the fractal quality of Buddhist ideas, each part containing the whole, especially the core idea of impermanence, that animates virtually every tradition. Part of the coherence is also the fact that, at a cultural moment rife with counterfeit gurus, Rosenberg only worked with those he considered bona fide masters. (Quoting the Hindu spiritual teacher Swami Chinmayananda, Rosenberg would say, "The longer the beard, the bigger the faker.") Early on, for two years Rosenberg immersed himself in Vedanta, an ancient Indian philosophy in which the goal is to manifest one's divinity. He spent five years studying Korean Zen, another five in

Japanese Zen, then he stepped back in the Buddhist canon into vipassana, which is rooted in the Buddha's original teachings some 2,600 years ago. It was a first-rate ramble. "My life had to unfold. I had to do all these different things," he told me, adding a *Neti Neti* twist: "This is not it, this is not it, this is not it—*this* is it."

Most of Rosenberg's mentors were foundational figures in modern Buddhism: the Vietnamese monk, Zen master, and peace activist Thich Nhat Hanh; the Thai monks Ajahn Buddhadasa, who taught an unornamented version of the original Buddhist texts, and Ajahn Maha Bua, whom many considered an enlightened being. Ajahn Chah, the Thai Forest monk who established branch monasteries in the West that hewed to his lineage's bare-bones, rigorous, but unscholarly approach, was a guiding light. Ajahn Munindra, a plainspoken Indian meditation teacher and scholar who visited the US, taught an unembellished version of self-observation. Hovering above this esteemed pack was Jiddu Krishnamurti, the Indian visionary who rendered Buddhist ideas and his own iconoclastic truths into a clear distillate.

Lest this pantheon look like a montage of male privilege, Rosenberg also worked closely with Vimala Thakar, an Indian social activist and spiritual teacher, and one of Krishnamurti's protégés. Like Krishnamurti, she viewed inner transformation as a social responsibility and traveled the world to share her insights. But Thakar aside, it was a male world and, in the case of Zen, of "dharma combat." Undeniably, Rosenberg was a man of his era. As he would, years later, tell his students, you start with where you are and the materials at hand.

On this odyssey, "Larry never lost his True North," Kabat-Zinn said. The walls of Rosenberg's meditation room at home—a simple, hallowed space with an altar, books, and a big damask reading chair—are decorated with framed portraits of his illustrious mentors. The Forest masters sit in full lotus position, their orange robes arranged diagonally across their chests, their arms and right shoulders bare, their faces often gravely serious; the Zen masters are well fed and richly attired, relaxed and laughing. As he once told a class, "I know that I couldn't have done it by myself. I know that I needed their help and that they gave it freely and generously."

Many of Rosenberg's teaching stories—and his best punch lines—come from his eclectic apprenticeships. His first serious Buddhist teacher, Seung Sahn, set up shop in Providence, Rhode Island. He had come from South Korea in 1972 and made a living here repairing washing machines for laundromats. He knew only ten or fifteen English phrases that often sounded like baby talk—but he wielded them like a scalpel: "Good." "Bad." "Broken." "Only go straight for the next ten thousand years." "Try, try, try, try." "If you don't make anything, then you can have everything." According to Rosenberg, "He was able to survive in a condition that was unpremeditated."

After work, Seung Sahn held meditation sessions in his Providence apartment, his underwear hanging from the ceiling to dry. Rosenberg asked question after question, irritating the other students. "Questions are good. Soon he'll exhaust himself and then he can start to practice," Seung Sahn said, defending his voluble pupil. The Zen master regarded Rosenberg with a kind of amused pity. "He merely understands everything," he would say, meaning that his obsessively inquisitive student, burdened with a PhD and a university mind, was filled with concepts and bereft of wisdom.

A long plane ride to Asia underscored the problem. Rosenberg and his teacher were en route to South Korea, where Rosenberg would be intensively meditating for a year in an ancient mountain monastery. He opened his carry-on bag and proudly revealed a stack of dharma books. Seung Sahn was unimpressed. "No reading for one year," he said. "No books of any kind. You already have too many words in your head. See what happens when you live and learn from your life."

The purpose of Zen, Seung Sahn often explained, was to vault beyond self-improvement to emptiness, nonconceptual knowing. For the first two weeks, Rosenberg suffered an intellectual's DTs—in his craving for language, even resorting to reading the ingredients on American ketchup bottles. He came to understand that the deepest intelligence comes out of the silent mind, the mind that is fresh, that has not accumulated facts or assumptions. As a teacher, Rosenberg often said that modern humans, drowning in words, have been educated out of unmediated, nonconceptual experience—the kind that Dogen, the thirteenth-century master who founded the Japanese Soto Zen sect, referred to as "intimate."

Later, Rosenberg worked alongside Thich Nhat Hanh. At Plum Village, Nhat Hanh's international practice center in France, Rosenberg received transmission as a teacher in the Zen lineage of Lin-chi, establishing him as a successor in that spiritual bloodline. What struck Rosenberg was that the gentle-voiced Nhat Hanh delivered tough-minded dharma. "It was a velvet glove with brass knuckles underneath," Rosenberg said. "And some of that rubbed off on me."

Rosenberg found his true spiritual home in 1982 in vipassana, the direct observation of mental and physical objects in their impermanence, unsatisfactoriness, and lack of an inherent, independent essence or self. It is the unadorned form of Buddhism still largely practiced in Southeast Asia and Sri Lanka. "That's what I love about Theravada Buddhism: it's a low-budget film," Rosenberg said.

Through vipassana Rosenberg learned *anapanasati*, or mindfulness of breathing. Initially this became the center of his practice and teaching. The idea is to use the breath as an anchor to calm the mind and in turn register feelings and mind states, which can bring insight and liberation. He plumbed the depths of this process with Ajahn Buddhadasa. Nearly eighty and ailing when Rosenberg met him, Buddhadasa gathered his students in a clearing in the Thai forest, as dogs and wild chickens wandered about. He showed Rosenberg that because the breath is so unassuming, it is undervalued. Rosenberg had been looking for a complicated path to enlightenment when this simple one would take him to the same destination.

When Ajahn Chah, the eminent monk in the Thai Forest tradition, visited the United States in 1979, Rosenberg jumped at the chance to learn from him as well. Chah was charming, impish, and crystal clear in his instructions, often poking fun at American students' attachments (what we might call "neuroses"). Though they worked together only briefly, Rosenberg felt a kinship with Chah. "A lot of the great meditation teachers in the Forest tradition were uneducated, from rural farming backgrounds, very direct and immediate. They could as well have grown up in Brooklyn," he said. Chah reinforced the idea that there are no bypasses to self-awareness; the only way to transcend suffering is to look directly at oneself. He also supplied one of Rosenberg's signature phrases. No matter what intractable problem a student described in class, the monk went through the performative gestures of giving it deep thought but always came up with the same answer: "Keep it simple and stick to the present moment."

—

Before Rosenberg's expeditions into Eastern philosophy, before his decision to become a wandering mendicant, even before he hatched an escape plan from the ivory tower, there was Jiddu Krishnamurti.

In the fall of 1968, the Indian philosopher spent the better part of a week at Brandeis, giving talks and being filmed. Rosenberg had heard about Krishnamurti's visit from a colleague, the sociologist Morrie Schwartz (who was later memorialized in Mitch Albom's book *Tuesdays with Morrie*). Schwartz knew that Rosenberg was disenchanted with academic life. "You have to meet this man Krishnamurti. He's an Indian gentleman I heard last week in New York, at the New School for Social Research," he told Rosenberg. "I didn't understand a word he was saying, but I know it's exactly what you're looking for." Rosenberg was dubious but decided to find some books by Krishnamurti at Mandrake, a high-toned Harvard Square bookshop. The only volume on the shelves was *Think on These Things*, selections from Krishnamurti's discussions with schoolchildren, which made Rosenberg even more dubious. But when he started reading it, he was enthralled. The words were plain, simple, natural—and seismic in their effect. He had never encountered anything like it before.

Most pointedly, Krishnamurti located wisdom in self-understanding. "You start with the ordinariness of what you see in yourself. He called that '*what is*.' It's an experiential fact of here and now, period," explained Rosenberg. "He said, 'By being fully with what is, you go beyond what is.'"

At Krishnamurti's first Brandeis lecture, Rosenberg expected someone in traditional flowing Indian garb to walk onto the stage. Instead, he saw an aristocratic figure with a handsome, swarthy, unlined face, dressed in a three-piece Savile Row suit and polished shoes, a British gentleman who looked like he just stepped out of *Masterpiece Theatre*. Krishnamurti was at ease and disarming in any social situation. But when he spoke about spiritual matters, he was on fire. In a photo snapped at a faculty reception, two professors in suits and ties and holding drinks look to be making light academic chitchat, amusing and self-amused. Krishnamurti, holding a cup of apple cider (he was a teetotaler), looks slight, abstracted, somewhat otherworldly. Rosenberg, wearing a Mexican serape and staring at the floor, looks quietly thunderstruck.

It's almost impossible to summarize Krishnamurti's remarkable life, which reads more like fiction than fact. He was born in 1895 in the southern coastal region of India to a Brahmin family. When Krishnamurti was fifteen, on a beach in Madras, his strangely vacant aura caught the attention of a high-ranking member of the Theosophical Society, an organization that preached a world religion and was steeped in the occult. Soon the boy was declared the group's next World Teacher and was whisked off to elite circles in Europe and England for an all-encompassing education—intellectual, philosophical, spiritual, and mystical. By 1929, though, rebelling against the role thrust upon him, he abandoned the Theosophists in a public speech that foreshadowed the themes that he would travel the world teaching until his death in 1986. "I maintain that truth is a pathless land, and you cannot approach it by any path whatsoever, by any religion, by any sect," he said. "I am concerning myself with only one essential thing: to set man free." In his prodigious speechifying and writing about the fruitlessness of any formal spiritual path, he evinced an austere intensity and a poet's gift for language.

At Brandeis, few people attended Krishnamurti's talks, and his schedule was open. Rosenberg spent every minute he could with him. What struck him was that Krishnamurti was completely relaxed, approachable, warm, friendly, clever, and a singularly attentive listener. Over the week, the two men walked in silence in the then-forested grounds of the campus. Rosenberg was keen to get instructions on how to meditate. Krishnamurti brushed off his badgering questions. Finally, on one of their last days together, Krishnamurti instructed Rosenberg to pick out something in the forest and simply look at it with full attention. Rosenberg chose a leaf. A half hour later, he was moved to tears, a city boy seeing foliage for the first time. Krishnamurti said, "When you go back to your apartment, sit down, get quiet, close your eyes, and look at your mind that way. That's meditation."

On Krishnamurti's last day at Brandeis, Rosenberg paid a visit to say goodbye. Krishnamurti urged Rosenberg to do his best as a professor and not waste time fighting the university administration. Then he advised, "Put your house in order first." At the time, Rosenberg enjoyed a bachelor style: clothes strewn on the floor, endless restaurant meals with friends, his refrigerator unplugged so that he could use its shelves as a bookcase. It was a kind of braggadocio: "See what an intellectual I am? I don't give a damn about conventional things." Rosenberg interpreted the instructions literally. "You mean my apartment—clean it up, put things in order, make sure the dishes get washed, things like that?" Krishnamurti tried to mask his impatience. "Okay, yes, you can start there. I'm talking about something else." He silently pointed to his heart.

Before they parted, Rosenberg asked for homework. Krishnamurti said, "Just one thing. Pay attention to how you *actually* live." The word *actually* carried a charge. "He emphasized *actually*. How do you *actually* live?" Rosenberg said. "Not how you think you live. Not how you should live. But how do you *actually* live, from moment to moment? He said, 'The key is in relationship: to people, to nature, to objects, to money.' And the word *actually* was burned into my skull when I left." As Rosenberg would later realize, the guidance is also a fair summation of the dharma path.

Though Krishnamurti's teachings about the beauty of awareness were shattering in their time, his name is not as well known today as it once was. One reason is that he didn't teach a coherent method—indeed, he spoke against method. But method—especially one well tested over thousands of years—creates a framework for carrying teachings over time. This is especially true in the absence of a charismatic figure like Krishnamurti, the rare human being born with a silent mind.

Krishnamurti offered little help to his followers except his magnetic presence; he taught solely from the summit of pure awareness. The Buddha also taught from the mountaintop but kindly offered ropes and ladders and pitons and grappling hooks—in the form of his voluminous teachings and myriad methods—to help the rest of us get there. In this sense, the Buddha was the better teacher. Rosenberg says that Krishnamurti's teaching helped him understand Buddhism and Buddhism helped him understand Krishnamurti. Comparing his two masters, Rosenberg alights on a New York subway metaphor: the Buddha is the local train, Krishnamurti the express.

Krishnamurti—and the Buddha, too—were almost certainly brain-wired differently from the rest of us, which may be why their teachings complement each other. One could say that Krishnamurti was an outlier, but also a gifted seeker and what might be called, in Rosenberg's original province of sociology, a "positive deviant," showing the way for others. These one-off individuals who move through the world with porous boundaries (as do many great artists) embody nonseparation.

Until Krishnamurti's death, Rosenberg kept up a strong connection, meeting with K, as he is known to his followers, whenever he got the chance. It's easy to see why. The same aversion to settled thinking that animated Rosenberg's journey also courses through Krishnamurti's talks and writing. "Is not discontent essential in our life, to any question, to any inquiry, to probing, to finding out what is the real, what is truth, what is essential in life?" Krishnamurti is quoted as saying in his *Collected Works*, "[T]he mind seeks very easily a drug to make it content with virtues, with qualities, with ideas, with actions, it establishes a routine and gets caught up in it. We are quite familiar with that, but our problem is not how to calm discontent, but how to keep it smoldering, alive, vital."

"Why did he help me the most? Because no matter where I thought I had gotten to, he cut it down. I never got one compliment in all the time I worked with him," Rosenberg said. "Was he perfect? No, he could be a real jerk. Yet he was extraordinary. Do I love him? Yes. Am I grateful to him the way I am to my own blood parents? Absolutely." As he puts it, "Krishnamurti was my first teacher and basically my last."

———

After years of wandering and absorbing lessons from the great figures of the era, Rosenberg returned to Cambridge. He taught meditation at Insight Meditation Society (IMS) and other established institutions. He also led classes at more informal venues: bookstores, acupuncture offices, art studios. At the end of talks, he would pass the hat. He gave individual dharma interviews at the Golden Temple Restaurant, a Sikh establishment in Harvard Square. Pre–social media, he posted notices on trees and lampposts of upcoming classes. He was spiritually wealthy and otherwise impoverished.

At a meditation retreat that Rosenberg was leading in the early 1980s, a middle-aged woman showed up. "I don't read auras, but if I did, she seemed gray. There was so much sadness and depression there, and the intensity with which she paid attention was overwhelming," Rosenberg said. The woman attended week after week, throwing her whole being into the effort and clearly benefiting. "She really got it." As they came to know each other, she was surprised to learn that Rosenberg was essentially living off charity. A person of means, she offered to buy a house that could serve as a permanent place for Rosenberg to teach and live.

At first Rosenberg was ambivalent. By then in his fifties, he was practically penniless but had always lived free as a bird and didn't relish the responsibility of running an organization. But the prospect of sharing the dharma won out. They bought a run-down, three-story Victorian between upscale Harvard Square and down-at-the-heels Central Square—an edifice that itself had seen previous lives, first as a birthing center, then as a rooming house. In 1985, Rosenberg founded the Cambridge Insight Meditation Center (CIMC)—still a hub of Buddhist instruction.

At CIMC, he intended to build a community of serious practitioners. It was an era of spiritual surfeit and easy access to every flavor of self-transcendence. Notices about meditation, yoga, Zen, Transcendental Meditation (TM), reiki, and massage vied for the attention of passersby. "Sufi dancing, insight meditation, four kinds of Zen, fifteen kinds of Tibetan Buddhism, eighteen million kinds of raja-yoga, Vedanta yoga, kundalini yoga, power yoga, powerless yoga," Rosenberg recounted in a class. "And people's minds are like the bulletin boards in Cambridge—one workshop pasted on top of another, photographs of smiling faces from all over the world. Who's smiling better? I should go to that person."

Rosenberg wanted to foster a group of doubters. He drew on the *Kalama Sutta*, part of the original Buddhist teachings. A group of people known as the Kalamas, not unlike the earnest seekers in Cambridge, were confused after listening to various gurus, yogis, and Brahmins plying their ideas. The Buddha's advice: trust your own experience. Blind obedience to any path or teacher is a recipe for failure.

Rosenberg worried that CIMC would lack a single, clear message in this college-town marketplace. A few months before it opened its doors, he had the privilege of an interview with His Holiness the Dalai Lama. How, he asked, could CIMC offer coherence in a metaphysical shopping mall? The revered monastic paused and rubbed his scalp, as he always does to signify that he is pondering a question. His advice: focus on the Four Noble Truths, the intersection of all schools of Buddhism.

Preserving Buddhist teachings has always meant walking a fine line between the conservative and the radical, between protecting what is timeless and adapting those timeless ideas to local cultures and a changing world. (As an homage to his own teachers, Rosenberg chose deep-green sitting cushions for the CIMC meditation hall, symbolizing Thailand's tropical forest, a fecund environment for Theravada Buddhism and his own training.) "We've engaged the same ancient forms practiced over the centuries—sitting, walking, and silence," said Narayan Liebenson, a longtime guiding teacher at CIMC. "Our mission was to make the teachings pertinent and relevant in these times without losing the beauty and the power of lineage." CIMC is believed to be the first nonresidential retreat center in the United States dedicated to the vipassana tradition. "Perhaps we've been a bit of a model for other daily life centers, showing that a nonresidential center in the midst of a city could embody breadth as well as depth," said Liebenson. "We've tried to offer a vision and a path that is grounded in our daily life experiences yet transforms those experiences into material for awakening."

Even as recently as 1985, meditation was off the beaten path. Making CIMC nonresidential was a critical decision for Rosenberg. He knew that it was easy for yogis to get calm and concentrated in a monastery or rural center like IMS, where three-month retreats carried a special cachet. But once the retreatants returned to their homes, families, and work, with all the attendant tensions and complications, their precious serenity often flew out the window. The raison d'être of CIMC was to throw people back into the messiness of their everyday lives.

Like all institutions, CIMC evolved. Founded by white teachers, it drew an overwhelmingly white clientele until quite recently—although its surrounding community was highly diverse. Unlike in the past, CIMC now offers affinity groups—sanghas, or communities, for individuals identifying as LGBTQIA+, elders, parents, people of color, people with disability and chronic illness, ages thirty-five and under, as well as a White Awake sangha. At first, Rosenberg resisted the change, arguing that dharma transcended identity—indeed, that its very purpose was to undercut labels and upend self-reification; in Buddhism, after all, not only are categories seen as constructions but human beings are likened to active and relational verbs, not static nouns. In recent years, though, as Rosenberg became increasingly dependent on others, his opposition softened. If belonging to affinity groups eased *dukkha*, or suffering, he was for it. Spurred by his own pain, "What I saw was, my goodness, there's no shortage of suffering in the world."

—

Though he authored three popular and widely translated books about the practice, Rosenberg steered away from spiritual celebrity, preferring to cultivate his small patch of ground in Cambridge and to focus on his own contemplative life. In his later years, he stayed within the ambit of a casual walking radius from his home. Declining countless invitations to appear as a headliner at faraway retreat centers, he never taught farther west than New York. "In the Indian tradition, some of the most respected masters don't travel or promote themselves. They just have small temples or live a regular lay life and fully attend to anyone who shows up," Daniell said. "Larry's like a temple priest. To me, that's one of his great contributions—he could have been a much bigger persona than he was."

In the early 2000s, Rosenberg had a shot at monster celebrity. His first book, *Breath by Breath: The Liberating Practice of Insight Meditation*, was selling briskly, and Oprah Winfrey invited him to her show. One dharma colleague urged him to say yes, arguing that Rosenberg's book sales would multiply a thousandfold. But Rosenberg declined, because the specified date landed in the middle of a long-planned winter self-retreat, a month of precious silence near the ocean. When he informed Winfrey's representative of his decision, the rep was dumbfounded, and said in a stunned, affectless voice, "You're turning down Oprah Winfrey." Rosenberg offered to appear on the show at another time. The rep informed him that with Winfrey, you only get one shot.

"It isn't narcissistic to want to do a retreat. It's very practical," Rosenberg told me. "The Buddha's main message is work on yourself. Anything you do for others is going to exhibit the work you've done on yourself. If you don't have a light inside of yourself, what are you going to be sharing with other people? Just empty words. For me, it wasn't complicated. I didn't even hesitate."

—

Decades ago, during a Wednesday-night dharma talk at CIMC, a student asked, "Are you a Buddhist?" Rosenberg looked down, closed his eyes, and pondered the answer—for a seemingly endless five minutes. Finally he looked up and said, "No." Half the room was speechless and the other half elated.

As he went on to explain, he didn't know the year the Buddha was born or died. He couldn't tick off the major Buddhist holidays. He didn't remember the names of the Buddha's storied attendants. But he could enthusiastically sign up for Buddhism as a guide to living, as a set of teachings to heal the troubled heart. When he got home that night, his wife, Galina, chided him with common sense. "You're confusing people," she said. "Just say you're a Buddhist." He took her advice.

For many years Rosenberg referred to a kind of self-torture around his spiritual identity—an odd affliction for one who teaches a tradition predicated on identitylessness. But he described the condition as, at times, "excruciatingly painful." Buddhist or not a Buddhist? Zen or vipassana? Buddha or Krishnamurti? In this restless, comparing state of mind, he came to believe that Krishnamurti was like Manjushri, the male bodhisattva often depicted in Buddhist iconography wielding a flaming sword, symbolizing the transcendent wisdom that slices through the veil of ignorance. By contrast, Thich Nhat Hanh was like Avalokiteshvara, the bodhisattva of infinite compassion, often depicted as a female. Which doesn't mean that Rosenberg was simplistically reductive; he knew from his own interactions that Krishnamurti had a tender side and that Thich Nhat Hanh could be hard as nails. On the dharma path, he says, those outwardly disparate qualities are integrated.

At another point, Rosenberg felt he was wrestling with two formidable father figures: Nathan Rosenberg and Jiddu Krishnamurti. His father's absolutist position against religion had put a lid on his ability to openly acknowledge devotion to any tradition. "He was the most *anti-religious* anti-religious person who ever existed," Rosenberg said, to the point where "there was nothing left." When Rosenberg set out on the Buddhist path, his atheist father was aghast. It took years for Rosenberg to admit, even to himself, that he loved the teachings of the Buddha and Krishnamurti.

Krishnamurti also opposed organized religion, but he was "the most *religious* anti-religious person I ever met," said Rosenberg. He asked the real religious question—Is there anything sacred?—and spent his life finding the answer.

Perhaps Rosenberg's antagonistic identities go back even further—to childhood, to the Jews he grew up with who had escaped the Russian pogroms and the Holocaust and were trying to learn how to be Americans. In his little enclave of Brooklyn, the question was "Am I Jewish or am I American?" Later, on the dharma path, the question became "Am I Jewish or am I Buddhist?" Oddly, it was the Indian meditation master Vimala Thakar who set Rosenberg straight. She assured him he needn't be at war with his heritage. "You have very strong roots. It gives you a source of strength. But is that all there is?" She reminded him that "if you meditate, you go beyond being Jewish or anything else you think you are." Rosenberg realized that the fourteen generations of rabbis that animate many of his autobiographical tidbits "are not the deepest part of me, and I know it."

So where does he think he belongs? To a larger tradition without a name. "I feel part of that lineage of people who care, who are trying to do something, who understand that unless you change inwardly, the outer is just going to be repeating itself over and over again."

Yet in recent years, Rosenberg seemed to return to his Jewish roots, becoming strikingly like his father. "To whom do I have the displeasure of speaking?" he would churlishly joke when I called. One day, he signed an email "Lazer (Yiddish name)." As he once confessed, "I don't see myself much visually. When I do see myself, I realize I don't feel old inside. But I look and say, 'It's an old Jew sitting there.'"

—

A number of Rosenberg's later-in-life classes were titled "Relationship as a Mirror." "It's obvious that you can get very good at sitting, and you can be very good at retreats," he said, "and still make a mess in your daily life."

Rosenberg's mirror has been Galina Rosenberg, his wife since 1991. Although she is his mirror, she is not his mirror image. Born in the Soviet Union, she spent her early life in Siberia, where both of her parents served as physicians in an army camp. When she was thirteen, her family moved to Moscow, where she was steeped in high culture. She earned a nursing degree in the USSR. In her thirties and soon to leave her marriage, she and her daughters emigrated to the United States.

"I spotted her. We went out on a date. And I was finished. My goose was cooked," Rosenberg said. He calls her "the love of my life"—his one and only marriage, a union he entered at the age of fifty-eight. As a wisdom teaching, he would often describe in class their carnivore-versus-vegetarian refrigerator skirmishes: Galina's repulsive herring, chicken, beef, and cheeses on one shelf, his pristine organic vegetables on another; sometimes the battle lines got crossed. He made broad humor of the fact that she is from Siberia and loves smelly fish. From this caricature, I expected Galina to look like a pre-Soviet peasant woman, with a long babushka, a heavy overcoat, and a raw, weathered face. So I was taken aback when I saw her for the first time—tall and regal, attired in an elegant flowered dress, her arm in his, the two of them walking *passeggiata*-style back from a restaurant before a class. She could have appeared in a Lancôme cosmetics ad: high cheekbones, dark-haired, sloe-eyed, with a warm and benevolent expression that offsets his more cerebral and appraising mien.

"If the world exists to set me free, Galina's been sent here from Siberia to set me free," he said with a smile. But he elaborated, in a more serious tone, "We are soulmates. Our bond is much more powerful than where we were born or how much academics we had." They have a natural affinity, sharing the Russian Jewish culture and emotional temperament—with vivid feelings close to the surface, easy and demonstrative affection, a keen sense of the absurd.

Rosenberg said that his deepest understanding of metta has come from his marriage. "How so?" I asked. "Just by living with someone with such a big heart. Not complicated," he replied. She often sweetly punctures his reputation as a dharma master, exposing him as a commonplace patriarch. One day at dinnertime, Rosenberg sat at his kitchen table, eating like a trencherman, oblivious to the rest of the world, as Galina and I and a Russian home aide named Olga hovered over him. "Today," Galina observed, "he has his three geishas."

—

As I was writing this, Rosenberg kept telling me not to romanticize him. "Don't make me into a saint," he said. "If I feel discomfort with something you write, that's okay. I'll get comfortable with the discomfort." But he brought this up so many times that I wondered if, subconsciously, he actually hoped I would idealize him. Was a strange kind of inverse narcissism at play? Finally, after the fourth or fifth reminder, I told him bluntly, "Larry, I never thought you were a saint." He said sheepishly, "That makes two of us."

For twenty-three years I came away from his classes inspired. But in our personal interactions, he was often deliberately imperfect, a bad boy testing the limits of civility, sometimes seeming to channel his father's surliness. One clear winter night when I was walking him home from class, Jupiter gleamed bright white in the western sky. I said, "Do you know what planet that is? It's Jupiter." He responded, "Who cares?" It was the same kind of exchange we would have when I would point out trees or birds by name—an enthusiasm for taxonomy, I suppose. Perhaps Rosenberg was implicitly teaching Dogen's notion of intimacy or nonseparation, the idea that words and labels create a distance from immediate experience—or maybe he was just grumpy from sciatica. Another nonduality lesson came up during our time together on the book. After I had turned off my voice recorder at the end of an interview, Galina appeared in the doorway of Rosenberg's meditation room and greeted us. To fill in some blanks in my reporting, I took the opportunity to ask a few questions about their life together. "Stop being a journalist," Rosenberg snapped. This time, his critique was spot-on.

Having had the privilege of observing his decline up close—of being allowed into his mind and world—was perhaps my greatest dharma lesson, a teaching about relinquishment and no-self. Sturdy and supple all his life, with a kind of droll pugnacity, he now looked solemn and gaunt. The indignities of aging have been Rosenberg's runway to death. He can't feel his legs and feet. The tremors in his hands make it difficult to eat—sometimes, an aide spoons food into his mouth. An attendant showers and dries and dresses and wipes him. An inveterate foot traveler, he now needs a metal walker and someone to steady him; soon he will be in a wheelchair. His pain scale never dips to zero.

Being older, Rosenberg remains Kabat-Zinn's "windshield"—but now, their rideshare is speeding through aging and sickness toward death. They still talk almost exclusively about dharma and the present moment. "Only. Only. Only," Kabat-Zinn said. "But we also check in and find out how the other is doing."

"Probably on my deathbed I'll be teaching if there's anyone who wants to learn this stuff," Rosenberg said. According to Doug Phillips, "He has made himself a vessel for the dharma and the dharma has worked on him pretty diligently. The dharma has done Larry as much as Larry has done the dharma." As he sees it, the foundation of Rosenberg's teaching and practice is "don't-know mind"—a mind that is emotionally and intellectually flexible, a beginner's mind, a mind open to everything, even in his final years. "To me," Phillips said, "that's truly the religious stance." Strangely, with Rosenberg's nearly bald head shaven, his cheeks pink from rosacea, his eyes wide and unblinking and appearing to absorb the entire scene at once, he often resembles an infant avatar of don't-know.

I once suggested using the term *master class* in the book's subtitle, but Rosenberg nixed the phrase because it implied that he was a spiritual master, which was far from the truth. Yet through every possible medical calamity and emotional impasse, he hasn't faltered. He has carried on through hospitalizations and rehab stays, respiratory infections and other close calls, total dependence on others, worries about finding home care, fears about Galina's health, his own deterioration—

everything. As Rosenberg once recalled, the Japanese Soto Zen priest Kosho Uchiyama Roshi was asked why he never allowed himself to be called a Zen master. He replied, "Because I don't think life can be mastered."

—

One day I read Rosenberg a quote from Thich Nhat Hanh: "Are you willing to arrange your schedule in such a way that you could die in peace tonight?" He had often said that, in his increasing debility, he feels both more fear of dying and more confidence that he will not be helpless when death approaches. "If you're really practicing, what you're practicing is the art of dying," he said. "Remember, it's direct seeing. All that will be different is that it'll be a moment when you're dying." During a hospital stay a few years ago after a small stroke, direct seeing taught him that when it comes time for him to die, he will not be able to count on anyone—not Galina, not his friends, not his teachers: nobody. All he could count on is awareness. "It's not something you grow or cultivate. It *is*. It *is*."

A central practice of Buddhism is *maranasati*, or death awareness. Monastics are instructed to imagine the human body in various stages of decay, a reminder that they, too, will perish and decompose. These teachings revolve around the inevitability of death, the uncertainty of when you will die, and the fact that nothing but dharma can help you at the time of death. Formal death-awareness practices are designed to help people edge closer to feelings that convincingly approximate the moments of actual demise.

In his physical decline, Rosenberg has often argued with his body, trying to talk it out of its infirmities, but now his body is talking back—loud and, he notes, with a Brooklyn accent. Rosenberg's severe spine-related pain likely goes back to a grueling physical regimen when he started out on the path. "Whatever I learned in yoga, I did at one hundred and twenty-five percent. It took me ten years to 'master' full lotus," he said. "I realized I wanted to be a picture-postcard-perfect yogi. It was striving. It was ego. It was ambition. Somehow I got this stupid idea that sitting in full lotus would take me to wisdom and freedom." In his helplessness, he is, perhaps for the first time, no longer practicing dharma from the top down but from the bottom up.

He says he has accepted "the limited round of life that I have." While he used to chant the universal prayers paying homage to the Buddha each morning before drinking his green tea—NAMO TASSA BHAGA-VATO ARAHATO SAMMA SAMBUDDHASSA—he has whittled that down to just one practice: awareness of what is, a statement that practice and life are the same. "I've experienced great joy in being house-bound," he said. Rather than seeing his condition as a prison, he has made it into a self-retreat. "I couldn't be deriving some joy from life if I didn't have an inner joy that's independent of conditions," he told me.

He watches movies. Brigades of friends and former students bring him home-cooked meals. He reads the books that became touch-stones on the path—Shunryu Suzuki's *Zen Mind, Beginner's Mind*, Ajahn Chah's *Food for the Heart*, Krishnamurti's *Commentaries on Living*, books by Dogen and the Japanese Urasenke tea tradition's Grand Master Sen Soshitsu XV. And he draws specific inspiration from his teachers—Thich Nhat Hanh, who lay in a coma for months before he died; Krishnamurti, who suffered agonizing pancreatic cancer at the end; Ajahn Chah, who was virtually paralyzed and unable to speak for ten years before he passed away.

Bedbound each day from about 9:00 pm to 9:00 am, Rosenberg passes the time meditating. At night, his cold hands shake so much that it keeps him awake. He reflects on Nhat Hanh, who once con-fided to Rosenberg that he couldn't sleep at night because he was depressed about old students and friends who had died in jail in Vietnam. "He'd just lie there and breathe and send as much love as he could to everyone," Rosenberg said. "When I can't sleep, that's what I practice with."

Rosenberg often says that old age is hard work and a full-time job, with so many appointments and phone calls and arrangements and caregivers. Sometimes he loses his mindfulness. "I'll realize, oh, I'm not practicing. The conditions have caught me." After a few minutes, his awareness returns and he has adapted to the new set of challenges. One day, I dropped off some pastry and asked how he was. He was calmly lying back in a recliner in his meditation room. "Pretty good," he said lightly, "for someone who is completely disabled." At other times, he seemed almost preternaturally still—not the stillness of old age and exhaustion but of alertness and attunement.

I've often told him that, in his physical incapacity, he has "walked the talk." He responds that it's just "waking up, waking up, waking up." That commitment is a training in "how not to have a head-on collision with the law of impermanence," he said. "The thing that has helped the most is a deep, deep—much deeper than I ever had before—understanding of the law of impermanence. Everything is impermanent and uncertain. I knew that years ago but not the way I know it now."

Even in the maelstrom of old age, Rosenberg cannot *not* be a teacher. If someone asks him a dharma question, he responds, "Don't get me started"—not because he is irritated but because once he begins answering, he won't be able to stop until he feels he has given a complete answer. Yet even when he doesn't answer, he manages to dispense wisdom. "I'll ask him a question every now and then, like, 'What's the most important thing you want people to know about what you teach?' Or, 'What's your practice these days, Larry?'" Phillips said. "He would look at me and give me one of those almost surprised looks and say, 'Nothing.' And we would both just howl. What a teaching!"

Despite these hints of proper self-relinquishment, Rosenberg continues to crave life—so much so that I've wondered whether he has actually made peace with death. "I want my life to continue—my wife, my friends, everything. Hey, I don't want to give this up," he said. "I shouldn't feel that way because I'm a dharma teacher. But I do." When Rosenberg spent weeks in a rehab hospital in late 2023, after breaking his hip in a fall, his face would light up when Galina brought thermoses of miso soup and green tea, when Daniell arrived with brown rice and tempeh, when friends fetched vegan food from his favorite restaurant, when I sent lemon-currant scones. Most of all, he fixed his attention on returning to Galina and his home and his life.

"He wasn't being transcendent. He was like, 'I want to do this as long as I can,'" Daniell said. "That's a lot of what Larry's teaching is: loving life. He doesn't care if it would be called clinging. He's being fully human, and that's his teaching." One day, after an interview at his home, I packed up my gear, leaned over his recliner where he was swaddled in blankets, and said goodbye. He clasped my hand. "I can't let it go," he said. "It's called attachment."

For Daniell, "There was a transmission quality in how he was saying, 'I'm going to go out in the saddle. I'm going out as I've lived.'" Oddly, not until Rosenberg was ninety-one years old did it occur to me to ask, "Larry, have you ever ridden a horse?" He replied, "A real horse? No." But as he himself might say, "Who cares?"

In his book *Lastingness: The Art of Old Age*, Nicholas Delbanco profiles trailblazers in the visual arts, literature, and music who held on to their creative drive and ingenuity well into old age. Most of these men and women, he wrote, "have tried for, if not constancy, consistency: the daily, weekly, monthly, yearly accretion of what can be seen, read, or heard. And there's something doubly moving in the image of an elder artist, bent to the page or the canvas or score, meditating the next mark." When I think of those artistic giants meditating the next mark, I also think of Rosenberg.

Among the artists who remained incandescent into old age was Katsushika Hokusai, the great Japanese painter and printmaker of the Edo period, who died in 1849 at age eighty-nine. As it happens, one of Rosenberg's favorite passages comes from Hokusai:

From the age of six I had a mania for drawing the form of things. By the time I was fifty I had published an infinity of designs. But all I have produced before the age of seventy is not worth taking into account. At seventy-three, I have learned a little about the real structure of nature, of animals, plants, trees, birds, fishes and insects. In consequence, when I am eighty, I shall have made still more progress. At ninety I shall penetrate the mystery of things; at one hundred I shall certainly have reached a marvelous stage; and when I am one hundred and ten, everything I do, be it a dot or a line, will be alive. I beg those who live as long as I to see if I do not keep my word. —written at the age of seventy-five by me, once Hokusai, today Gwako Rojin, The Old Man Mad About Drawing (1835)

I asked Rosenberg why he loved that quote. He said, "Because for me, the verbal teachings are so neat and tidy. But I've always felt that life is messier than the teachings, and I will continue doing this practice until the last breath."

—

Rosenberg often says, "The deepest healing happens in silence." But what exactly does that mean? What is the healing and what is the silence?

His accounts of two profound healing experiences in his own life give a sense of this process. The first was during a six-month self-retreat at Insight Meditation Society. It was winter. He had already been there several months, and his mind was quiet, tender. One afternoon, meditating in his room, he was disturbed by the commotion of other retreatants entering the building with their boots on, stomping off the snow. The racket set off a skein of memories from his childhood. "Suddenly—and I don't know how to describe this except as an extremely vivid set of images—I was in Nazi Germany, and those stomping boots were the SS troops coming to get me," he recounted in *Breath by Breath*. "I felt a kind of terror that I had never experienced before, and haven't since. The horrifying visual images that kept coming to mind seemed utterly real. I was trembling, nauseous, sweating, weeping, going through deep physical as well as emotional pain. It was an extremely complicated and convincing mind state." Looking back, he suspects that this depth of fear would not have arisen if he hadn't been ready to touch it with calm concentration, the fruit of years of practice. He brought full attention to the images and to his physical and emotional state. He'd be mindful, his mindfulness would slip, and he'd turn to the breath to bring him back to the moment. He lost track of time. Finally, his attention became unwavering. "There was complete intimacy with the energy of fear, observation without the separation of a self-conscious observer," he wrote. After minutes, or hours, everything broke apart. The terrifying images vanished. He wept and fell into a deep peace.

In our conversation, he added a caveat: "Relative peace. I don't know if I'm done with it." He realized that his lifelong obsession with the Holocaust was what psychotherapists call "counterphobic": a consuming intellectual interest rooted in buried fear. He understood that this disabling fear was an energy that could be dissolved when he held on to mindfulness and didn't identify with his physical sensations.

The second major healing hit closer to home. After Rosenberg's father died, sadness overwhelmed him. Nathan Rosenberg was his hero, his exemplar, his first wisdom teacher. When Rosenberg scattered his father's ashes in the Atlantic Ocean around Plum Island, a friend lent him her cottage for a personal retreat. Rosenberg, then in his late sixties, thought he had finished grieving. But what came up, to his surprise, was a burning resentment against his father for unkind words about a non-Jewish woman Rosenberg had dated decades earlier—wounding hypocrisy from the man who had always expressed contempt for religion. Just as he taught his students, Rosenberg started with the resentment and stayed with it. His mind turned to the pain and suffering that his father's family had endured to emigrate to America. "But I didn't get there by trying to get there. I got there by acknowledging my deep disappointment in him for judging her, because I knew she was not an anti-Semite or anything resembling it." Then his emotions took another unexpected turn. He felt immense sorrow, the pain of loss that he hadn't permitted himself to feel. A wave of vulnerability and betrayal swept over him. "My consciousness got transported right into the fact of vulnerability—it wasn't an idea."

In that tsunami of feelings, the Buddha's teaching changed for him. "Even though I'd read it, studied it, practiced it, even taught it, it went dramatically deeper," he said. "The notion, which I didn't know I was carrying even until my father was ninety, was that my father was invulnerable. He was a very strong personality, physically and otherwise. My notion was 'Daddy is always going to be here.' I didn't know I still had traces of that. When I finally got the full impact of 'Bye-bye. Gone. This is it,' I felt betrayed by my own ignorance, my own gullibility, my own refusal or inability to face exactly what was happening. This was a childish kind of delusion, which I still had as a grown man.

"I allowed myself—allowed myself? I *felt*, and *what is* took me there. K's teaching is brilliant. You've got to keep being with 'what is, what is, what is, what is, what is, what is,' and it takes you somewhere—it takes you to truth. What came out was a tremendous pain of loss of my father, whom I loved. And then I had a good cry. And then I was done."

A few months later, after he shared these stories, I asked him if the dramatic healing experiences were, in the popular jargon, breakthroughs. "I don't think in terms of breakthroughs anymore," he said. "I think in terms of just being with what is, period."

MADELINE DREXLER

October 2024

# 1

## The Art of Meditation

MEDITATION IS A GEM for the human race. It's not a luxury item. I don't narrowly mean *vipassana*—insight meditation—or any of the other wonderful forms that exist. I mean just setting aside time in silence to be with yourself exclusively. It's not narcissistic pampering or self-indulgence unless you're intending it that way. Don't even use the word *meditation*. Just sit silently for a certain amount of time each day, where the only job you have is to be with yourself and be in touch.

Continuity is more important than sitting a lot one day and then letting four days go by and forgetting all about it. Keep that flame going every day. It's a mnemonic device that reminds you how important awareness is. Start the day off by sitting. Even days when you literally have no time, you can usually find five minutes. If you know that meditation is valuable and you have a sense of what that value is, then you will look at your life and find ways to reorganize it so that contemplative time is protected. It takes real intention.

Some days you won't feel like sitting. Some days you will feel resistance. You may wonder: Why meditate? Why bother with all of this? What's the point? Don't march yourself at gunpoint onto your cushion. It's not cod liver oil. It's you taking care of yourself, setting aside time where the only thing you have to do is attend to how it is for you to be alive at that moment. On this path, I don't think we can simulate urgency. It's like falling in love or getting a joke—sometimes we genuinely don't have it.

On the other hand, we have many, many minds. If you only sit when you feel like it, you're only going to get to know the mind that likes to sit. One piece of advice that was given to me very early on by a Korean Zen master—Seung Sahn Sunim, may he rest in peace—was "Keep the mind that decided to practice." Of all the different minds, stay with that one. In the Tibetan tradition, there are ways of lighting a fire under your behind. Reflecting on how short life is and how precious the human birth is—and how it is slipping through our fingers. Out of that can come a rush of energy: I can't afford to dillydally. In the teachings of the Buddha, there's no ambiguity about the purpose of meditation. He said it's about one thing and one thing only: the elimination of suffering and sorrow from the human condition.

The bedrock of Buddhism is inquiry. The Buddha loved questions that came from suffering and pain. But there were a lot of questions he didn't answer—he felt they didn't lead to the end of suffering. I feel the same way, that I would be doing a person a disservice by getting into idle, philosophic, ontological discussions that go nowhere. They're good for coffeehouses or when you're courting, but they don't take you out of suffering. So the Buddha was extremely practical when he said don't turn away from what is, don't turn away from the facts of now.

The facts of now lead to perhaps the most important instruction: start with where you are. Years ago, two Western monks and I were in Korea. As soon as we arrived, we got sick. For weeks we couldn't hold down food. When the retreat started, there was a koan—a phrase that helps to arouse great doubt and great energy. You take up the question and ask it of yourself, not in words but as a deep pondering. The koan that we were working with was "What am I?" We could barely crawl along and get to the meditation hall, let alone ask the question "What am I?" Our question was "What am I doing here and how can I get back to the good old United States of America?"

We went to one of the teachers, and he said, "It's true that an ardent yogi asking the question is ideal. It's wonderful to be on fire with the question 'What am I?' But when you're sick, it can just be a small 'What am I?' not a big 'WHAT AM I?'" You use a sick person's energy. You're in it, you're going with it, you're floating with it. You haven't given up, you're not lost in it. At the same time, you're not unrealistically pushing yourself, because you'll just be more exhausted. Work with the energy you have, because that's your life in that moment.

I'll introduce another term, the *kilesas*, sometimes translated as "mental afflictions." These include greed or that in us which is always wanting something, which feels something lacking and wants to correct that lack; hatred or aggression or aversion; and delusion or confusion or unawareness. Those three energies, according to the teaching, are embedded in the human heart. It's not saying that we're bad people, only that we're suffering people.

You probably didn't even know you had kilesas until today. Now you have a new affliction. You're going to go home and say, "I have three kilesas. I thought I only had an eating problem or a drinking problem—but they're kilesas!" If you can see that, you don't have to slavishly go after everything that turns up in the mind, clutch it, and be taken on a trip by it. Why do we keep doing something that doesn't work?

Here, I'd like to disinfect a certain word, which I think is a beautiful word but has been misused since the Korean War: *brainwashing.* We know that soldiers were captured by the Communist Chinese and Koreans. They brainwashed the American soldiers into having views that weren't their own. If you can disinfect your own mind for the moment, just hear the term—it's beautiful, it's extraordinary: *brainwashing.* Could we really wash the brain clear of all the stuff that's in there? It's a description of what we are doing. In the Tibetan teachings, the kilesas—greed, hatred, and delusion—are called the three poisons or toxins. This is a way of cleansing the mind of those toxins, of those ways of viewing life, of inhabiting the present moment in ways that turn out to be destructive.

We have to be warriors with ourselves. Now, the warrior metaphor can be tricky: some people like it and other people hate it. To me, it has nothing to do with ego or being macho—in fact, it can be quiet and unassuming. It has to do with inner strength. It has to do with refinement, softness, compassion, love—but also honesty and clarity, which give it its warrior-like aspect. In this tradition, you may have seen statues in which a meditating yogi holds a sword that cuts through ignorance; sometimes there's a flame at the tip of the sword.

Our practice centers on perfect seeing, and that seeing is our weapon—because what the kilesas hate most of all is light. They hate being looked at with interest, with a discerning eye. They hate balanced, open attention. They hate being understood. One of the reasons they hate it is because they lose their energy when you examine them.

## We Are Subject and Student

When you look at your mind, you are enacting the essence of this practice, which is learning how to live. Here I should briefly explain the Buddhist definition of "mind." The Sanskrit and Pali word *citta* is often translated into English as "mind," but that doesn't quite do it justice because in English, "mind" has a cerebral connotation. A more accurate translation of citta is "heart-mind," because it includes emotions as well as thoughts. In the Theravada tradition, citta is the subjective mind, the mind of our inner experiences. So when you see the word *mind* in this teaching, you would not be wrong to substitute the word *heart* because that conveys the richer Buddhist sense of the term.

With that said, it takes tremendous humility to look at your mind or heart-mind, because you have to admit that, in important ways, you don't know how to live. That's very hard for so-called adults to do, maybe harder for men than for women. If, like me, you're from a Russian Jewish culture, you're always correct. I myself have never been wrong in my entire life. My father, he never made a mistake. Amazing what a lineage I come from.

We think we're independent, but actually we're in thrall to our minds. It's an epic struggle, like any of the classic struggles. Here, the struggle is between the kilesas—which have the upper hand in a human being, especially one who is not on any spiritual path—and wisdom.

In dharma, *wisdom* has a meaning different from its conventional meaning. In English, the word *wisdom* usually means worldly wisdom: knowing enough to put on a raincoat when it's pouring, knowing enough to set aside money for your retirement. In other words, there are ways in which you arrange life and act that are beneficial and not harmful for you and others. But the deepest wisdom, the kind of wisdom that we're talking about—the Pali word *panna* or the Sanskrit word *prajna*—is a form of intelligence.

Here, too, we are using the word *intelligence* in a way that varies from its usual meaning. Often, the word conjures up bad memories of high school, where intelligence meant your grade or score on an IQ test; some numerical index. What I mean by intelligence is not intellect or the rational mind, although intelligence can certainly draw on that. Nor is it the use of thought or logic, as wonderful as those qualities are; it's good to have a mind that works, that can add and subtract and figure things out—it's an asset. Intelligence, as I'm using it, goes well beyond that: it is awareness and discernment in the midst of living.

Our practice is a kind of school. Our subjects are not mathematics or physics or literature but loneliness, restlessness, silence, hunger, whatever. We do not study the subjects as an external academic topic. Rather, we are both the subject and the student, and we are in the process of the awakening of intelligence—that which knows. It knows how to live, it knows what to do, it knows what's right. Wisdom delivers its truth to the heart so that the heart has no choice but to let go of the destructive patterns that do nothing but harm it, scorch it.

In a famous discourse called "The Fire Sermon," the Buddha said the whole world is on fire with greed, hatred, and delusion. This was long before the nuclear age. But even in the nuclear age, the real problem is not nuclear weapons—it's the minds that create and operate those weapons. There are some who feel that in the modern world, the kilesas have become extraordinarily powerful because of the breakdown of the family, the breakdown of religion—it's a field day. I'm not interested in speculating, because what's most important is for each one of us to take our own condition to heart, to examine ourselves and to see in our own life, from moment to moment, the ways in which the heart issues directives, feelings, which we follow and which produce suffering.

## An Inventory of the Mind

As the mind becomes stronger, clearer, more stable, it accesses deeper levels of wisdom. This discernment can be profound. At one point, the Buddha was asked, "How are these *arahants*"—people who have finished the journey—"different from the rest of us?" He said, "One way is that they know that everything that arises passes away." Maybe we would all say in unison, "Well, we know that." But do we?

How do we strengthen the wisdom factor? How can we make it so strong that the heart can't fail to get the message? *Samadhi*, or concentration practice, is needed. When you listen carefully, you'll hear what the mind is preoccupied with, how it spends its time. I've often asked my mind, "How do you spend your day? What do you do?" Sometimes I conduct an inventory. It's ridiculous how my mind spends its time.

Perhaps we feel angry or depressed or deprived. We feel confused or in conflict because something came up and we latched on to it and made it real. It's like blowing air into a balloon and then believing what's written on it. Or like painting dragons. An ancient Chinese artist who was an expert in painting dragons one day did such a good job that he walked into his studio and ran out terrified; he was frightened by one of the dragons that he himself had painted. That's what we're doing. We believe in our own stuff. It's a one-person show. We're all monologists creating things that we run away from. Then we need techniques to help us cure the problem that we've created.

As you become better able to carry out the instructions, you learn that you have a kind of sanctuary. As the samadhi, or intense concentration, gets deeper, it becomes like a home. It's a resting place, which we desperately need. We need to rest from all of the turmoil that the mind throws up and has been throwing up for many years—some would say many lifetimes. As the capacity to stay with one object develops, we create a place of stability that we can go to rather than be taken on a journey by these destructive tendencies. Once we do that, the energy of the kilesas is weakened.

Samadhi provides us with not only stability but also a place to heal, because it nurtures a certain happiness that's necessary for human beings. It's a happiness that's not dependent on external conditions. With this happiness, no one has told you that you're handsome or beautiful or intelligent. No one has given you a lot of money as a present. It isn't necessarily a sunny day. You look around and you can't account for it. "How come I'm so happy now? I shouldn't be this happy. I'm not entitled to be this happy."

Once you begin to realize that there is already a wealth inside you, you relax. There are still many wonderful things in the world and they're to be enjoyed, but you no longer approach them as a beggar desperately looking into people's eyes to see if you're all right, searching for some kind of confirmation. We all do it—until we don't. We find out that there is a fulfillment intrinsic to being a human being. It's a portable, internal happiness waiting to be tapped.

Let's say the heart has tasted a bit of joy, a bit of peace in dropping into this place of stability. You're in a much better situation or condition to investigate, to probe into yourself, to find out all the things that you say you want to find out. It's self-inquiry, self-understanding, self-knowledge. We work with fears, loneliness, boredom, anxieties, and moods that we don't like. If the heart can get some degree of happiness from its samadhi work, then it has a fighting chance to look at these difficult states.

Years ago, it struck me as quite hilarious that the practice of developing samadhi was to get me to be happy enough to look at my unhappiness in a way that I could do something about it. Strange, but I guess it's necessary. Unless there's some degree of fulfillment or stability, every time loneliness or fear comes up, we're blown away, we're swallowed, we drown in it.

Then investigation takes place, and that's the work of vipassana—to probe into the body and mind to see impermanence, or *anicca*, at work. If there's suffering, to be able to see it. If there's emotional resistance to our suffering, to be able to see that. To examine what we mean by "self." What is the whole planet devoted to satisfying? Someone's self, lots of individual selves. What is this "self"? What is it really? In answering that, we're doing the work of wisdom.

## Dog versus Lion

When we observe the self, we can't help noticing that the self is self-obsessive. We're like a dog running after a bone. This has always intrigued me—seeing someone throwing a bone or a piece of wood, and the dog runs right after it and brings it back. Throw it again, the dog runs after it. It goes on indefinitely. Dogs seem happy to run after whatever you throw; the thrower gets tired before the dog does.

But the lion doesn't run after an object. The lion just sits there—powerful, stable, with dignity—and looks at where the object is coming from. Can you feel the difference? The lion doesn't unthinkingly run after a bone or whatever object crosses its field of vision. It watches: Where did that come from? It looks at the person who threw it. That image is wonderful for what we're doing. We all have dog mind. "The dog runs after the bone" means that the mind is constantly throwing things and we're constantly running after them. With lion mind, we stay at the source. We stay right there at the mind while all kinds of tantalizing thoughts claim our attention—a memory that makes us feel bad, a worry, an anticipation, and nice fantasies, too. We do a lot of running after the bone.

How can we become a lion rather than a dog? We begin by seeing how active the mind is, how preoccupied. If you're new at this, it can be quite discouraging, especially if you have a well-paid and highly respected job. Perhaps you have an advanced degree and are an excellent brain surgeon or accountant. Suddenly you see that your mind is totally out of control. You're the president of a bank and you can't even follow one in-breath. When you come down to it, the world is being run by people with minds like this.

If you have the stomach to stay in the lion mode and begin to see this, you can attain something. It's called "attaining the cascading mind." A mind that's cascading, like a waterfall, is wild. You might say, "Well, what kind of attainment is that?" It's an attainment because we see our predicament. We see, "Oh, this is the way my mind is"—the mind that's signing checks, deciding to get married, raising children, leading governments.

Sometimes the cascading mind perseverates—entertains the same thoughts over and over again. I have a homemade remedy that you won't find in any Buddhist book. Let's say you have a compulsive thought. You have it again and again. Start counting each time you have the thought. "He said, then I said.": One. "He said, then I said.": Two. When you get to seven or eight, you can't help but have a good laugh at your own expense. It is so ridiculous because nothing good comes out of it. It's draining, it's tiring. One time I got to nine, and I couldn't stop laughing at how stupid it was. Realizing the futility of perseverating helps siphon off the energy being squandered on thoughts that are harming you and that are not doing the other people in your life any good, either.

## The Way Out Is In

The First Noble Truth says, "There is suffering." It's not saying that life is suffering. It's saying that part of being alive includes suffering. One of the beautiful aspects of this approach is how ordinary and mundane and simple it is, how available to everyone. You believe in God? You're a Christian? You're a Muslim? You're an atheist? Fine. Do you suffer? Yes. Okay, then you're eligible, you qualify. You're authorized personnel, as they say in the military.

The Second Noble Truth is that there is a cause of our suffering. If there were no cause, then we would be stuck with it. And if you can't see that cause and understand it, how can you get free of it? All too often, we project the cause of our suffering onto our situation or other people. There's no denying what we call stressors. The world is not an easy place to live in; the body ages and develops afflictions and inevitably dies. But we have a stake in how we relate to what's happening to us.

The Third Noble Truth is that there is healing, well-being, cessation of suffering. And the Fourth Noble Truth is the Eightfold Path, which is a guide to the end of suffering through ethical conduct (*sila*), concentration, and wisdom.

Let's start with the First Noble Truth. Do you understand that you're suffering? When I've taught this, some people, believe it or not, have said, "Oh, I'm not suffering, I'm okay." You have to really worry about those people. It means they're totally blocked or have some kind of commitment to never feel anything painful.

Wisdom is seeing with the eyes of the dharma rather than with the eyes of ignorance. Wisdom is in the service of the art of living. Yet we don't seem to have much interest in that. We're interested in our standard of living, how much we earn—but not in the quality of our life. At this point, most human beings take better care of their car or garden than they do their own heart and mind.

Today, there's increasing interest in questions like "Is there life after death?" Many books on the subject have been published—on reincarnation, rebirth, previous lives, death visions. Mediums report back from the dead. It's on talk shows, books, videos. Is there life after death? It's a fascinating and worthwhile question. But what we're taking up here is a different question: Is there life before death? And if so, what quality? Is this life the way we want to live?

Dharma practice is an attempt to turn our present priorities upside down. It says that we're fully responsible for our own happiness and unhappiness, and that we've got to see how we harm ourselves through greed, anger and aggression, and ignorance. If we don't learn how to live, then this is what the world looks like. We can't complain when there's so much suffering because it comes about through ignorance. Here, ignorance does not mean lack of knowledge or information. We're ignorant of ourselves, ignorant of how our own heart works.

With wisdom you begin to see that there are systematic ways in which you're inattentive, that in certain realms of your life you seem to be highly unmotivated to pay attention. If you see you're inattentive, there's a good chance that it has to do with anxiety, perhaps harking back to an early experience in life. Psychiatry has documented that beautifully. Sometimes when you see attachments to experiences that no longer exist but that rule your present life, those are clues to areas you need to take on as training, as a practice for special attention. We each have different areas of vulnerability, circumstances where we tune out. You probably know yours.

The Buddha is telling us, "Look inside." Thich Nhat Hanh, one of my teachers who is sorely missed, would say things like, "The way out is in." In other words, if you want to break out and be free, go inside. We tend to look for freedom outside. That counts, too—human beings should have the freedom to voice their views, to vote, to assert themselves politically and economically. But the deep inner freedom—the way out—is in. You have to see whether you are free outwardly and enslaved inwardly.

## The Man with the Adams Hat

When I was growing up, there was a commercial: "I go for a man who wears an Adams hat." I couldn't wait to grow up so I could get an Adams hat. Does it make you wise? No, it just makes you someone with an Adams hat. I was the same jerk with or without the Adams hat.

Bone-deep understanding of yourself comes from intimate and often sustained seeing. Sometimes it's just a second or two. It's not necessarily dependent on time, but it's certainly dependent on clarity, intimacy. There's no separation between you and your experience. It's a deeper kind of learning, transformative learning. It's the art of facing yourself, learning how to stop running away. From what? From yourself.

The cutting edge of vipassana is the ability to widen our capacity to receive our own experience—widen it, deepen it, broaden it, stabilize it. I find that fascinating. We're learning to receive our own experience, not someone else's. And we seem to need a lot of help just to be with the way it is for us in a given moment. That sounds odd—you'd think that would be easy. But it turns out to be one of the most difficult things in life. We're most afraid of what's inside us.

In Buddhism, people talk about "enlightenment." I prefer the term *awakening*. The Buddha was known as someone who was fully awake. We're practicing being awake from moment to moment. We have a moment where we wake up to a breath, to a step, to a bite of food, to our job, whatever. Then we fall asleep again—we see with ordinary eyes, judging, preferring, getting caught. Then suddenly we wake up again.

We're learning how to see with what is called "the wisdom eye." It's interior looking, and it takes courage and humility to be willing to look inside, because that's the source of all our difficulties. It's also the source of our greatest riches. The journey of seeing isn't passive, fatalistic, "just walk all over me." Seeing sets in motion a dynamic energy that moves us internally. Once you start to be with what is, you transcend what is. You'll find that what we call the mind is vast. The Buddha didn't talk about it too much except to say that the original nature of the mind is luminescent. Each one of us has this capacity to flower.

Sometimes I ask people, "How's your practice going?" Very often the reports are instrumental. "My blood pressure has gotten lower." "I have more energy." "I'm more efficient." "I'm more effective." "I don't get as upset as much." It takes a while for the person to realize that there can be a certain perfume in the practice. In other words, any moment of awareness is a great way to be alive. You don't need a quasi-medical enumeration of benefits to document that this is okay to do and then have it proven by scientists for millions of dollars. You know it yourself, in the moment. There's a kindness and a lightness. In that moment, there's a different flavor to living.

The Buddha's teaching is all about waking up into freedom. We're liberating ourselves from ourselves—kind of weird. In an age that is increasingly filled with darkness, greed, hatred, and delusion, we're bringing wakefulness and light into our own life. Is it possible to be sane in a crazy world? I think it is.

But to do that, there's a certain hardiness—you could call it a spiritual hardiness or a dharma hardiness—that we need to develop. Now, hardiness here doesn't mean commonsense hardiness: you have a stocky build, a lot of energy, a kind of peasant vitality. That's nice, and if that helps you to do some of these practices, that's fine. But you can have a frail body—it has nothing to do with the body. The hardiness that I'm talking about is a willingness to enter into life, and it begins with awareness. It's opening up to just what's there. What does it mean to be alive?

Let's say there's a flow of coming and going moods, bodily conditions, thoughts, and images of the past and the future. In the Buddha's teaching, it might be three seconds when you are neither grasping nor pushing away, not escaping, not fighting, not drowning in it. In those three seconds, you're practicing being free. Sometimes this is called "the practice of liberation through nonclinging."

When we hear "liberation," we think, "Way down the pike, some-day, I'll be free." There will be a rainbow at the end, *nibbana*, nirvana, bells will go off, Steven Spielberg special effects. But ours is the *practice of liberation.* From moment to moment we bind ourselves psychologically. As soon as we see it—that grasping, that tight fist—something happens. The fist opens. The thought is just what it is. Everything is what it is. In that moment you feel freer. Then you lose it. Then you come back.

If you keep doing it, liberation grows. Sometimes there are dramatic breakthroughs—no denying it. But a lot of it is blue-collar work. Keep your denim shirts; don't throw them out. It's laboring in the vineyard, sitting after sitting.

## A Thought Is Just a Thought

When you follow the practice day in and day out, you'll soon realize that you're imprisoned by your thoughts. We get so caught up in thinking that the thinking is doing us. Thought, of course, is a magnificent, beautiful thing. But the mind does a lot of compulsive thinking. If you watch your mind, listen to how thought is being used. You're talking to yourself and you're convincing yourself, "I'm okay, I'm not okay, I'm okay, I'm not okay." It's tremendous self-obsession. It's not creative, it's not constructive, and in the extreme, it's delusion, because the mind makes up stories about anything it wants and then we believe it.

Let's say you're watching a basketball game on a large-screen television and you happen to know everything there is to know about basketball. You sit there and are perfectly able to understand what's going on. But a TV executive has decided that you need someone else to tell you what's happening. They're called play-by-play commentators, and they're paid a lot of money to tell you what you're already seeing. So while you're watching the game, someone else—in a sense, an actor trained to evoke certain moods in you—is narrating what's on the screen. If they're for the home team, they choose certain words; if they're for the visiting team, they choose other words. What you experience is a blending of images that you can see perfectly well yourself, plus voices of the announcers with their enormous enthusiasms. If you don't investigate, the outcome is an excited mind state that goes unexamined.

Instead, try turning off the sound and watching the game. It's a different experience. Then turn the sound on again and listen to the announcer cooking your experience. Turn the sound off. Turn it back on. You see that the commentators are making up stories about what's happening. Those commentators are like your mind, constantly painting word pictures about every experience and encounter.

When you're mindful of thoughts, the thoughts fall away, collapse, because thoughts are not substantial. A thought is just a thought. Did you know that? That's all it is—it's a thought. But without mindfulness, a thought is like a dream, which we then imbue with reality.

An ancient Chinese master had a deep awakening—it was obvious to everyone around him. Someone said, "What did you learn when you woke up?" The master replied, "I learned that the grass is green and the sky is blue." Now let's shift it. What if that awakened seeing was seeing into the nature and the cause of your suffering?

Liberation doesn't come from a cloud. No teacher can give it to you. There's no guru or savior. If you find one, good—I haven't, and I've had a few I consider great teachers. One of the things that was great about them is that they each made it clear that my happiness was my responsibility. My first meditation teacher was Jiddu Krishnamurti, from India. One time a woman stood up at a gathering and said, "Krishnaji, I've been listening to your teaching for thirty years, and I realized that what you've been saying all along is that you can't help us at all!" And he calmly said, "Exactly, madam." Of course, he was helpful, because after giving a teaching, he constantly and tirelessly brought you back to yourself. He helped the mind learn how to take care of itself, by itself, from itself.

### Suffering Is a Doorway to Liberation

Krishnamurti's emphasis on self-reliance aligns with the Buddha's. The Buddha said that suffering is a noble truth, but not because suffering itself is noble. If that were so, the poor world, with so many suffering people, would be crowded with nobility. It isn't. Suffering is suffering. It wears us down, it's discouraging, it ages us prematurely, it cuts off creativity, it creates all kinds of problems. But in this approach, suffering is a doorway to liberation.

The great Indian yogi Shantideva once said the greatest obstacle to spiritual progress is the absence of obstacles. Can you imagine if it were all just a breeze? The point is not whether we have obstacles but finding a new way to regard what seem to be obstacles: if only this didn't happen, if only that person didn't treat me poorly, I could have a good life. The practice is to constantly come back to the facts. We need something to go up against to bring out the best and worst in us, and to see it so that we can genuinely free ourselves from it. From this point of view, the world exists to set us free. It sounds strange, but the attitude is that whatever happens to you can help you get free as a human being. Free of what? Suffering; living in repetitive, compulsive ways that have proven to be unfulfilling or unfruitful.

Our practice is the art of pure observation—including observation of our minds. With that idea in mind, let me suggest things that are *not* observation when a difficult state arises: denying it or drowning in it, getting lost in it, identifying with it, being swallowed up by it, burned by it, bitten by it. There are all kinds of subtle escapes that don't seem to be escapes but are postponement. As things come up, we don't look at them directly. Instead, we cope with them—sometimes for years. We human beings have an amazing capacity to delay, postpone, hesitate, cope with, until finally, when we've exhausted everything else, when we have nothing else to escape to, we come to wisdom—kicking and screaming as a last resort: "Okay, I'll look at my suffering directly."

Why do we keep doing things that don't work? If your house is burning, you don't enroll in a workshop and study with a teacher to get encouragement about what steps to take next: you run out to save your life. The dharma attitude is just as urgent. Why don't we stop doing what brings us misery? Again, it requires learning how to live. But bear in mind: there is no escape from suffering. I'm not saying there isn't an end to it—I'm saying there's no escape from it. If you've seen yourself wiggle this way and that until there's no more wiggle room left, it can give you tremendous energy to get on with it, to practice.

From the Buddhist point of view, if something is true, then it can help you get free. The reason we're suffering unnecessarily is that we're not living in truth. We're living in delusion, in our imagination. Now *truth*: that's an interesting word. There's conventional reality—we all know it: red light means stop, green light means go. But our practice is beyond Buddhism, beyond any *-ism*. There's a truth that has nothing to do with any ideology or culture or point of view; with Buddhism, Christianity, Islam, inner meaning, outer meaning—that's all man-made, human. This practice, by dealing with the relative truths of our daily life as we find it, can help take us to that which is beyond constructed truth—what I would call real truth or ultimate truth.

For now, though, let's stay close to the ground. We all know the happiness that's a mind state. People are nice to me, I'm happy. People are not nice to me, I'm unhappy. I make a lot of money, I'm happy. I lose on stocks, I'm unhappy. That's up and down, and it's a hard way to go through life. First of all, it's tiring—you're spending your life between oscillations. You're also vulnerable because anything can be threatening. Our path is learning how to become comfortable with discomfort, how to not be afraid of fear, how to not be tyrannized by moods that drift through the mind.

As you examine the full range of human experience, you arrive at a place that's beyond plus and minus—and that's the whole point. Your practice takes you to something deeper. I wouldn't even call it happiness. What the Buddha is talking about is deep peace, inner peace. It's not the happiness of ecstasy, which comes and goes—and when it comes, enjoy it.

For me, there was a turning of a corner where, at a certain point I realized that even in looking at my suffering, this practice was the best thing I could do for myself. It's not because the books said so or some teacher said so. I just knew that this is the best thing I could do. Maybe there was no person called "the Buddha," maybe science will do carbon dating and find out he never existed, maybe Buddhism came out of an ancient think tank of twenty bright people. If so, I would still keep doing this—not because I'm a fanatical, ideologically committed, true-believing Buddhist but because a life of awareness and learning is the most sensible way I know how to live.

# 2

## Dharma in Daily Life

FOR MANY YEARS I lived on Ellery Street. One of my closest friends lived down the street. So I passed up and down, walking into Harvard Square, walking back up Ellery Street, walking into Harvard Square, walking back up Ellery Street. Apparently my mind liked that route. But there came a day when I looked around and, my God, I felt so dead. What was dead? The sameness of it. The same yellow fence, the same dog barking, "Bowwow, bowwow." Same neighbor coming out and saying, "Hot enough for you?" Same cars parked in the same spots. I'd seen it countless times. When I passed my friend's house—same door, same address, again and again—I realized the obstinate familiarity of memory. We're not experiencing life directly; it's conceptual experience rather than immediate, intimate experience.

Many of us don't realize it, but we're quite content with conceptual experience—even in these teachings. We hear the Four Noble Truths, we feel we understand them. Sometimes we apply them, but we apply them mainly with thinking. Real transformation is unmediated by ideas. It's to just be awake and learn. Watch what's happening in the mind and in the body—it's experiential learning.

In this case, I opened up to a kind of boredom with Ellery Street— and suddenly the street came alive. Then that feeling spread. Of course, it wasn't about Ellery Street; it was about me. And it turns out to be about life.

## Endless Paying Attention

Meditation is a way of living. It's an open inquiry into our life as we live it, from moment to moment. Sitting helps that inquiry along—quite dramatically. Long-term retreats can be enormously helpful, whether alone or in a group. But wherever you are is fine, because meditation is total respect for our own life as we live it. It's also one of the hardest things to learn. I encourage you to make the most use of this extraordinary posture and activity called sitting meditation, without throwing out or ignoring anything else in your life.

While you're sitting, you're not eating, you're not in relationship, you have no task. Your job is just to be—and that's not a small thing. To sit is also an expressive act. When you think of an expressive act, you may think of dancing, figure skating, playing a musical instrument. When you sit, it's a subtler expressive act: with dignity and composure you are simply sitting, dropping everything in order to be with yourself, using a physical posture that supports that objective. The posture itself is a statement: you are temporarily relinquishing everything but this.

Here is something that the Buddha said 2,600 years ago:

Whether going out or returning, the yogi acts with full attention. Whether looking ahead or looking around, he or she acts with full attention. Whether bending an arm or straightening it, he or she acts with full attention. . . . Whether defecating or urinating, he or she acts with full attention. Whether walking, standing, or sitting; whether resting or awake; whether talking or silent, he or she acts with full attention.

In other words, everywhere, everyplace, every posture—nothing is too trivial. Everything that we encounter is our life. Meditation is designed to bring an increasingly sensitive and clear seeing to those moments as we live them. Urinating or defecating—this is not in any way sacrilegious—is not inferior to sitting on the cushion, eating a meal, taking a walk, putting on a coat. Essentially we're learning how to live. But the art of living is not something that I give to you or that anyone else gives to you. It's not a recipe or formula. The art of living is something that each one of us digs out of our self through alert attention in the midst of our life.

We're starting to take a look at how we actually live—*actually*, how we *actually* live. It's very helpful if you can, for the moment, set aside all the theories and explanations, including the Buddha's. Just be empty-handed, real, innocent. Self-knowledge hangs on every second. The small things of a day reveal so much to us if we're willing to look and learn: the way we relate to objects, the way we dress and wash. Take a look at how you tie your shoelaces, how you walk, your annoyance with people for doing certain things, pleasure when they do something else. The art of living develops as we come in direct contact with how we actually live, because if we pay attention to how we actually live, certain things can't be done anymore. It's not so much cultivating idealized styles as much as seeing those aspects of life that don't work: our emotional states; particular ways relating to our body, to nature, to food, to other people. It's endless paying attention.

Awareness of unawareness is a high level of awareness. Noticing that you're not noticing is really noticing. The practice gets to be quite exquisite. Vipassana is gentle, but also ruthless. If you hear the teaching, you realize there are no loopholes, no exemptions. There's no way out.

Words like *practice*, which we all use a lot, imply a distinction between your practice and your life. But it's really—always, at all times, wherever we are—our life.

## No Sacred, No Profane

The best statement that I've heard on the relentlessness of dharma practice comes from a movie that I saw called *The Adventures of Buckaroo Banzai across the 8th Dimension*, which I walked out on after about twenty-five minutes. But there was one line that stays with me: "No matter where you go, there you are." It's easy to make sitting, and the special places that we go to sit, stand out over and above everything else. It's a delicate line, and personally I find it a difficult one in terms of teaching. When I emphasize daily life, then people don't sit so much, or they use the instructions to justify not sitting, or they forget to sit. So then I'll shift over and talk about how important it is to sit, and then daily life becomes sloppy.

If you are going to become a full-time meditator, or a nun or a monk and live out your life in a monastery or some equivalent environment, no longer having to deal with that stuff out there, then full speed ahead. But most of us will be spending most of our time in what we call "daily life": at a job, in relationships, with a family, with children, in a school. This leads to a kind of nonhospitalizable schizophrenia. We go away to retreat centers and our practice of meditation gets stronger. We isolate our experience at retreats, dip it in bronze and put it on our mantel. We come to think of it as sacred—perhaps enlightenment or God realization comes out of it. But it also means that everything other than sitting in this posture is nonmeditation, discredited. Then we have a split between the sacred and the profane. We see daily life as something lesser.

What we need is a practice that embraces all of life, where nothing is divorced or separated, where there is no sacred and profane—either it's all sacred or none of it is. And the sacredness comes from you, from what you bring to each encounter with a person and with nature. If you walk into a church, even the most magnificent, it's not sacred. It's a high-class, dramatic stage prop. This can be useful because it inclines the mind toward certain aspirations. But when you look at the building itself, it's made out of the same cement as a urinal. It's no more sacred than a Greyhound bus terminal. It's just something constructed by human beings. It may be more beautiful, and there may be sentimental memories attached to it, but how much real sacred activity is going on inside churches? I don't mean to single out Christianity, or any religious institutions; that's not my intention.

In a retreat center, you walk into a large meditation hall, and at the front of the hall is a statue of a person sitting up there peacefully. We've come to symbolize meditation as a person sitting still, cross-legged, quietly. It's one way that has been found through thousands of years of experimentation to be extremely useful, to bring everything to a halt. But it isn't meditation—it's sitting meditation. If you become attached to this particular position, you'll think of it as being what meditation is.

The Buddha never said that the only proper form of meditation is sitting cross-legged with special garments and a certain posture. That iconic posture has gotten singled out; it's come to stand for the entire journey. When you go into a museum, you don't see a statue of some-body vacuuming, with a sign saying this is the Buddha. Or two people making love, with a sign saying this is Mr. and Mrs. Buddha.

Let me give you an example of the split we face. This is the most concrete and vivid example that comes to mind, even if it's trivial. A young man I knew came to a class some years ago and started to do this meditation, and he took to it. Eventually he did weekend retreats and two-week retreats. I was present on one long retreat that he attended. He did the eating meditation with exquisite attention: each bite taken with total awareness, total sensitivity, the body fully there—in other words, contemplative eating. Then walking meditation: tremendously graceful, fully in the walking, slow and mindful. He was doing a beautiful job of it. If awards were given, he would win Number One Walker and Eater. I was impressed. I thought, "This person has grown a lot. He's got a very concentrated mind." I felt I played a small part in that as a teacher.

A couple of months later, I was heading to a party and I happened to run into him on the way. We walked together to the party and I noticed that his walking was totally wild. His head was one way, his arms were another. It was awkward, poorly coordinated bodily movement. This guy looked like he was becoming unglued. His mind and body were not in the same place, not even close. It seemed strange to me, after I'd witnessed his almost ballet-like gracefulness. We went to the party and we were all eating and having a good time, and his eating was just as wild, grabbing things and gulping them down and getting food all over his clothes.

At a certain point, I couldn't resist anymore. I went over to him and I said, "You know, when we were at the retreat, your movements were like a work of art. How come now it's so different?" He didn't know the answer, but we explored it. He was an open person, fortunately. Then we had a huge laugh. It turns out that at the retreat, he had sanctified eating and walking. "I'm walking with awareness—that means I'm a yogi, a meditator, headed toward enlightenment. Now I'm eating with aware-ness—meditative, contemplative eating." But when he left the retreat for the outside, it was the same old jerky walking and careless eating.

There's no sacred and profane. When you have a split where spe-cial people do spiritual work and go to special places and wear special clothes, remember that they've created a hothouse environment in which to practice. I'm not putting that down, because out of that expe-rience can come extraordinary developments. Some people, precisely because they've given everything up, can go deep inwardly and come to God or Buddha-nature or whatever language you feel comfortable with to mean "freedom."

But that isn't our situation. As laypeople, we will live out our days like this, wearing Birkenstocks and stretch pants and all the rest of it. Does that mean we're less spiritual? The Buddha's deepest teaching has nothing to do with any form. It has nothing to do with whether you're a monk or a nun or eat vegetables or don't eat vegetables. It has to do with the inner meaning of what you're doing. We talk about renunciation, but you can be hungry and it's not particularly a virtue—it's terrible, it's awful. Anyone who's experienced even a little hunger knows this is the case.

If you take on any of these meditation practices and see them as special, you're not going to get the fullness out of them. Because full, real meditation is living wholeheartedly. It has nothing to do with a particular form. It has to do with the sense of who's in there, who's doing it, and how you're doing it. Dogen, a great Japanese Zen master, was once asked what the awakened mind is like. He said it is "a mind that is intimate with all things." But typically we insert thinking in between us and the actions that we're carrying out. We're not fully present. The practice is not to strong-arm your way into intimacy. You can't. It's to notice separation.

*Intimacy* is a word that we use only for good things: intimate with the person that we love, intimate with our family, et cetera. But can you be intimate with suffering, *dukkha*? The Chinese word for dukkha translates as "bitter," and their word for the Pali term *sukha*, which means happiness, translates as "sweet." Life is both bitter and sweet. It's what they call the ten thousand joys and the ten thousand sorrows. Can you be intimate with all of it?

The capacity to not separate ourselves from our experience means we learn about all the ways in which we avoid the rawness of the present moment—the actual, naked, wild, raw, present moment. We cook it in concepts and live much of our life in notions. The practice is to see that and very gently but decisively start living a real life. It's easy to be in touch with our experience when we feel love or there's a beautiful sunset. But what about when we hate something or we don't like being here, or we're bored or feel irritated? From the point of view of practice, that's no less useful. Everything is practice because everything is life.

You can use relationship as a spiritual vehicle or absence of relationship as a spiritual vehicle. You can use money as a spiritual vehicle or lack of money as a spiritual vehicle. You can use eating food or not eating food, special clothes or no special clothes. It's not what you do but how you do it. By "spiritual vehicle," I mean a way of growing, learning, freeing yourself. What I'm endorsing is for you to live the most significant life you can.

## Life Is a Mosaic of Trivial Moments

Every activity, large or small, can be seen as a spiritual vehicle. Have you ever tried just taking a shower? You get clean. The arms go like this and the shampoo goes like that. You're healthy and everything gets done. But where were you when it happened? In dharma interviews, U Pandita, a Burmese master, would often ask, "Were you mindful when you got dressed? Did you notice anything? Did you learn anything?" The question comes from the Buddha, in a simple, unadorned teaching called "The Postures of the Body": be mindful while sitting, standing, walking, and lying down. At first, if you can squeeze ten conscious minutes out of the week, that counts as a success.

If you're taking a shower, take a shower. If you're getting dressed, get dressed. You'll see that it's not easy to do, that your mind is running off into the future or reminiscing about the past or worrying about this or that. It's amazing that we get through life as well as we do, since we're hardly ever where we are. Try to gradually turn that around. Don't make it a grim project: "I've got to pay attention to everything I do." You'll be exhausted by noon. Give it a lighter touch and be prepared for losing it.

The problem with habit is that, often, we're asleep. We know how to brush our teeth, and we may even get into all the cracks and hit the gums the right way and do everything the dentist suggested. But in the meantime, we're solving Einstein's formula of relativity. People often say, "Why do I have to waste my time on such a trivial thing as brushing my teeth? I could be planning out my day."

But there's something to be gained from being with the brushing of the teeth—bringing that meditative state to bear on the activity that you happen to be carrying out. In and of themselves, little behaviors like brushing your teeth are trivial—not from a dental point of view but from a consciousness point of view. Why not fantasize or go through the motions or plan what you're going to make for breakfast? The problem is that our life is like a mosaic—it's composed of small, seemingly trivial moments. Where does it stop? Taking out the garbage, that's also trivial. Making the bed is trivial. Washing the dishes is trivial. Before you know it, you realize, "My whole life is just a big bore; it's all routine. Except on Saturday night, or during summer vacation, or on the three-month retreat—everything will be different then."

This practice is designed to uproot that fractured way of living and bring awareness into each moment. Precisely because an activity is ordinary, it has tremendous learning potential—because that is your life at that moment. Your life is made up of routine activities, one after the other. The degree to which you can be fresh and alert and alive in them is a profound statement of the quality of your life, rather than having particular outstanding moments, ecstatic experiences, that come around once every few months and stand for your life.

## Wholeheartedness

Often the most penetrating awareness happens when the gears of our mind are disengaged from any task. I've always loved to do nothing—absolutely nothing. It's an art. There's something about surrendering and having no agenda that makes me happy. It's probably some rebellious streak, that I don't want any authority. But the point is that there's something in surrender that gladdens the heart. I can feel it, independent of what turns up.

The three main Buddhist traditions all have some version of this, with their own characteristic language—whether you call it Dzogchen or *shikantaza* or choiceless awareness or *mahavipassana*. Sometimes it's not called anything special—maybe that's best of all.

Relax, open up, surrender. You're learning to let go of the supports, the motivational structure that you take for granted as normal in your life, which is to go after what you want so that you can get it and be happier—in short, willful action, which takes tremendous energy. The art is to be present with whatever turns up and to give your full attention to that, simply because it's there. It's the art of allowing, to have no preferences, and it's one of the hardest things for us humans to do. One Chinese Zen master said that picking and choosing is the real suffering. Life would be easier if we didn't.

In this surrender you're learning how to live with uncertainty. You're learning how to fully be with what turns up, with what life presents you. It's learning how to be wholehearted in what you're doing, supple and flexible, so that you can be available for what's next, whether it's hugging your child, driving a car, playing tennis, sitting, giving a talk.

Wholeheartedness is not easy. Try to remind yourself periodically during the day or pause before starting an activity like washing the dishes or making your bed, and form the intention to do it wholeheartedly. It's not simply a concentration exercise. Samadhi emphasizes one-pointedness and stability of mind, but wholeheartedness is more than just one-pointedness and stability—it has calmness in it. A rich dimension is being tapped when the mind is steady.

Another way to put it is that you're more fully alive. That's why people sometimes report feeling great while doing the most "trivial" things, like chopping vegetables or riding their bicycle. The magic is not in the vegetables or the bicycle. It's that we're alert, and when we're alert, we're more alive. A buddha is someone who's fully awake, fully alive.

Many activities are not done in a wholehearted way because we think they're beneath us. Cleaning the toilet bowl—well, let's just get it over with. But there's a lot of wisdom in toilet bowls. If you can do it and see your aversion to it, see how trapped you are, see how you can't go into that bowl, see the games you have to play in order to do that, then you learn something about yourself. So often we're not alert because we consider our activities trivial or negative or mundane or routine. In social encounters, we're not alert because we define certain people as not being worthy of full respect or full attention. Special people, important people, people who control money or gratification: they get full respect, at least sometimes. But there are a lot of people who just pass in and out of our lives. There's nothing in it for us, and they become nonpersons, objects. Put another way, wisdom is abundant. It's growing on trees, just waiting for us to pluck it.

The Chinese used to say that when you're divided—when you're not wholeheartedly doing what you're doing—it's "killing life"; when you are at one with what you are doing, just doing what you're doing, it's "giving life to life." If, while you're drinking a cup of tea, you're longing for champagne or even thinking of champagne, you've killed both tea and champagne. You've killed life in that moment because you're not fully drinking the tea and you don't have champagne. You're neither here nor there. Check to see if there isn't a fair amount of that division in your life.

In the late 1970s, I was eating lunch and watching TV, a program about the Flying Wallendas. They were a family of tightrope walkers. The star was the founder of the troupe, Karl Wallenda. He was performing in Puerto Rico. He was supposed to walk on a high wire strung between two towers, but there was a huge windstorm. He was advised not to go up because it was dangerous. They tried and tried to convince him, but he wouldn't relent. Finally he went up. I was eating my sandwich, and right in front of me he was walking on the high wire and blown to his death. They quoted from an interview years earlier where he had said, "For me, life is walking on the high wire. Everything else is just waiting." In dharma, we believe just the opposite: life is only in this moment.

Those of you who have practiced for a while, you know that there's a different quality to being alive when you're mindful, when you're awake, when you're aware. It's not that it necessarily leads to liberation: if I do enough of this, then I'll be a sane person who's free of suffering. No, it's that the benefit is right there in the moment. There's a certain fragrance to a conscious moment, fully lived. It can be the most ordinary activity. One of the jewels of practice is that you come to enjoy tremendously the ordinariness of life, instead of always waiting for something incredible, fantastic, amazing to happen to you. Your life will be real and fulfilling. Anything will do it.

I did a sweat lodge once. My memory is that it was quite useful and valuable. But it was a dramatic experience—not something I do every day. In living a meditative life, on the other hand, there's a quality of sensitivity and wakefulness and intimacy with your normal, routine experience. In this everyday meditative life, special experiences only happen by accident—they come uninvited. Yet some of the most beautiful things arrive just that way. I don't think that you can make enlightenment happen, but you can lay the groundwork, you can open the windows. Whether or not the breeze comes in, it's out of your hands.

Some years ago, a professional cook in one of our practice groups, about the seventh or eighth week of the class, came in very excited and said, "This morning, I finally understood what everyone's been talking about, all these books and the Buddha." "Well, what happened?" "I was chopping broccoli"—I remember the vegetable—"and suddenly, it was the most beautiful activity in the world. I was totally clear. My mind was not ahead of the broccoli or behind the broccoli. It was just receiving life in the form of broccoli and cutting."

The person was full of tears. Suddenly they felt so alive. Now, does that mean we all run out, buy broccoli, and start chopping it? The beauty is not in the broccoli. It has nothing to do with broccoli. It has to do with the quality of mind that was brought to a rather ordinary activity.

Dramatic things can happen in meditation—what we call "breakthroughs." I'm not denying that. But the practice is that in each moment, we're either enslaved or free. When we're caught up, identified, attached, or averse to what we're doing, lost in what we're doing, we're enslaved. In a breath or in a moment when we see what's going on, suddenly there's a clarity and an awakening, it's a moment of freedom. This practice of freedom is ongoing, moment to moment. There are big freedoms, undeniably, but small freedoms and small slaveries are what our life is made up of. As you stay aware, like anything else, it becomes more natural, and you wonder, "Why did I ever live any other way?"

In ancient China, a meditation master was asked, "What is enlightenment?" He answered, "Eating rice and drinking tea." It's a profound statement and can be looked at in two ways. One is, just eat your rice and drink your tea. It can be a spiritual endeavor. To just eat rice and to just drink tea is shorthand for just doing anything, really. But it's also a statement about the depths of enlightenment experiences, breakthroughs, in our practice. When people attain varying degrees of enlightenment, then eating rice and drinking tea becomes enlightenment. That is, there's nobody there. There's no one who's eating the rice, no one who's drinking the tea—and the food has never been more delicious.

When you wholeheartedly do what you're doing and finish the activity, let it go and move on to the next thing. Fully exhale the situation that's over so you can fully inhale the next situation. You'll find that you have moments when the self goes into abeyance, when you forget the self, when there's just doing. And because the doing is wholehearted, there isn't someone who's doing it—we call it "doerless doing."

Those are precious moments, where self-preoccupation is either weaker or completely absent. The Zen tradition is rich in examples of this sort. That is, if there's awakening, then awakening is manifest in whatever we do. The practice of enlightenment is not that you get enlightenment—some static object—and you frame it and sit on a throne for the rest of your life. Rather, you bring that clarity of mind into life as it is. You fall down and get up and fall down and get up. I call it continuous awakening.

## Wrecking Our Samadhi

We live in a time and culture in which wholeheartedness is at peril. You know the bumper stickers that read "I'd rather be golfing" or "I'd rather be fishing"? The whole society wants to be somewhere else. Either golfing or fishing or dancing. Or we're walking down the street wearing earbuds connected to our smartphones, tuning out what's right in front of us. Walking down the street in the middle of Central Square, Cambridge, but we'd rather learn Spanish in thirty days or stream a curated playlist or have a conversation with our best friend on another continent.

Or let's say you're watching CNN or another cable station. You're watching the main newscast and while you're watching it, a crawl along the bottom of the screen tells you that the president said this yesterday. So you're watching that. Then there's a different report in the upper right-hand corner. Then you're back to the main program, and the anchor is telling you that two or three guests will be coming on. Meanwhile, the crawl says that if you want more detail about the real story, go to CNN. com. Sometimes you get involved in the crawl and just as it's getting interesting, the newscast switches off for a commercial break.

When I first saw this, I thought, "People are getting paid to dream this up, as if it is an advance in media." Then I thought, "Do people actually enjoy this?" After reflecting on it, I realized they do. And the reason is obvious: our minds are like this. They're at home with it.

I'm not at home with it. As Ajahn Chah said, "Keep it simple, stick to the present moment." Unfortunately the whole society is designed to wreck our samadhi. The point is to never be where you are. It's always to be fishing or golfing. Our practice can't change that. But can you be simple inside, learning how to take each thing in turn?

The paradigm in dharma practice is breathing in and breathing out with awareness. If you stick with it, you may see a certain beauty. It's not an idea. You actually experience the beauty of it, the refinement of moment-by-moment awareness, of dedication to the task at hand. It's like a craftsman working on a piece, refining it over and over and over again. There's a joy in doing one thing well. We need to bring that quality back into our lives.

## Infinite Respect

Some years ago, a Zen archer performed at the Naropa Institute, in Boulder, Colorado. There was a large gathering and the target was set out. Archers have special gloves and a beautiful bow. There's quite a ceremony preceding the event, chanting and bowing.

Finally, the archer was ready to let loose the arrows at the target. We in the audience held our breath. We'd all read *Zen in the Art of Archery*. We had Hollywood Zen in our heads. We were ready for him. After finishing all of the prostrations and bowing to the Buddha, the archer pulled the arrow all the way back, for what seemed an eternity. Then he suddenly angled the bow upward and aimed the arrow at the sky and let it go. Everyone was completely disoriented, shocked. What is this? We questioned him, and he said that he'd hoped we learned. Of course, we hadn't, so he had to spell it out. He was saying that the target is everywhere, that there's just no place where the target isn't.

It's the same message in the Hasidic tradition, Jewish mysticism—this notion of infinite respect. Each person, every human being, is entrusted by God with a small piece of the universe. It might just be a corner candy store or your family or a hobby—anything, it doesn't matter. That's your little piece of the universe, and you're in charge of it. What's suggested is that you treat it that way, that there's a certain dignity in every situation and that you pay attention. No matter what the setting—whether it's a palace or a humble shack—you're entrusted with life, beginning with your own life, and you infuse all your actions with life. That's done through undividedness.

If famous people are around or there's a large formal gathering, we're spiffed up and meticulous in everything we do, because we're chained to convention and status. Usually there's something in it for us—money or approval. When those conditions are not present, it's amazing how our attention falls away. Why should we pay attention? What's the purpose of it? No one's watching.

Hasidic Jews say God is always watching, that there's no backstage. In most of our lives, we have front stages and backstages. If strangers are not going to see how we live, then it's okay to toss our underwear in the air and wherever it lands, it's all right—until we find out that some famous Tibetan monk is going to visit us. Then it's amazing how our garments and everything else magically fall into place: infinite respect.

There was a Cartesian Christian monk who did a three-month retreat at the Insight Meditation Society some years ago. He fell in love with vipassana, even though he remained a Christian. He even led vipassana retreats for Catholics. When people asked him, "How do you reconcile vipassana with Catholicism?" he would say, "Do you believe that God is everywhere?" "Of course." "Well, the instructions here are to be mindful all the time, right?" "Yes." "Well, it's the same thing. We're paying attention because God is everywhere. There's no place where that presence is absent." It's a slightly different angle on the same idea.

Infinite respect is having respect for everything you do, which is another way of saying having respect for yourself or respect for life or respect for God, if that's your frame of reference. No matter what your situation, no matter how humble your job or living situation, that's what you're supposed to care for right now. If you do that, it builds a momentum. When you meditate, some of that momentum transfers to the sitting practice. It's the steadiness of sticking with something.

## The French Enlightenment

At times, of course, we stick with an activity far beyond its expiration date. Some years ago, everything French was in. It was in fashion to spend your junior year abroad. If you went to college in Paris and if you knew how to pronounce "croissant," you were considered sophisticated. There was one French patisserie in Cambridge, and all of us would go there with our berets and our *New York Times* and drink French coffee and eat French cheese and croissants.

One day, a woman came to a practice group and she couldn't stop laughing. She said that for ten years she'd been eating French cheese. Then she tried the meditative practice of eating slowly and carefully, really tasting the cheese, and she realized, "I don't like this cheese, but I've been eating it for ten years!" For ten years she'd been eating a concept.

So little of our daily diet has to do with food. When we eat a meal, our cravings are stimulated by a pleasant taste and then a holding on or attachment. This attachment may show itself in terms of how much we take, or whether we go back for seconds, or whether we feel almost a sadness when the meal has come to an end. But it's possible, through awareness, to experience joy in eating without attachment. It's similar with sex and with money. The problem isn't in those energies; it's that we don't know how to use them. We either destroy ourselves with too much food or not enough food, too much sex or not enough sex, too much money or not enough money, too much power or not enough power. It's a rare person who can learn how to use these beautiful energies.

Some spiritual traditions set up an opposition because we don't know how to use the energies of food, sex, or money. In those traditions, we just stop it, cut it off, regulate how we eat, become celibate, avoid handling money. That's one solution to the problem: simplify life and keep those stressors out, because we know that if we let them in, we're vulnerable and will fall apart. We build a fence around ourselves. That's often the strategy in monastic settings. Here, we use a different approach. We're in the world, we eat, we have sex, we carry money, et cetera. Our practice is to enjoy things fully while we have them, and when they're over, to learn the art of acknowledging what's true: that it is over. It's living based not so much on deficiency but on trust that each situation is adequate.

When you're eating, it's important to tell the difference between the body and the mind. In the Buddha's sutra on arousing mindfulness, there is the phrase "observing the body in the body." In a sense, there are two bodies. There's the body-body, the literal sensations that are happening. And there's the mind-body, which could be cravings or body image. If you can tell the difference, it's a major step. The pure sensations that come with eating a meal is the body in the body. But when the mind has reactions and concepts, it colors the act of eating.

Sometimes you'll see that the body is positioned to augment the devouring mind. That's a primitive behavior, as if you're ready to pounce on your food. I remember the first time I tried meditative eating. After a while, I noticed that I was eating bent over. I would lower myself to the food, but I would never come up. I would stay close to the food to get the next portion and the next and the next. With awareness I could feel the organs in my body, because with this extreme bending over they were scrunched together. It was very uncomfortable. Apparently I'd been able to eat that way for years.

When we eat, taste often becomes so predominant that we negate other signals coming from the body. This is an important element in eating: body signals. Every time we put a substance into our mouth and chew it, as it goes down, the body gives off signals—some of them strong, some of them faint. The signals are tied to temperature, pressure, or the shift of weight. The body is telling us how it's experiencing what is happening. You experience the dominant body signals as disruptive or harmonious, even after one bite. You may feel well-being or buoyancy, or heaviness and lethargy, even early in the meal.

The antidote is to slow down so that you bring awareness to the food. Place a morsel of food in your mouth. Perhaps taste it before you start to chew. Then chew. Watch to see what happens—a whole bunch of sensations will arise in the mouth. If you pay attention, you'll see that two things are going on. One is the pulverizing of the food, which uses the teeth. Some people who say they love to eat—and by all evidence, do love to eat—when they start to examine this process, they find that the main thing they enjoy is not so much the taste as the pulverization of the food. It's a release of aggression, in which they're using tremendous force. Part of why they eat so much is that their aggressive need gets satisfied.

The second experience is tasting. Just as some people are primarily pulverizers, others are primarily tasters. Now, taste is a delicate sense. If you pay attention, you'll see that there's a rich universe of sensations going on in the mouth. If you become aware of those sensations, you may discover that you don't need to eat as much food, because it's more fulfilling to simply taste it. You may notice that in the past, you had been eating food without tasting it. What I've discovered in this practice is the power of anticipation: "Oh, that piece of cake will be delicious." But then I eat it and I stay with my awareness. Is it really that good? Often it's just okay. I chew on. Yeah, just okay.

Pay attention when your plate is empty. Your body will say it's had enough. Your mind may disagree and overrule the body. A civil war breaks out. At that point, become quiet. You can even close your eyes and allow that war to rage in full fury. Sometimes the conflict gets resolved in favor of the mind's craving rather than the actual needs of the body. You may feel tremendously guilty—you flagellate yourself for hours, which can be much worse than the overeating. Observing that reaction is also part of our practice. To see aggression and how you turn it toward yourself requires great sensitivity, staying alert, staying present, observing it dynamically.

Say you don't want to stop eating something that you find delicious. It's called greed, the wanting mind. The mind is saying, "I know that I should stop right now, but I can't. It's so good." Watch at that moment. Because at that moment, the mind becomes desperate. It's like the planet is about to annihilate you. You are the most deprived, pitiful figure who ever lived, because you have to give up that taste and texture. Keep watching. Sometimes a little bit of reason breaks in. "Is it true that I can't stop?" No, it's not true. The Four Noble Truths were not meant to die in a book. The First Noble Truth is: there is suffering in human life. The second is: it's due to craving and attachment. You're attached to that food. You see for yourself the fact of impermanence—that a meal has to end and that if you're attached to it, you're going to suffer. Watch that process, don't try to stamp it out. Notice how you try to prolong the meal, perhaps because you don't want to switch into whatever the next activity is. All this is self-knowledge; the food, in a sense, is incidental.

If you do overeat, run the movie backward. What were you feeling just before the meal? What was your mood? Was it anxiety or fear or anger? Was there something that made you vulnerable to grabbing food when you were no longer hungry, as a comfort? If there was, then go to that. The practice constantly pushes us toward the roots of our problems. Perhaps the ultimate root is self-cherishing—this incredible part of the mind that is humorless and totally preoccupied with its satisfaction.

Even after the meal is over, sustain your contemplation. Body signals convey messages about what was helpful physiologically and what wasn't, independent of taste. Something could taste good and not be received by the body well. If you observe this cause-and-effect relationship, you're learning a major lesson in this practice: how you can become self-reliant and liberate yourself from your own limitations. That understanding can have tremendous momentum and power.

You see that there's a relationship between what you eat, or the quantity of what you eat, or the quality of what you eat, and consciousness. If you eat certain foods in certain amounts, you may find the mind inclining toward dullness or agitation. If you eat less food or other kinds of food, you may find the mind fresh, buoyant, alert, calm. If you're feeling tired and sleepy after a meal, there's a good chance that you're overeating—by your body's standards, not by any expert standards or dietary program. That means a disproportionate amount of your blood is being used to digest the food and you don't have enough for the brain. Identify that pattern.

### King Pasenadi Goes on a Diet

I'm not trying to raise some austere moral principle: do not betray your understanding around food. Nor am I advocating some kind of food moralism or natural health puritanism. It's rather that if these patterns play out, making your life less fulfilling, then examine them. Investigate why you do things that are not in your best interest. I'm not only talking about food. It applies to everything else: relationships, choice of work, where to live, friendships, how we practice meditation—everything.

At the time of the Buddha, there was a king who tended to overeat. It's an actual discourse, called "King Pasenadi Goes on a Diet." This king was a disciple of the Buddha, and one day he started eating and eating. He ate a whole bucket of food and gorged himself, panting. He couldn't even sit up—he needed to lean over on one side. He asked the Buddha for a teaching. The Buddha told him, "From here on in, be mindful of how you eat and see if your practice is correct." The king said, "What do you mean?" So the Buddha spelled it out. It's not just about eating, as you'll see.

The Buddha was hoping that in teaching mindfulness of eating, other qualities of mindfulness would also be developed. He told the king, first of all, stop everything else that you're doing. Just sit down and take a morsel. When the food reaches the tongue, what are the sensations? Is your chewing thorough? Are the digestive juices activated? What about the aroma, the flavor, the liking of it or not liking of it? He went into great detail. Finally, of course, how does it feel when you overeat? In the sutra, it's mainly the amount of food that is discussed, because that was the king's problem.

A young man was standing by, and the king said, "From now on, every time I eat, remind me of what the Buddha said and I'll pay you." The young man took it on as a job. Every time the king would eat, this young man would recite the Buddha's instructions. "How does it taste? Are you chewing thoroughly? Slow down, you're eating too fast." In the sutra, the king not only loses physical weight in terms of poundage but also ego weight; the awareness accomplishes two things at once. In the sutras, it's always a happy ending.

We live at a time when we're bombarded with different diets. But this sutra is not just about diet; it's not an extension of WeightWatchers or the usual nutritional advice on the internet. All of the Buddha's teachings put us on a wisdom path. They are meant to help us wise up, and wisdom is the art of living. Mindfulness is being alert and sensitive, and watching what happens.

In daily life, why do we keep doing things that we know are harmful, again and again and again? What I've discovered, in myself as well as in hearing other people, is that we haven't yet fully seen the dukkha—the suffering. It has not sunk deep enough into us. How many more times do I have to do this before I stop? There comes a point—in eating or spending or relating to others—where you see quite starkly: I don't want to live this way and feel this way ever again.

# 3

## Uses of the Breath

THE BREATH IS often referred to as a concentration object. To me, that trivializes this rich form of meditation. It makes breath awareness like practicing piano scales or rehearsing dance steps. Remember: if the breathing weren't there for you to contemplate, you wouldn't be here. You're contemplating life and death itself. We're literally hanging by a breath. That's why another term for our practice is "remembering to breathe."

Following the breath is not a means to an end. It's not intended to achieve a deeper samadhi (a state of intense concentration), to reach the *jhanas* (advanced concentration practices), or to find equanimity. A moment of free breathing is simply a moment of joyful living. You're not caught up in the productions and concoctions of the mind.

The *Anapanasati Sutta*—mindfulness of breathing—begins with something as ordinary as breathing and ends with the total transcendence of everything, including breathing. Just be with the in-breath and the out-breath. The instructions are on the level of Donald Duck and Mickey Mouse. They are so simple that we may miss the fact that if we can stay with that simple practice, the outcome is profound. The reason it is profound is because the operation is so simple.

Perhaps you have had a taste of that joy in small, humble moments, sometimes only for a few seconds, when the burden has been put down. A taste here, a taste there, an easing up of something we're holding tightly, an untying of a knot, all moving in the direction of full disentanglement, full cleansing of the heart. The Buddha used the breathing technique to help develop *samvega*, the sense of urgency: we don't have forever. What do you want to do? How do you want to spend your days on this strange planet? The big joke is that *anapanasati*, the full awareness of breathing, has nothing to do with breathing. It has to do with developing liberating awareness, the awareness that sees through all of our attachments.

### Horse and Rider

All Indian yogis, without exception, have put tremendous care and attention into studying the breath. In the first four contemplations of the *Anapanasati Sutta*, we contemplate the breath in the body. What we see is that the breath conditions the body. The original way in which the breath conditions the body, of course, is that it conditions it to be alive.

When you drink alcohol, you know that this substance has an impact on your system: the mind is altered, the body changes. What we don't understand is that every substance that we put in the body—every food, every drink—has an impact. And the breath is a form of food. Thought is another form of food. If you're having lots of certain kinds of thoughts, you're conditioning the body in a certain way. But the breath is even subtler than that. It nurtures the body, nourishes it, sustains it. Yet for some reason, many people are not interested in following the breath. It doesn't seem to have enough of a story to it. In fact, we don't even think of the breath unless we fall sick or get the wind knocked out of us. People who have asthma are likely to be more sensitive to what I'm talking about. Most of us, however, take the breath for granted.

Think of the breath and body as a horse and rider. If the horse is jumpy, it's going to be harder for the rider to hold on. If the horse calms down, the rider calms down. Or put it the other way around. If the rider is a relaxed, highly experienced rodeo rider, the horse will be relaxed. If the rider is agitated, the horse will be agitated. Horse and rider condition each other.

With breath awareness we see that as the breath gets soft and deep, the body gets soft and deep. If the breath is rough, the body is uncomfortable and unsettled. If the breath is shallow, the body is low energy and slumped. What you're witnessing is the process of cause and effect—everything being conditioned by something else. Right now, we're examining it from the point of view of the breath affecting the body. We could equally look at the body and see how it affects the breath. But we have much more control over the breath—in an instant, we can change the quality of our breathing just by paying attention to it, and immediately the body will follow. As you see the interdependence of breath and body, the whole notion of cause and effect and conditioning becomes palpable and real.

Here's what's most significant: we're studying a law of nature. As we become attentive to breathing, thought becomes unruffled. If we're inattentive to breathing, thought is all over the place—imagining this, worrying about that, planning something else. In turn, the breath is cramped by the distracting effects of thought. In dharma practice, this is a profound connection. Toward the end of a three-month retreat, the Buddha went into detail about breathing with awareness—more than anywhere else in the teachings. Apparently this was the practice he used during his own enlightenment. Even after enlightenment, the Buddha would go off by himself for an extended period of time and sit and watch the breath.

In breath awareness, you follow your breathing in an open, natural way. Not confining it, just letting the breath go its own way. You're following the breath and experiencing it. "Is this breath long or short?" As you begin to know that, you notice differences between the in-breath and the out-breath. You see that certain qualities seem to accompany different kinds of breathing.

In describing the breath, the Buddha singled out deep and shallow, long and short. What's so special about these attributes? As you get to know them in an intimate way, you see that as the breath becomes fuller and deeper, it also becomes smoother and freer. When the breath becomes shallow, it grows coarse. You may discover the influence of the breath on the body, that there's a close relationship between the state of the breath and the state of the body. In fact, the term *kaya sankhara* means that the breath is a powerful body conditioner. Of course, the breath also sustains life itself. This clay that we are made of is breathed into and suddenly there's life. When we contemplate the breath, we're contemplating something sacred.

I have an old technique that I call "Brooklyn yoga." Works every time. Close off your nostrils and seal your mouth tightly and see how long you can practice. You'll soon find out how vital the breathing process is. What you're attending to is not some random object of concentration—it's life force itself. As the breath becomes fine and deep, the body calms down and something magical happens—you can sit in a posture that before was full of aches and pains. The breath naturally wants to be full and free, just as a healthy body wants each organ to do what it's supposed to do. Awareness changes the breathing in an extraordinarily beneficial way.

If you can remember to turn to the breath, you have a way of developing happiness in the moment. This happiness doesn't depend on anything external to you. You see how sensitive the breath is. You see how emotional problems interfere with and constrain the natural and full working of the breath and body. One negative thought and you feel the breath and body change, tighten up. Now you have a medium through which to immediately shift the state of the body. You see how the breath influences the body and how the body influences the breath—it's a two-way street.

There are a number of ways to enliven both the breath and the body. One is that while you're breathing in and breathing out, you sweep your attention through the body. Sweeping is like a body scan. You start at the top of your head and take a tour through the body with awareness, but not losing touch with the in-breath and out-breath. Another way to enhance bodily sensitivity with the breath at the center is to make the whole body the field of attention in the sitting posture. Sometimes it feels like you have poured mindfulness into your body. That is, your body is permeated with awareness and sensitivity as it fully experiences each in-breath and out-breath. As that capacity develops, there's no separation between breath and body.

If you keep paying attention to those same old boring in-breaths and out-breaths, if you keep doing it for years, the breath becomes a rich universe, as do the mind states that come out of it. In fact, the practice is really not about the breath. We're using the breath—it could be any object—to unify the mind. You may find that once you get beyond a certain threshold of calm, you can sit and follow the breath for hours and not be bored or cast about for preoccupations that had dominated your mind for years. If you find breath awareness monotonous, you're not in the present. Monotony comes in when you're not mindful—that is, when you're living from memory. Let's say you follow twenty breaths. If you're not fully alert, the twentieth breath is being measured against the nineteen that went before. But when you're in the moment, each breath is fresh; it's born anew and dies anew.

### Where to Follow the Breath?

Should you follow the breath at the nostrils, the chest, or the abdomen? There are differences of opinion. I used to be prejudiced against the nostrils. It seemed too artificial and limited, while the whole breath sounded more romantic and holistic, New Age. Early on, it became almost ideological within Buddhist circles: all the stodgy, narrow-minded people stick to the nostrils, but the free spirits (like us), they're with the whole breath, because it's more natural. Overwhelmingly, the opinion of expert commentators is that the smaller the region that you're focused on, the more concentrated you can get quickly. Which is not to say that whole-body breathing is worthless—it's beautiful and valuable.

The instructions are to let the breath happen rather than to make it happen. That flies in the face of our tremendous training and conditioning to orchestrate, control, direct everything. We're terrified of chaos; terrified that if we don't put everything in its place, our life will fall apart. Most of us are very good at controlling. The mind likes to grab the steering wheel and put its foot on the brake and edit what's happening, because otherwise we're afraid of what might turn up— it may be embarrassing, it may threaten our self-image. The instruction here is to allow the breath to happen naturally and just see it, notice it, examine it, experience it, and know how it is—its quality, its characteristics.

When we do that, the ego suddenly wakes up. It didn't know there was any cash value in the breathing, but now it tries to not control the breath—and in doing so, paradoxically, it controls the breath. Learning how to surrender to the breath just as it is now is key in all spiritual work and dharma work. If we can learn to allow the breath to unfold naturally, without tampering with it, without in any way controlling it, then the question becomes: Can we allow the mind to do that in other circumstances, to empty itself of whatever is there without interfering? Some of the free association techniques in psychoanalysis get at a similar goal: complete letting go.

By allowing the in-breath to be the in-breath and the out-breath to be the out-breath, we're planting seeds, learning something that will help us come to freedom. In this practice—the practice of full awareness of breathing—the mind liberates itself. My own view is that the practice is about coming to see your original nature, your true nature—it's the same as nirvana. It's pointing to a place that has nothing to do with conditioning. It's an invitation for everything that's inside of you to surface.

As you keep coming back to the breath, you learn that you have more options than you ever thought you had. One main option: you don't have to go along with the stuff in your mind. We've had a lot of practice doing that; we're highly developed in that way. Most of us come from complicated lives where we have endless choices, conflicts, decisions to make—sophisticated, complex, nuanced decisions. But this practice is utter simplification. That's the challenge and the beauty of it.

Samadhi practice is a form of renunciation during the time when you're sitting and watching the breath. If you can turn to the breath, make that your sole interest while sitting, you're letting go of the world. The only way you can do that is to stop grasping at the world in your mind, the images and moods that keep coming up. As samadhi goes deeper, you let go of everything. Now, this is not training in becoming breathomaniacs, even though it may seem so. All of the disparate thoughts in the mind—all of the "I want," "I don't want," the tremendous scattering of energy—all of that is gathered together, collected, and unified around the breath. Samadhi practice goes beyond the breath and comes to a place where the knowing, right now, has one object: the breath. At a certain point, even the breath falls away and it's just pure knowing. It's a state of extreme wakefulness.

As you keep doing this, it becomes subtler. With that subtlety, the heart starts feeling happier, the body starts feeling lighter. There's an increased sense of well-being. You could say that the heart gladdens itself as it drops stressful preoccupations and just settles in. To get there takes patience, dedication, and interest. Calling these "moments of quiet" or "stillness" is another way of saying happiness. It's also a way of saying strength. The mind has to be strong for spiritual work, otherwise the practice is just superficial, sentimental, fanciful. A strong mind is a mind that's peaceful. The mind becomes strong as it empties itself of thought, because it's thought that wears it out, exhausts it, creating confusion and conflict.

## Are You a Snake or a Mouse?

Full awareness of breathing can become quite illuminating. The in-breath can take five seconds to reach the lungs, or it can take thirty to forty seconds. The in-breath can be long and the out-breath short, or it can be the other way around, or it can be that they're both long and short. Get comfortable and learn to discern and recognize a long breath when you have it and a short breath when you have it. As that becomes easier and more natural, you learn from it. See if, when there's a lot of thinking, the breath is different from the breath when there isn't so much thinking. You may find that when the mind isn't feverishly thinking, the breath relaxes and becomes long. Or you may notice that when the mind gets busy, it interferes with breathing. You may find that the more continuous your observation, the more you're able to bring close attention to the in-breath and the out-breath, and the breath gets longer.

The ancients closely observed the way animals breathe. They saw, for example, that snakes and elephants take long and slow breaths, but mice and rabbits breathe shallowly and rapidly. Which one are you? Are you a snake or a mouse?

As you watch the breath, the body becomes transparent—you feel the breath wherever it is. As the breath becomes more available, it's easier to gracefully turn to it during the day. Don't make it into a grim "I've got to be with my breath." Everything will backfire and you'll soon stop doing it. Just slowly introduce the breath into your life, unite it with a variety of activities. Not simply while standing or waiting for an elevator or sitting on a bus, which are obvious places where you can easily do this, but in social interactions or relationships, where it can be helpful.

But remember: breath awareness shouldn't make you more of a misfit than you were before you ever heard of this practice, becoming even more of a square peg in a round hole and calling it "spiritual." Some people use breath awareness in the wrong situations. If you're driving a car, first and foremost, drive the car. Forget the breath—instead just focus on steering wheel, left, right, green light, red light, passing lane. That's your correct action, overwhelmingly. It's not to become involuted, preoccupied with the breath while the world passes by.

It's tempting to become obsessed with the breath as a method, to become preoccupied with the breath in and of itself, constantly trying to improve the quality of the breath, analyzing it endlessly. Your life turns into the Breath Olympics, where competitors set the world record for continuous mindfulness of breathing. "I went for one hundred hours without missing one breath." Fine. Are you any wiser?

Some people use the breath to tune out other people, just sitting there and being with the breath, getting nice and calm and happy inside. Obviously I don't favor that goal; we practice in order to make the breath of a piece with life. A better option is to use the breath to reach a soothing, balancing effect—and while you're doing it, listening to the people that you're with, talking to them, responding to them, so that the soothing, balancing effect of breath awareness is helping you in the moment. By contrast, if it's an unpleasant situation, the breath can help you stay awake in it. Here, what you're learning is how to maintain your composure and equanimity in a situation not of your liking. It's true that you can easily go into a disappearing act using the breath. But you can also immerse yourself in any situation, using the breath to take it on. That's how you train yourself to be at home in the world.

When you are attuned to your breathing, you weaken the tendency to grasp at things in a destructive way. You weaken the kilesas because you're not feeding energy into them. Instead, you go to the breath and come to a place of repose. In the process, you decondition the tendencies to suffer. When you come out, the underlying sense of well-being and joy permits you to investigate unpleasant states.

Put simply, every time you decide, instead of rolling in your stuff, to make a conscious choice to go back to the in-breath and the out-breath, aiming your attention at and fully experiencing the breath, you increase the possibility of awareness in the future. You're establishing a place of strength, a place to come to inwardly. It's an inner strength—you could use images of a house or a fortress. You turn away from whatever is demanding your attention and drop into a place of peace.

### Breath as Nature

Following the breath is taking the medicine of dharma. Often the heart doesn't want to take its medicine. It wants to play with the kilesas. Or sometimes people will set conditions for breath awareness—they have an easy time being alert and awake, say, in nature, taking a walk in the woods or alongside the lake. Nature has a hold over their mind and they're motivated to attend to the breath. But in everyday situations, the breath itself is not that interesting.

I guess you know what I'm about to say: if the breath isn't nature, I don't know what is. In fact, in Buddhism, one meaning of dharma is "nature." A good attitude for practicing meditation is one of a naturalist. Let's say you like to watch birds, the ocean, or the sky; you get delight from observing the natural world in its many forms. It isn't that you are outside of nature or that nature is only trees and birds and fish. It's that there's *only* nature. Nature is happening, and you're it. Likewise, the mind is part of nature. So when you observe the breath, observe it the way you watch birds or gaze at the ocean. Understand that it's your own mind that you're watching.

As you get to know long and short breathing, you develop the ability to unite awareness of breathing with whatever activity you're doing during the day. If you're washing the dishes, wash the dishes fully knowing that you're breathing in and you're breathing out. Walking down the street, be aware of the body walking while breathing in and breathing out. In short, the breath becomes your friend in everything that you're doing. This is an ancient principle in samadhi work.

The main way samadhi—or, in Pali, *samatha*, a calm abiding, a steady and concentrated mind—is developed is that you take one object and wholeheartedly work with it, coming back to it over and over and over again in the face of much distraction. In this case, the breath is in the background, serving as an anchor. It helps keep you awake. It minimizes unnecessary thinking. It keeps you from forgetting to be in the present moment. The Buddha is saying: if you can surrender to the breathing, that can help you surrender to the mind and heart. Eventually it becomes total surrender and freedom.

One of the important uses of samadhi practice is to learn how to get out of harm's way. Harm, in this instance, means the many negative things that the heart churns up—thoughts, emotions, attitudes, intentions to act that are destructive, painful, that lead to suffering. To use a prosaic example: you're irritated because there's a long line at the supermarket. You could look directly at your irritability. Or you could turn to the breath because it's relatively uncomplicated. You exchange feeling irritable for the breath. In other words, you swap objects of attention. If you go to the breath instead of the irritability, you don't feed the irritability or the tension. Instead, you enter into the in-breath and the out-breath. As that ability gets stronger, it can exert a calming, stabilizing, fulfilling effect right there in the moment. It's not suppression or repression or avoidance; it's just a skillful use of our own nature.

This is what we're doing in the sitting practice. Normally all these objects in the mind compete for our attention. A thought comes through: "Look at me, I'm wonderful." We grab it, and feelings and bodily states ensue. In samadhi practice, we exchange all of those many possibilities for one possibility: the breath. As our ability to stay with the breath deepens, we have an option that we didn't have before. Before we had to struggle, deny, repress, intellectualize, act out our mind states. Now we get out of the way and enter into the in-breath and out-breath. As awareness gets stronger and we let go, we can prevent mental proliferations and short-circuit our suffering. We realize that we don't always have to be taken on a painful journey.

It's an art, turning to the breath. I'm not advocating that you avoid your problems because, as you know, the heart of vipassana is looking at what's there. Before I learned about the breath, whenever I had a problem, I would duck into a movie or call someone up or put my head in the refrigerator or read a book, absorbing myself in something else so I wouldn't suffer so much. I know that trick. And it's true that there are times when we're not able to look at something that's difficult. If so, breath awareness is a handy way of giving the mind a rest when it's exhausted. After all, no one can investigate forever. You can't do vipassana twenty-four hours a day. Constantly examining phenomena to see how they're impermanent, to see how you're suffering, to see how mental formations are not self—you'd get a big headache.

As breath awareness develops, you create a kind of inner sanctuary. It doesn't belong to anyone else, and it's portable. You can drop into peace, allow the heart to heal itself and regain its energies, and then look at whatever it was that you didn't feel up to. The Buddha said that the method of being fully aware of breathing, if practiced continuously, "will have great rewards and bring great advantages" or "great benefits." For example, when you are in a conversation, aware of your breathing, notice if the quality of your listening is better when you speak or when somebody else speaks. See if you can, while listening, allow the breath. At first, the breath seems to recede to the background. Try to be in touch with the in-breath and the out-breath. It may feel awkward, like you're trying to do two things at once, but eventually it becomes graceful. It's comprehensive attention that includes both breathing and listening.

### Breath as Friend

I learned the hard way how the breath can act as a peaceful refuge. Some years ago, I was practicing in Thailand with Ajahn Maha Bua at the monastery Wat Pa Ban Taad. I found myself in a little bamboo hut in the middle of the jungle. The huts were separate from each other, and though there were paths connecting the huts, you couldn't see anyone else. There were all kinds of animals and sounds that, until that point, I had only heard in the movies. And there were things that went slithering by—I think they're called snakes. As if that weren't bad enough, I had dysentery; I was constantly throwing up. A tooth broke literally in half, and there was no dentist for hours. I was in the middle of nowhere, trying to follow my breath. It was awful.

After about the fourth or fifth day of this misery, I had taken everything from an armory of herbal medicines that I had brought with me. The Thai monks looked at me with compassion. They were giving me everything they had but nothing worked. So finally I had this meeting with Ajahn Maha Bua, who was a tough old bird and a wonderful teacher, very kind. He was a blend of the United States Marine Corps and Mother Teresa. I don't know how, but those two personalities were happily married in him. You got confused sometimes as to which one you were dealing with.

He looked at me and he saw right through me. He said, "Okay. We've used up all our medicines. You've used up all your medicines. Let me reassure you: If we felt that you were going to die, we would rush you to another town where there is a doctor. But if you're not going to do that, what are your choices? You can go home and tell all your friends about your wonderful week at a Thai Forest monastery and use it at parties"—he was sophisticated—"or you can try the Thai jungle school way of getting better."

That way was simple. He said, "Right now you're probably thinking, 'If only I weren't sick, then I could practice.' Big mistake. The sickness *is* your practice, only you haven't gotten it yet, so stop fighting it. As you breathe in and breathe out, be totally aware of the life of the body, whatever it is, and be sensitive to the way the conceptual mind, the thinking mind, is starting to make up stories: self-pity. Right now, the most important thought is *me*. This is happening to *me*. This is *my* pain, poor *me*. Once *me* comes in, you're in big trouble." And so, the practice was attempting to stay close to the isness of the illness. The isness: Do you know what I'm trying to say? There's no concept in it at all. Even the word *nausea* isn't nausea—it's what that word points to. Or that funny feeling in my gums because I had half a tooth.

He was right. What helped me get through it all was the breathing. Because the breathing can become like a good friend. It's holding your hand and soothing you. "Breathing in, I'm aware of how miserable I am. Breathing out, I can see it's a total nightmare." That's the gist of anapanasati; that's it in a nutshell. If you practice breathing with awareness, the breath becomes a reliable resource. Finally, anapanasati is not even about the breath. It's about awareness. It's about our ability to deeply see into ourselves.

### Breath as Metaphor

When we use breath awareness to see deeply into ourselves, a certain stillness or silence of the mind emerges. Does that have value? Absolutely, because when you come out of that state, as inevitably you do, the mind is stronger, there's more inspiration to do this stuff. But it's also dangerous, because you get attached to the joys that come from a concentrated mind. Ajahn Chah, an extraordinary Forest master from Thailand, called it "stillness with delusion." Why delusion? Because you're not dealing with your afflictions, with those toxins. They may go into abeyance, but only temporarily. Stillness with delusion means that you're not wising up, you're just feeling good, you've merely gotten concentrated.

In this sense, the breath is a wonderful metaphor for the whole practice of how to live. We need oxygen to keep us alive. We use the oxygen and exhale the waste—carbon dioxide. If you think about it from a physiological point of view, when we exhale, we're getting rid of stale air, old stuff. That makes room for fresh energy to come in. It's a metaphor because the challenge of living is: Can we meet the present moment and behave appropriately? What is correct action in a given situation? When that situation is over, can we exhale it? What we're learning is how to fully be here and then exhale the experience when it's over, so that we can fully be with what's next, because the mind is fresh.

*Zen Mind, Beginner's Mind,* by Suzuki Roshi, nicely summarizes the transcendent possibilities of breath awareness. When we practice zazen, our mind follows our breathing. When we inhale, the air comes into the inner world. When we exhale, the air goes out to the outer world. The inner world is limitless, and the outer world is also limitless. We say, in quotes, "inner world" or "outer world," but actually there is just one world. In this limitless, boundaryless world, our throat is like a swinging door. If you think "I breathe," the "I" is extra. What we call "I" is just the swinging door, which moves when we inhale and when we exhale. When the mind is pure and calm enough to follow this movement, there is nothing: no I, no world, no mind, no body—just the swinging door.

It's a beautiful statement of what we're doing. As Suzuki Roshi pointed out, when you look carefully at the breath coming in and going out, especially as it becomes more calm, there's no question that breathing is happening. But can you find any breather? I defy you to do that. There's no breather, there's just breathing. Breathing is happening now.

Ultimately vipassana ripens into no technique whatsoever. You have to travel light, jettisoning even the breath, breath mantras, counting breaths, the endless thousands of breathing techniques. At a certain point, the practice naturally grows into a place where techniques are a burden. It's like carrying suitcases when you've already arrived. You don't need them; you can put them down. We're developing ways of looking at life with respect and openness.

In Buddhism, this arrival has been called many things—choiceless awareness, free attention. Not only do you drop the breath but you drop everything. There is no agenda. There is nothing whatsoever that is held up above anything else as being important to attend to. The only goal is attentiveness itself. It takes a certain faith and confidence to do that, because you don't know what's going to turn up. When you drop the agenda, you also drop a guiding technique like the breath, which gives the ego something to grind its teeth on, so to speak; something to work with. You're learning the art of letting go.

With breath awareness, we touch upon *anatta*—the Pali word for "not-self," the absence of a solid self doing anything. The universe is a process and each one of us is a small universe. There isn't a separate entity known as "me" doing the breathing. There's just this undivided process. Contemplating the breath is a way to contemplate emptiness, both the emptiness of the breath and the emptiness of everything else.

# 4

## A Few Words about Silence

WE DON'T KNOW what silence is. Our culture has neglected the human need for a contemplative dimension. We've been brought up in an age of action, doing, getting, achieving, competing, becoming. We are busy running around, assembling things, breaking things down, putting up new things, thinking, analyzing, jumping, dancing, singing, shouting—just look around, our world is very dynamic. We don't know a whole lot about what happens when that frenetic activity stops.

Above all, we're drowning in words, the continuous radio in our head. It's nonstop thinking—blah, blah, blah, on and on, even in our sleep. I'm not saying that's bad or good; it's just true. We forget that the ability to stay silent for a period of time is a kind of nourishment, wonderful and necessary.

There's a dimension of living called "silence" or "stillness" or "emptiness." When we use those words, we think of their dictionary definitions. But those definitions don't convey what I'm describing. Stillness doesn't mean that the refrigerator has stopped rumbling or the TV is shut off.

The elusive state for all human beings, in the Buddha's time and now, is inner silence, infinite spaciousness. It's sometimes called "the deafening silence of the dharma." A mind that's calm and clear can see into itself and all that's other than itself. I won't say where that leads—

you find out. You might think, "Whoa. That's a bit much. I only took up this practice to calm down."

But you're already practicing coming to this silence. After all, the Third Noble Truth is cessation or well-being. There are moments when we deeply appreciate the ordinariness and extraordinariness of life.

### Silence Is Shy

There are many ways to quiet ourselves, all of which are valuable. There's a silence that comes from reading a book filled with magnificent ideas. There's a silence in seeing beauty in any form—in nature, taking a swim in the ocean or a walk in the woods, or just being in solitude. But I'm talking about a measureless kind of silence that grows out of the practice. You could say it's the heart of the practice because the deepest essence of our innermost being is silence.

This silence is shy. You can't find it through the intellect. You can't reach it with your emotions. In fact, you can't search for it—the search itself would cause stirrings, movements, vexation. You can't order it, expecting to receive silence by command. That would be like commanding love—we all know you can't force love into existence. Silence likes humility, gentleness, innocence. It likes to be valued for itself. Thought goes into abeyance gently, gracefully, peacefully, without a struggle, without any bloodshed.

When you enter into silence and you're grateful for it and it has been healing and rejuvenating, even for just a few moments, you feel a tremendous energy. In Buddhism, we have concentration techniques where, temporarily, you might reach a certain silence, but that's a silence held in place by effort. There's still separation, a doer, an observer. The silence that I'm talking about is here right now. Allow yourself to soak in that spacious kind of silence. Let it operate on you. Let it work on you. If you recognize it and appreciate it when it's there, the chance that it will return increases.

This silence is not a rarified experience. Stillness or silence or emptiness is not reserved for mystics who live high up in the Himalayas, wear loincloths, eat one grain of rice a day, sit cross-legged for weeks while freezing cold, or stand on one leg for ten years. It's part of the human constitution.

The emptiness I'm talking about is not dead; it's not a vacuity. When the mind gets silent, you're tapping into the energy of the universe. Though we're part of the universe, we typically just receive it in little drips—drip, drip, drip, like a faucet that's not fully turned on. When we let go of who we think we are—all the notions, concepts, images, and delusions—we channel the energy that animates the whole universe. Silence is an energy that's packed with life. It's highly charged.

## Silence within Speech

I studied in Asia with a teacher who explored with us right speech, which is part of the Eightfold Path. Conventionally, right speech means you pay attention to your speech, noticing if there are occasions where you are not exactly being truthful, you're being harsh, or what you're saying is divisive. Or maybe it's just idle small talk, not amounting to much.

My teacher said, "This is all good. But what will help you most of all is to taste silence." I asked him why. He said, "When you learn how to live in even a little bit of silence and feel the beauty of it, the sacredness of it, then as soon as you open your mouth, you realize you're wrong. No matter what you say, even if you use the most refined speech, it's a crude instrument for expressing the deep experiences of being alive."

The more you listen and become sensitive to your speech, the more you taste silence. And the more you drink and taste the beauty of silence—real stillness—sometimes you don't even want to speak. If you do speak, you want to say something that, in a sense, doesn't sully the silence. Put another way, you hear when your speech is off, when there are false notes. You become more sensitive both in noticing what is not true and in being vulnerable, fragile.

Silence is what spiritual life is about, at least this version of it. Behind all the commotion of our lives there is an unfathomable silence accompanied by unlimited space—an endless dimension. We're psychonauts, whether we know it or not. Ours is an inner orbit. The Tibetans put it plainly: the cognizing power of emptiness. In silence, there's an awakening of a kind of intelligence. Great healing, the most important healing, occurs in silence. In silence you find you're more compassionate, wiser. All the *metta*, or loving-kindness, you could ever want is in silence.

As the mind empties itself of its own content, it brings you to a place that is prior to thinking. Silence has nothing to do with culture. It has nothing to do with your conditioning, family, job, or bank account. It is opening up to what is before culture, before thinking. In this sense, mindfulness is preconceptual. It can only happen in the present moment. You can get pretty good at experiencing silence for extended periods of time on the cushion. The real challenge becomes: Can you bring this profound silence into your daily life?

In vipassana, we're learning how to rest in silence. I can't say I live there, but from time to time I have had access to it. It's unbidden. It can even take you by surprise. You can be walking in Times Square and suddenly come upon that mysterious place.

# 5

## Self-Knowing

THE JAPANESE MEDITATION MASTER Dogen, when asked what these teachings are all about, said, "To study Buddhadharma is to study the self. To study the self is to forget the self. To forget the self is to be awakened by all things."

To study the self, in the sense that Dogen is using, is not something you do in the library. You can't get self-understanding from a book, other than the "Book of You."

To forget the self—does that mean we are training to lose our memory? No. To forget is to let go. When we observe all the conditions that come and go and flow through the mind, we see the law of impermanence at work.

To be awakened by all things—that's a beautiful aspect of these instructions, because it gets at the power of emptiness, *sunnata*. All you could ever want is here, right now. But we obscure it with our worries, preoccupations, fears—and the tremendous conditioning that has been put into our brains—centuries of it, in some cultures thousands of years of accumulated ideas.

The whole point of vipassana is to liberate ourselves from who we think we are. That includes all the notions, images, and conclusions that have been handed to us by others and that we've taken on and embellished. In this sense, self-knowing is learning about the old mind, the ancient mind—some of it even preceding what our parents inherited, farther and farther back in time. Now it's our turn, and it's not working. Discovering that truth through various meditation methods—here, we emphasize direct seeing—you find that something happens when awareness accompanies your accustomed reactions. Another way to think about it is that our practice is to become simple. We are awakened by all things when the mind becomes clear and empties itself of itself, all the notions secreted by the brain about who I was, who I am now, who I could be.

Many years ago, a cartoon in a Japanese newspaper showed a Zen monk walking along the beach, hauling a huge bag. He was bent over, with a grimace on his face. He left deep footprints in the sand. Printed on the bag was the word *me*. What he was carrying around was himself. "Selfing," a term I like to use, is when the mind attaches to something as being "me" or "mine." We expend an enormous amount of energy in creating, protecting, enhancing, or degrading the sense of me—putting ourselves up, knocking ourselves down, sustaining ourselves, reinventing ourselves, modifying ourselves, editing ourselves.

When all that gets quiet, the mind is a kind of stillness, an emptiness. Empty of what? Empty of attachment to "me" and "mine." To be clear: Real emptiness may still include some thinking. But you have a new relationship to thinking—you can use it as you wish. With meditative training, you can disarm its power over you.

When selfing ceases, the healing and rest in the stillness is something I don't even have words for. You hear it called our "original nature." In the Thai Forest tradition it's called our "original mind." Ajahn Chah described it as a "holiday of the heart," where we give ourselves a break. Often we don't even realize we need a break.

When the thinking part of the brain is quiet, there's a different kind of knowing. It's not intellectual—it's intuitive, direct. If you need a good intellectual understanding about this nonintellectual way of knowing, so that you can feel reassured, it's going to be a slower trip and a bumpy ride. Some people need intellectual explanations about themselves. Or they need to write a short story or poem, publish a journal article, desperately holding on to the world of thought and explanation. You could spend years psychoanalyzing yourself, stuck in introspection. But the skills that we're developing are quite different.

Our practice is open inquiry into our lives. In this practice, intimacy is important. Now, when we think about intimacy, we think of being intimate with another person. But do we want intimacy with loneliness or fear or anger? Instead, we get excited about brilliant explanations of, say, loneliness: the existential theory of loneliness, the psychoanalytic theory of loneliness, the Buddha on loneliness, Kierkegaard on loneliness, Larry on loneliness. You can sit in your library surrounded with books on loneliness—just being lonely.

Ours is a wisdom path. In trying to understand ourselves, we often use wisdom grudgingly, as a last resort: "Okay, I've tried everything else. Let me try wisdom." But when we do, something shifts. Little by little, our capacity to attend improves. Little by little, we have more faith, more confidence, more trust. We are able to edge our way toward different states—perhaps, at first, with binoculars from a mountaintop. Eventually we start to touch loneliness or fear or anger, and our energy is not being wasted on all the escapes that don't work. Face it, we're all escape artists. If our escapes worked, none of us would be drawn to this path.

I think of self-knowing as a quiet passion. You need to be interested in understanding yourself. But once the habit gets going, it can be incredibly satisfying. Full of joy, full of love. Intrinsically so worthwhile that you don't need anyone like me telling you that it's good for you. Once you set things in motion, you see that you have, and only you have, the capacity to straighten out your life.

## The Problem with Problems

Typically, when we begin to pay attention to our mind, all we see are problems that need solving. There's always an "I" and a "mine" in it: "I have a problem. It's my problem. What can I do about it? How can I get rid of it?" We treat problems with great annoyance and disappointment: "If only this problem weren't here, I could live happily." The dharma attitude is that only the dead don't have problems. In other words, life includes problems.

One meaning of *dharma* is "the way things are." It's a natural order, a lawfulness. Things aren't random. In the Buddhist scheme of things, everything is nature. In dharma, we hand everything back to nature—not as an ideology but as a heartfelt truth. We begin to understand that there isn't anything in this world that we own, least of all ourselves. What we call problems are all opportunities to learn, grow, and develop. There's a tremendous amount of energy trapped in what we call a problem. If we can open up to it, in a sense crawl inside the problem with mindfulness, the solution is obvious.

Many problems fall away when you look at them closely. When awareness gets strong, you don't solve problems, you dissolve them—they're simply not there anymore. Sometimes words can be a prelude. But you'll find more and more that you don't need words to arrive at the answer.

If something comes up over and over and over again, such as anger, there's probably a good chance that inquiry is needed. Usually there's something that you should be doing but are not doing, or something that you should stop doing but are doing. It could be a conversation that needs to take place, a bill that has to be paid, a job that must be quit. When you find yourself suffering, sometimes it's useful to pause and, whether or not with words, ask, "Why am I suffering right now? What is this?" It's not chronic introspection or trying to think it through, because the old mind will give you answers that come out of memory, or solutions that you've gotten from psychology textbooks or advice from the internet. It's more simple listening: "Why am I suffering right now?" Then just let the suffering tell you.

The Buddha said, "This practice liberated me. But it won't solve your problem—you have to do that yourself. You need firsthand knowledge. You have to do what I did: examine yourself. And in order to examine yourself, you must equip the mind to be fit to do that." That's why this is a training, a journey. We're willing to go through all kinds of training to climb a mountain, to dive into a pool, to dance. Do wisdom and liberation require anything less?

It's the most difficult thing that's asked of a person. We're being asked to face ourselves. In this practice we're doing it in a gentle, gradual, sustained way, and there's only one direction. Once you're on this path, there's no turning back.

## Self-Knowledge versus Self-Knowing

Self-knowledge and self-knowing sound synonymous, but they're not. Knowledge is something we acquire, and often it takes time. It becomes part of our computer, our memory bank. Here, I'm using the term *self-knowledge* to mean information that you store up about yourself. That information may come from looking at your life. It may also come from what families, friends, teachers, and psychotherapists have told you. It is accumulated and static—your big fat book of insights.

Self-knowing is nonaccumulative. It's just in this moment. You're seeing the way it is right now, and then the insight is dated, obsolete, over with, archaic, useless. It's an impediment because if you hang on to it, you will be seeing the next moment through the authority of your accumulations. What we're trying to develop is a freshness from moment to moment.

In self-knowing, when you learn what has to be learned in the moment, it often coincides with action. That is, directly seeing the situation as it is can be the action itself, because there's clarity and sensitivity. Every time you meet a challenge in life directly and don't veer from it—that is, you are vulnerable, you have opened yourself up to it—you become more sensitive. If you act in accordance with a clear perception of what's happening, that quality of self-knowing in turn is deepened, leading to wiser, more direct action in the future.

## Meeting Life Anew

Self-knowing unfolds in the moment. As Buddhist teachings emphasize, there's only the present; it's fresh all the time. But we don't necessarily meet the moment freshly but rather through yesterday. One account that has helped me understand the importance of meeting life anew appeared in a Boston newspaper some years ago. Perhaps because it happened to an animal, it was even more stark in terms of guidance for us humans.

There was a bear in a zoo in Austria. According to this newspaper article, the bear was tormented. It was kept alone in a small cage with no companions. The food was bad, the water was dirty. Children used to put broken glass into food that they would slip under the bars. A life pattern evolved where the bear would just walk around and around and around. It had a certain home range, and that's what it would do when it wasn't sleeping. It just walked around the perimeter of the cage—so much so that it dug a deep rut into the ground.

Some enlightened zookeepers from another zoo in Austria saw this and were appalled. They purchased the bear and transferred it to a new zoo, a kind of modern bodhisattva-type zoo. There weren't even metal bars. It was a ravine where the animals could play. There were lots of companion bears, good food, fresh water—a totally different experience. As it turned out, the bear was delivered to this new zoo in a cage and at first wouldn't leave the cage. Eventually the bear did leave the cage, but it continued to walk within the same dimensions as its old cage. When the article was written, it was approximately a year and a half after the bear had been transferred, but this pattern had not changed. The bear, obviously traumatized, still had a cage in its mind. That story knocked me over because it's so arresting. Our cages are much subtler, but they also keep us in place.

In the practice of awareness, we're encouraged, in an unrelenting way, to pay attention to our conditioning, to all the cages that we've stored up. Often in the spaciousness of silence, our cages become transparent. You see that it's you who keeps remaking your situations over and over and over again.

In order to practice this kind of learning, a certain humility has to come into play. The best image of the challenge for us as adults comes from children. When young children ask questions, they genuinely don't know the answer. They ask a totally sincere question and in their sincerity is complete ignorance—and they feel no shame about the ignorance; they haven't been poisoned yet. It's the famous "don't-know mind" that the Zen masters talk about, which may be the highest form of intelligence: the willingness to acknowledge that you don't know.

Learning about yourself requires not only that childlike quality but also a certain nonattached attitude, which is not the same as a detached attitude. Detachment has a connotation of pulling away from life and just watching it all go by. Nonattachment is to learn how to live fully in the moment. It is an open awareness, not pushing away or holding on. At a certain point, you understand that the world doesn't care about you. It just keeps rolling on the way it wants to roll on, and you can get flattened by it. You can't change the world, but you can learn how to use the practice so that, in effect, it's a different world.

### Self-Knowing Is Bad News

Self-knowing is often bad news. What you find out about yourself, you often would just as soon not know. But that's a beginner's attitude. In fact, self-knowing is very good news. If it's true, if you've been walking around with all these limitations and concealments, and you start to find out that you're not quite what you have represented yourself to be, either to yourself or to others, and these self-images get shattered— well, isn't that why we're here?

You might have had an image of yourself as being generous and kind, and discover that you have a certain stingy quality and are capable of cruelty. Or you may discover that you're a judging person, that you've had a lifetime of practice at it, that your judging muscles are strong. Is it a wonderful way to live, to be judging people all the time? Find out. How do you feel when you're doing it? What is the price you're paying? The key is the quality of the seeing. It's a sustained quality of attention, and there's an affection in it. You experience judging in the body, you feel how the breath suddenly changes, you feel shifts in the quality of the mind. Most of us banish those facts from self-awareness.

Lin-chi, a Chinese meditation master and one of the great Buddhist teachers, was asked, "What is enlightenment?" or "What is full awakening?" He said, "To become a true person of no rank." A true person of no rank? Is he talking about a military career?

All of us measure ourselves against others. Much of our suffering comes from the comparing mind, where the ego is always on the line. "This person is better than me." "This person is worse than me." In Cambridge, Massachusetts, people do a lot of "We're all equal." But we are the ones making those comparisons, and so it's still me, wanting to be something. We make rank, we make superiority, we make inferiority, we make equality. When you begin to see this pattern, you don't feel superior, you don't feel inferior, you don't even feel equal.

Instead of making the judging mind into a problem, turn it into a practice. It's an opportunity to explore, learn, grow, and get free. We're always with people, even when we're not actually with people—in our head, in our sleep. If you are a true person of no rank, that means you've tapped emptiness. You've tapped silence. Because in silence you're not superior, inferior, or even equal. You just are—and everyone else is, too.

As one teacher told me, "If somebody's a monk and is walking along all day long thinking, 'I'm a monk, I'm a monk, I'm a monk,' they're not a monk. But if a layperson walks around not thinking anything, they're a monk."

## The Mind's Addiction to Self-Images

As all these examples attest, there's something in us that loves to be me. The mind is addicted to self-description, endlessly narrating itself to itself, trying to convince itself of its own worth. Self-images are attempts at security, but they turn out to make us more insecure because of the constant need to protect and maintain these images and construct new ones. The way of wisdom or self-knowledge is seeing these images and our need to perpetually reinforce them to ourselves and others. Even when the self-image is painful, we hold on to it because, although it's a depressing drama, at least we're the star.

Self-knowing reveals us to ourselves. Perhaps you've had some glimpses. It could be something you already knew about yourself, but with sustained attention the insight is deepened. It could be small aspects of your personality, things you dislike or like: "Oh, I didn't realize I was so impatient or harsh, or so nostalgic or sentimental." As the practice evolves, we discover not who we are but who we aren't—namely, all of our self-images. Dharma practice is subtraction, not addition. The end point is personal identitylessness. The time comes when you have recited your story so many times, and from so many different angles, that you begin to get bored.

I have seen *Gone with the Wind* five times. I know about the fire and the railroad station, I know that Scarlett O'Hara decides to love Rhett

Butler when it's too late. So I've had enough of *Gone with the Wind*. I've had enough of *Lawrence of Arabia*: four times. But what about Lawrence of Brooklyn? The process of self-knowing is seeing how all of these images, all of these cinematic representations of ourselves, are insubstantial. They arise and pass away. The more we see that, the more easily we can let go of them.

The major spiritual traditions all recognize that suffering is usually due to self-cherishing, creating a sense of separateness and prizing that over and above anything else. These traditions are concerned with the problem of the ego. Jesus said, "It is easier for a camel to go through the eye of a needle than for a rich man to enter the kingdom of God." The inner meaning of his words has nothing to do with money—the rich man is someone whose ego is filled up.

The Buddha put it this way: birth is suffering. One interpretation is that it's painful for a child to be born. Another is that to be born, to have a body and a mind, to be here on earth, is to put yourself in a field where suffering happens. But the meaning I prefer is that suffering is the birth of the ego, the "I." It's a mental birth, from moment to moment. Every time the "I" is born, every time selfing happens, every time something in us appropriates what's happening and takes it on as being "I" or "mine," then that will lead to suffering. What we're learning is, to use a modern term, deconstruction. We're deconstructing what we've so laboriously built up—this sense of me, starring me. In other words, freedom is liberation from our story.

"Letting go. Letting go. Letting go." In dharma centers, letting go is the coin of the realm. But our letting go isn't so much "Cut!" as feeling the disconnect between words and images that tell you who you are and how life actually is. You might say, "Well, what about my uniqueness, my personality?" From a dharma perspective, personality is quicksand. It's always changing, and life keeps changing as well. Self-knowing is being fresh right here and right now. Of course, the ego doesn't like when it hears what I'm saying. It's terrified because now it's out of business, it doesn't reign supreme anymore.

When we protect our precious self-images, it masks the moment-to-moment, detailed unfolding of experience, which is far more complex and unpredictable than any of the simplifications in our minds. In fact, a lot of self-knowing is getting to know the mind itself—all the stories, reassurances, doubts, memories, plans, and worries. These images crumble or are tarnished, they turn out to be rather limited representations. Even negative self-images do not fully represent what or who we are and cause their own type of suffering.

Sometimes letting go provokes fear: "Oh, my God, why would I want to give up everything I know about myself?" That's the old mind, the me-making machine, the ego. Maintaining our fragile self-image is like carrying around an ancient Ming dynasty porcelain. It's quite valuable—at least, we think so—but it could break at any second. One wrong step, we drop it and it shatters. When your self-images shatter, that's when the big trouble begins—or to put it in a positive light, that's when spiritual work begins. However it comes about, the shattering of our self-images can give rise to an immensely creative time in our lives. Sometimes, when trauma or crisis destroy images about ourselves that we didn't even know we had, we feel released.

One of my teachers, as his last instruction, gave me a calligraphy: "Don't make anything!" During our time together, he sometimes elaborated on that idea—and this is one of my favorite teachings of his: "Don't make anything. Then you can have everything." It is a statement of possibility.

Is it possible for a human being to live without self-images—or without attachment to self-images? Would we go insane if we didn't have pictures about who and what we are? Would we not know what to do? Would we be lost? Or would it be quite the contrary? Would letting go of attachment to our images enable us to live for the first time in a fresh way?

## The Waiter Who Was a Writer

In the realm of work, self-knowing is actually quite practical. We have a certain number of years on this planet. How are we going to use that time? If each moment is precious, what are we doing with those moments? What is our work, really? What does it amount to? It's common for people who are drawn to meditation to either have left an occupation that they're disenchanted with or, if they're younger, not having found an occupation or a way of channeling that energy. They come to meditation as a kind of life raft.

In this situation, as in so many others, try to begin with the child mind—a mind that is not embarrassed to say it doesn't know, that's willing to look at something without preconceptions. Instead of reading books about various occupations, start with the state of your mind. Inquire whether it's confusion or fear or the need to live out certain kinds of experiences or expectations that have left you baffled or ambivalent about work. It requires complete openness. It's not a kind of superficial vocational guidance but rather an integral part of self-knowing—to seriously attempt to find out what your true work is. Of course, your original job is to get free.

I remember a waiter in Cambridge. I ate at his restaurant. He was distracted at times. You could see him holding back a lot of grumpiness, even hostility. It was obvious he was not having a good time waiting tables. As things happened, he started to meditate. We got to know each other, and he made it clear that he was really a writer, not a waiter. He saw waiting tables as beneath him; he was a writer, a talented and gifted writer saddled with a menial job. This inner conflict turned up in the quality of his work and in the quality of his life because he was spending many hours a day at the restaurant.

I asked what I thought was a simple question: "How long have you been waiting tables?" He said, "Sixteen years." I said, "You're a waiter.

You're a waiter who likes to write. And when you're waiting, you're harming yourself."

Fortunately this person was drawn to practice. He was interested in meditation and self-awareness, and he understood that his mind was divided. What came out of his practice was the ability to see that he was hurting himself by living in that divided way. The truth is whatever you encounter is your life. Each moment spent waiting tables, that was his life.

He went another step, which was quite wonderful. He saw that when people meet in Cambridge for lunch, it's often an important part of the day. It might be a break from work, it might be meeting a friend. It has a certain excitement. If a waiter comes to that situation in the right frame of mind, there's nothing menial about the job because what he's doing is helping to enhance and facilitate the quality of customers' lives in that moment. If status consciousness creeps in, the experience is polluted, poisoned. He would start resenting people who seemed to have enough money to be his customers, while he didn't have enough money to go out to eat. He would wait on them and before he knew it, he got into social-class warfare.

With self-knowing, the waiter started to see that he could rewrite or reinvent his job so that the new description made it a lot more pleasant. He realized that what's important is the principle, the attitude, of how fleeting and valuable life is, so that whatever he was doing, it deserved the highest quality of attention.

People often fixate on the question: Should I stay at my job or move on? Often we know the answer, but we're afraid to acknowledge that we know because it could mean a change in our life, and it could be disruptive in ways that are frightening. When the mind gets clear, the answer becomes obvious. If the answer brings up fear or apprehension, then that's what you practice with. We humans want security. We prefer an old shoe, even if it pinches.

Here's something that when people hear it, especially Americans, it drives them crazy: the clearer the mind, the fewer the choices. When the mind is clear, what you don't want is so obvious that you actually have fewer options, because you're not wasting your time on things that are petty, trivial, irrelevant forms of old conditioning. Life is simpler—not in the sense of sacrifice or restriction but because it's clear what you don't want to do and what you do want to do.

## Identifying with the Body

In our appearance-fixated culture, many of our most distorted self-images have to do with the body. The Buddha used the phrase "the body in the body." It sounds odd in English, but in this practice, "the body in the body" invites you to just experience the raw body—the body that's not cooked or steamed or fried or boiled by ideas and notions about what the body is. It means pure, naked bodily life, not body image. Most of us experience the body through images: we're too fat, too thin, too out of shape, too old, et cetera. At first it's difficult for us to separate bodily sensations from body image, from attitudes for and against it, from reactivity about anything that happens to our body, ranging from alienation to narcissism.

The body in the body means you're learning how to be intimate with your body. If you're thinking about your body, just that bit of energy taken up by thinking removes you to some degree from the direct experience of the body. Perhaps you like your body, how it looks, how it appears to others. You work hard at feeding it, massaging it, exercising it, moisturizing it. But what you need is to rub some wisdom into it. The reason you need wisdom is because we all get old. No one wins. Those with good bodies don't win. Those with bad bodies don't win. Pain or self-pity are also notions piled on top of the bare experience of bodily life. If you attach to your body—if your weight isn't exactly what it's supposed to be in this culture, if your features don't match the way the latest models look—then you may walk around with a tarnished self-image; you may think there's something wrong with you.

I learned this in the most dramatic way with a yogi some years ago. This yogi was a woman who had been coming to retreats and interviews for a long time, and we'd had many exchanges. She had had one arm since childhood, and she identified herself with her body and the fact that she had one arm. Whatever we talked about, it always came back to the fact that she had one arm. For her, this identification led to lots of depression and self-doubt, awful feelings that she had about herself. I tried everything, but nothing seemed to help. One day—I don't know if it was out of wisdom or exasperation—I said, "This may sound crazy, but I think you're the biggest egomaniac I've ever met."

At first she was taken aback. Then she was delighted. People who have a handicap often are treated gingerly—strangers and even loved ones are overprotective; they tiptoe around them. No one would say something like that: "You're an egomaniac." What I meant was, "Okay, you have one arm, I understand. But are you going to destroy your whole life because you were born with one arm? Is that the only thing that you can say about yourself?" She was quite a lovely, intelligent, sensitive person.

From that experience I learned a lot. I learned how fiercely we can get trapped by an identification. To some degree, what I said was helpful for her—to understand that her attitude was egotism. We tend to think of egotism as a positive self-image. But the flip side of egotism can be an incredibly negative self-image, including about the body. It's the same game, the same trap.

As an aside, I remember from my years in academia that many scholars identify less with their bodies than with their ideas. In the university, to disagree with somebody's ideas is like trying to kill them, because their ideas *are* them. Their ideas are their creations, their babies; they gave birth to them. But what they actually gave birth to, from the dharma point of view, is selfing. The "I" organized itself around a particular body of thoughts, "my theory," with a proper name in capital letters. Anytime we grab onto something as the basis for forming a sense of ourself, we suffer.

### Identifying with One's Profession

At Buddhist retreats, our tenacious self-images inevitably surface. This is especially true when it comes to our "yogi jobs." On retreats, we have two jobs: one is the yogi job itself, and the other is learning about ourselves. Often they are the same thing.

Some years ago, an oral surgeon showed up. What yogi job was he assigned? Cleaning the toilets. He refused. He said, "I didn't come here to clean toilets." The office negotiated with him and tried to persuade him to clean the toilets. He still refused. He said, "I came here to learn how to meditate." They threw up their hands and sent him to me.

So he came in, highly articulate, very presentable. He said, "Look, it's simple. I'm not going to clean the toilets." I said, "But that's part of the practice, to take whatever job you get." He said, "I'm an oral surgeon—I'm not just a dentist. I've gone beyond that. I'm an oral surgeon, and you're asking me to clean toilets." I said, "I am. And it sounds like it's getting more valuable for you by the minute. Go on, the meter is running." We went back-and-forth. I have to admit, I had the temptation to give in. I was wavering inside, but I didn't let him see.

I said, as nicely as I could, "You either have to help clean the toilets or you can't participate in the retreat. We'll give you a complete refund." He stalked out. I didn't know how it would turn out—he was ready to go home and he wasn't ready to go home. He fought with himself, he struggled. He was pacing in the hallway.

Finally he gave in. He spent the retreat cleaning toilets as his yogi job. At the end, we had a long exchange. He said, "Look, I had low self-esteem—that's why I became a dentist. But even being a dentist wasn't enough—I had to become an oral surgeon."

I said kind of jokingly, "Well, where does it go from here? What's the next rung in your profession?"

He went on: "Cleaning the toilets felt threatening to my image. But I didn't know I had a self-image, and I didn't know it was that brittle. So I was furious with the assignment—it pushed a button. But I started to see that to clean a toilet, you just take a brush and you go like this and pour in some of that and you're done. It's a simple human activity, and a necessary one."

There is a dharma aphorism: a bad situation is a good situation. Look at what your mind makes out of a bad situation. Self-knowing and learning how to live are two sides of the same coin.

### Who Are You?

Bodhidharma was a monk who brought Zen Buddhism from India to China. He had a clipped, direct, and kind of inscrutable way of speaking. When the Chinese emperor, who was a big supporter of Buddhism, asked him a series of questions, Bodhidharma's answers were almost impudent—he kept undercutting the emperor's desire to be praised and gain merit for building temples, copying sutras, and ordaining monks. The Chinese emperor finally asked, in exasperation, "Who are you?" In other words, "Who are you to be so rude to me?" Bodhidharma's answer was, "I have no idea."

Does that mean Bodhidharma was lost? Just the opposite. It means he knows he's not an idea about himself. He just is; there's a beingness or isness. If you start watching your mind, you're going to see how many fabrications—*sankharas*—the mind makes up about itself. The subtlest and most deceptive one is "I'm nothing"—in other words, I'm like Bodhidharma. You can forge even extreme humility into an identity.

The "I" is not a solid entity that has a core. In a sense, the "I" is born and dies many times during a day, part of the ongoing process of greed, hatred, and delusion. We're greedy because we want something to enhance the self. We're hateful in order to protect the self or punish the person who has undermined our sense of ourself. We're confused or deluded in endlessly enacting this routine.

*Self* is just a word, after all. There's a kind of a current in us, a feeling that there's a solid person, like on a motion picture screen. But in reality, we are more like a rapid succession of frames that give us the illusion of a continuous being. As you get to know your mind from moment to moment, you'll see that it forms self-descriptions through images and words, all of which seem convincing.

The idea that the self is hollow is hard to stomach. In my practice, in a rare moment of honesty, I was able to admit that I don't care if the Buddha and Nagarjuna and the Dalai Lama and Thich Nhat Hanh and all the other masters and all the books said that there is no self. I felt like, "Damn it, there *is* a self! There is a coherence! I am a self! I'm filled with myself! They're all wrong!"

Somehow, getting that out of my system brought me to just looking at the seeming solidity, coherence, homogeneity of this entity that is me. Of course, it didn't stand the test. I was just a bunch of thoughts and feelings, often contradictory, inconsistent, flying by a mile a minute. Whatever the self was, I couldn't hold on to it. I started to see my mind endlessly describing itself—I'm a this, I'm a that—almost feverishly. Why was it working so hard? What was it trying to prove? If the self was so solid, what's all the fuss?

Before that, I would think what was ideologically appropriate in my Buddhist circle—that there is no self. For me, this deeper insight into anatta was a turning point. It was only when I could allow myself to fully feel a sense of defiance that I started to see, "Oh, the self really isn't solid." So self-knowing is not a lofty philosophic principle—that's not what the Buddha was all about. The main test of the teachings is whether they help us get free.

Emptiness of self actually turns out to be a good thing. It means that the self is interrelated with everything else. In other words, the materials that make up what we think of as ourselves come from the culture, our friends, our parents. We use the materials at hand. There's no autonomous and independent entity doing all of this alone. As we get quiet, we see that our self is just an ocean of process.

Now, suppose that were not true. Suppose there really was a solid core self. You'd be in bad shape. It would be hopeless. You wouldn't even be able to practice. You would be stuck forever in just the way you are. "I'm a this. I have to go through life as a this." The fact that things are ever changing means the possibility of freedom.

### The Alchemy of Awareness

In ancient alchemy, base metals are transmuted into gold. In dharma, our base metal is ourself at this moment—our personality, our way of living, our character habits. The gold is spiritual states that are healthier, freer, more loving, more compassionate. The movement from base metal into gold comes about through fire, but the fire has to be sustained, and it has to burn in a hermetically sealed container. Through the application of this flame, we burn away all the problematic energies that have brought us here.

It takes courage, humility, and a bit of maturity to be a yogi who seeks to be free. The humility is the willingness to take a look at yourself and see what's there, no matter what. Sometimes it yields suffering that you wouldn't have had if you hadn't been exposed to these teachings. But this is the kind of suffering that frees us from suffering. While renunciation is big in spiritual circles, to me there's only one renunciation: to renounce the tendency to identify with everything that happens as being me.

The end point of self-knowing is awareness, emptiness. But having an empty mind does not mean you develop amnesia. It's not a prefrontal lobotomy. The "me" has been put together by a lifetime of concepts, thoughts, experiences, memories, aspirations, yearnings, failures, successes, and hurts—all in memory and woven together. Liberation comes when we turn away from those fabrications.

In China, a Taoist monk discovered ancient caves that had been inhabited a few thousand years ago. Here's what was written on the walls—it's a distillation of the practice of self-knowing: "Throw away all notions about yourself."

# 6

## Relationship as Mirror

IN THE 1920s and '30s, there was a Russian philosopher named George Gurdjieff. A lot of his teachings were similar to Buddhadharma. I studied in the Gurdjieffian tradition, but I found it grim, joyless. It was called The Work, and that's exactly what it was. The teachings were modeled after Buddhism but with modifications. Because it was a mystical tradition and the Russian Revolution was underway, Gurdjieff had to move his school from Russia to the outskirts of Paris.

One student there was a supreme *nudnik* (a Yiddish word for "nuisance"). This man was annoying, demanding, irascible—he drove everyone crazy. He was, far and away, the most unpopular person in the whole community, universally detested. One day, he left. He had had enough, too. Gurdjieff asked, "Where's Mr. X?" "He's gone. He went back to Paris." Gurdjieff ran after the man, caught up with him, and paid him to come back.

In other words, you have nudniks. They can teach you more than anyone, including the Buddha. But you have to see it that way.

Relationship is a mirror. All day long, when you're in the presence of your fellow workers or bosses, your friends and neighbors, and of course your families, children, parents, partners—the whole rich array of relationships that make up life—you have reactions. These reactions are, for the most part, mechanical, repetitive, conditioned. They just happen; they're not under your control. They come out of your upbringing, your school system, your wounds, your joys. You have an archive of experiences and conclusions in regard to each person. When you meet, you might try to be nice, tolerant, sensitive—that's part of being socially polite. Maybe some of that is necessary; if we all told each other exactly what was on our mind, the world would look worse than it already does. But dharma practice is to throw away attachment to all of your accumulated experiences.

Let's say someone is difficult for you. When you're in their presence, you react in a predictable way. I'm not advocating that you curb your reaction or impersonate a saint—in fact, you're learning how not to do an impersonation of anyone. Instead, you learn who you are, honestly and accurately, from moment to moment. Transformation can come out of that—out of the irritability, the resentment, the anger. Liberation can come out of it as well. All the energy trapped in fighting with that high-handed colleague at work or that noxious neighbor—quarreling with them, wanting them to be other than the way they are—is not available to you for anything useful. Even if you're outwardly temperate and pleasant, trying to make the best of it, inside you are seething.

Most of us live out our lives from a reactive place. We've not spent a lot of time being aware of our reactions—we're too busy reacting. And we're proud of our reactions; we worship them. By worship I mean we give immense authority over to our reactions as being true, good, right, worthwhile, justified. We dwell in the dimension of good/bad or right/wrong. The Buddhist attitude is more about understanding—and not just conceptual or intellectual understanding. It includes the clear seeing that helps you see yourself.

Just before you are about to meet somebody who pushes your buttons, try following two or three breaths, which will put you in a wiser and kinder place. And be prepared for the old machinery to kick into gear because of years of conditioning. It's not that you're using this person as an object to practice getting liberated. It's that seeing your reactivity can actually improve your connection with them, because you're going to be more authentic and honest.

In the great ancient teachings—Hinduism, Taoism, and, of course, Buddhism—there were people who went deeply inward and came to see the nature of what it means to be a human. But if we look around today, it's clear that their lessons haven't taken hold. We still haven't learned how to live together. So, a critical undertaking is relationship itself. Relationship becomes a means of self-discovery, not so much self-improvement. If you're busy patching up your ego, trying to make it a kinder ego, a gentler ego, a nonviolent ego, a vegetarian ego, there's no question that meditation can help you do that. But the ancient image is still a good one: self-improvement is decorating the prison cell. Dharma is to be free.

In relationship, we're learning the skill of being simultaneously attentive to the other and to ourselves as we live out our life. Having done this for some time, I have found that nothing unearths selfing—the self-centered preoccupation that we all have, the sense of the self being a solid, enduring "me"—like relationship. Relationship shows you right in your face the truth of what's going on inside you, what you will verbalize and what you won't, what you'll share and what you won't, what you are prepared to sacrifice or rethink or change about yourself.

### The Marxist and the Buddhist

In a practice group in Cambridge, there was a professor of political science who was something of a militant atheistic Marxist. The woman that he was involved with had taken up vipassana meditation. He started to feel a gap between himself and her, and that was his only motive for signing up for the class. He told me right at the start that he thought meditation was a bunch of nonsense, but he wanted to understand what she was learning so that their relationship wouldn't be damaged. To his credit, he had the energy, determination, and openness to explore his own mind.

In the same practice group was a Buddhist doing postdoctoral work in Buddhist studies. He merely knew everything about Buddhism. This class met for ten weeks, two hours once a week. By the seventh or eighth week, the fellow who said he was a Marxist was starting to taste all kinds of new things in meditation. The man who was officially a Buddhist was having a very hard time because of all the concepts that he kept tripping over; for him, it was two steps forward and ten steps backward.

Now, why was the Marxist able to open up? What enabled someone that skeptical to change? It was because the Marxist was willing to look at his mind, and to start by focusing on his breath. Gradually his mind calmed down and he could examine thoughts and feelings and bodily sensations. He started to see and experience parts of his consciousness that he had never known were there. It was pure seeing, direct. And, of course, it challenged a lot of his strongly held beliefs.

What does this have to do with relationship as a mirror? In order to listen deeply to another person, you must listen deeply to your own mind. Your relationship to yourself affects your relationship to everyone else.

### See Your Part in the Equation

In quite a few of his talks, the Buddha said that the hardest thing to let go of is attachment to views and opinions. If you look carefully, you might find that your views and opinions give you a feeling of identity, a sense of worthiness. Sometimes we've toiled hard for a cause that is vital to us. Maybe you've spent all of your life working to develop a certain point of view and protect it, maybe a political view. Then suddenly somebody close to you disagrees. You might react with a kind of grieving. What can come out of that? You can either get lost in hurt or anger or treat it as a dharma door to help you get free. The Marxist had the inner strength or confidence to challenge his own beliefs.

Not surprisingly, reactive and conditioned behavior is often to blame when people are having trouble in relationships or marriages. Sometimes they should get divorced. Sometimes they can stay together and learn how to live together in a new and wonderful way. Awareness will show you which it is—that's the beauty of it. What's revolutionary in this teaching is that the Buddha said, in effect, "Spend your energy not on trying to fix others but on trying to understand yourself." The whole point of the Four Noble Truths is to turn everything around and see your part in the equation.

In the quest for intimacy, the main thing to be intimate with is yourself. If you're not intimate with yourself, then how are you going to be intimate with someone else? A common problem in relationship is that people who are not intimate with themselves desperately want intimacy with others, who also are not intimate with themselves. Both of you are carrying each other's projections on top of who you actually are and who you think you are. How can real intimacy come out of that?

Here's where the dharma attitude can be helpful. You want the other person to make everything that's off in your life okay. But no one can do that for you. In this practice, you begin to see that the other person suffers and that they are impermanent, they lack self; they're not unified—and neither are you. Two ever-changing entities wanting some kind of deep fulfillment and certitude cannot provide it for each other. This is not to say you're condemned to being alone. But there's a deeper level to which all spiritual paths are directed. When you don't expect a person to deliver something that they can't possibly deliver, suddenly it can be a more fulfilling relationship, where you see their humanness and they see yours. All of us, whenever we're in each other's presence, are teaching one another.

This attitude of giving space to others is not always easy. I often hear from yogis: "Buddhism talks about nonattachment, but how can

I love someone and not be attached?" You fall in love with someone, you live with someone, you marry someone—aren't you attached? If Buddhism says no, well, it must be a cold, totally unrealistic teaching. The truth is that when we get involved, of course there's attachment. We were lonely. We met someone. "Oh, thank God, finally." We all know the variations on that attachment. But if we have an ideal of perfect attachment—in other words, what would it be like if the Buddha got married?—it's not going to work out too well.

Here, as elsewhere, start where you are: there's attachment and possessiveness in love. So work with that. Now, it's best if both people are willing to work with each other. But even if you are the only person on the path, there's no question that you can loosen your attachment so that it's not strangling you, so that you become less possessive. Instead of, "Where are you going? When are you coming back? How long are you going to be away?"—after a while, you see that every time you say that, it feels terrible to you, and the other person hates it, too. The letting go comes not from sprouting wings and flying out of your attachment but from getting to know what attachment is. It takes courage and patience; it's not easy. You are coming to understand, "Oh, this is what attachment feels like."

Buddhism speaks of nonattachment. But what if, say, you are a parent? How can you be true to your heart and stay on this path? A student once told me that a mother can only be as happy as her unhappiest child. Maybe. But here's the problem, as I see it. When you read the Buddhist texts, they're ideals. Much of the literature comes from the monastic tradition, people who have never had children. So we receive the general teaching that attachment is suffering. But motherhood is a primal attachment—no getting around it.

Still, there's a difference between attachment and love, and it's subtle. As the mind gets quieter and begins to know itself, it can feel a distinction between holding on and love. I'm not saying that the pain goes away when your child is suffering. But often with awareness, some of the pain can be eased.

No matter what your children are going through, try to keep doing the practice. It will help you. As you pay attention to your suffering, often what you see is repetitive thinking, which throws logs on the fire and makes the suffering worse than it needs to be. This is not to say get rid of thinking, whether or not you're a parent. But you can learn something by seeing if there's a lot of extra thinking, repetitive thinking, the same thought over and over again.

One of the benefits—and it's not a small one—is the realization that if your child is in pain, you aren't obliged to encase your own suffering in cement. "I have to suffer because she or he is my child." Be open and see what unfolds. What I've discovered in people who sincerely do this is that the pain of being a parent may never go away but you learn how to take care of it with more equanimity. That enables more clarity, which gives you the possibility, the potential, for being more helpful to your child in ways that you may or may not be able to imagine.

### Heal the Wounds in Yourself

Repetitive thoughts are habit energy, and they seem to accompany almost every emotional wound. Say somebody close hurts you. You find that you can't forgive them. Start with where the dukkha is. You've been hurt. Who got hurt? You'll see that it's "me." What is it that got hurt? What balloon got punctured? Again, the sense of "me." Forgiveness is important, and it's good. But start with the wound itself, which is in you.

The beauty of the Four Noble Truths is that we start with what is rather than with what should be. One of the habits that's hardest to unlearn is the human tendency to blame our suffering on something exterior. It's not to deny that how someone relates to you may be off, even cruel or toxic. But forget about the other person, because you're the one who's suffering.

Say you feel resentment—not the word but the energy that the word points to, the actual living energy that's boiling in you, which you will make up a word for. Understanding comes from your ability to become aware of the energy of resentment without pushing it away, drowning in it, explaining it, or just spending so much time resenting the person who's treating you this way. We're learning how to help the mind heal itself.

Here's what I've discovered in my life. If you can heal your own wound, then when you're with the person who hurt you, something happens in them without their even knowing it. Say they mistreated you and you have resentment. Even they can feel your resentment and so they mistreat you again, back and forth, and it builds. Finally you don't even talk to each other. I know a father and daughter who haven't spoken in twenty-five years. Ridiculous. If you heard the reasons, you'd say they're trivial—but apparently not. Neither one can give an inch. So we're not waiting for the world to change. We're taking charge of ourselves and taking care of ourselves.

I'll give you an example of how the practice of mindfulness can help transform what seems insurmountable. Some years ago, a woman was trying to get love from her mother, over and over. Ever since the woman was young, the mother wanted her to be a model. The woman was beautiful but she didn't want to be a model. It went on and on, and she never could get love from her mother. Finally the woman became successful, wealthy, and respected in her field. She bought a home for her mother, even though her mother continued to be cold to her because she was disappointed that her daughter hadn't become a model. But even before the woman had become successful, she had always taken care of her mother without getting much in return. Eventually, the mother was dying. The woman came to me and said, "What should I do?" I said, "Tell me what you're feeling." "I'm feeling anger toward her. I don't even want to be with her as she's dying." I said, "No, that's not an option. She's your mother, but be mindful of your anger." And she did. She was a committed yogi, had a mature and strong practice. It's not that she overcame her lifelong anger, but she went to the hospital, stayed with her mother, held her hand, and before the mother died, she held her mother. The mother held her, hugged her, and they both started crying. The mother said, "I love you. I've loved you all along. I've been a fool."

This may sound like a sentimental Hollywood ending but it points to a serious truth. As dharma practitioners, we heal ourselves in order to help others in our life. The support of a sangha—a community of like-minded people—is essential. In this case, it was me, the woman's teacher, who encouraged her to do something that she resisted after a lifetime of conditioning (though any dharma teacher would probably have given the same advice). Ultimately this woman was able to take care of her own emotional wounds after a life of being mistreated by her mother. This self-healing enhanced her dharma practice, which in turn enabled her mother, even as she approached death, to grow emotionally, to reach deeper into her own heart. If the woman had never gone to the hospital and held her mother, we don't know how her mother would have died. The point is, we never give up on anyone. We never cast anyone out of our heart.

The Dalai Lama once said that if it weren't for the Chinese, he wouldn't have learned real patience. His practice is to try to get his country back but not in a violent way. He could walk around feeling endlessly bitter, but he has freed himself from that. He doesn't put the Chinese down. His approach is to be intelligent and skillful but also to keep his own heart pure, because otherwise he could be the loser in the relationship. Decades ago, I was in the audience when the Dalai Lama was interviewed by a conservative commentator. After the formal interview was wrapped up, the commentator remarked with some astonishment that, during the entire conversation, the Dalai Lama didn't express any anger toward the Chinese. As I recall, the Dalai Lama replied, "Isn't it bad enough that they stole my country? Do I want them to steal my mind as well?"

Notice how much you suffer by harboring negativity toward anyone. See how you are the loser in it. Reflect on how unskillful it is to maintain anger, grudges, ill will. It's a kind of inquiry. You grasp the fact of what you are losing in harboring vendettas and grudges, an eye for an eye and a tooth for a tooth.

Another approach to soften resentment is to develop compassion for the other person by reflecting on them. Sometimes you can see that if they are a particularly negative person, they're already suffering a lot. In the Buddhist concept of rebirth, when people live in a negative way, not only are they destroying the quality of their present life but they're creating future rebirths that will be negative. I don't know if you believe in that or not. I don't think belief is required—this life is proof enough. You can see the ripple effects of their negativity, and sometimes that dilutes your anger a bit. Then you can try to send metta, or loving-kindness, to that person.

When we feel aversion, we see people as being worse than they are. We tend to feature that negative picture, blow it out of proportion, and in our mind the person becomes a reductive conclusion. Try to remember that this is a whole human being. Try to complicate the storyline by seeing them as a complex person who at one time was cruel to you but also perhaps at one point was kind to you or someone else—or maybe you simply caught a glimpse of them feeding a pigeon in the park.

As they become a real person in your imagination, it becomes harder to sustain a black-and-white morality. The main thing is for the melting to happen, the softening, seeing how harmful your animosity is to the quality of your own life. The other person may never change. They may continue to be cruel. But we have the possibility of freeing ourselves from that burden.

In dealing with difficult people, you may set up an ideal, trying to make yourself compassionate or cultivating a quality that you feel you're weak in—say, you're violent and you want to be peaceful. There are meditations that can help you change your attitudes and behaviors. In this tradition, metta is part of a package of trainings that include compassion, joy for the well-being and success of others, and equanimity—the four *brahmaviharas*, or divine abodes. I'm all for that. Sometimes people so lack a certain quality that cultivating it is beneficial. I don't know if this product exists anymore: Adolph's Tenderizer. It kind of softens up meat. The brahmaviharas are a bit like that but with our minds.

The metta meditation, in particular, nurtures a quality of all-embracing loving-kindness and sends it to yourself, to others, to all sentient creatures. In reciting one of the many variations of metta—such as "May I/you be happy." "May I/you be healthy." "May I/you be safe." "May I/you be at ease."—the mind becomes more concentrated, calmer. When the mind is concentrated, it's happy. Loving-kindness is used to develop a one-pointed, steady, concentrative meditation. Or if we turn it around, the more developed and concentrated the mind becomes, the broader, deeper, and more powerful metta becomes. In our culture, the word *love* might be used for a kind of casual sympathy or good feeling about someone. But the expansive feeling of metta is of a different order.

Here's my caution: cultivating metta, beautiful as the feeling is, is not the same as wisdom and direct seeing. I'm not setting up a cultivation practice like metta against vipassana practice. But as you hear many times in dharma or any wisdom path, you start where you are. That's the beauty of it—and, in a sense, the austerity of it. With the never-ending challenges of relationship, instead of doing an impersonation of a compassionate person, start with your lack of compassion. This is a tried-and-true method.

## How to Love a Nonmeditator

I'm often asked, "How should I relate to people who don't practice?"—in other words, most of the world. I'm an expert on this subject.

If you keep meditating, part of what you learn is how to live in a world of nonmeditators. But even making that distinction is a mistake. They're just human beings, all trying in their own way. Let me be more concrete—I'll be personal. My wife doesn't meditate. She's a political émigré from the Soviet Union, and she speaks with a thick Russian accent. She eats Russian fish and all kinds of other things unmentionable. I'm an American. I teach meditation. I'm a health faddist. I've been vegetarian for more than fifty years. And so, I've had to create segregation in the refrigerator. My nice, beautiful, sweet, smiling vegetables are over here; and the pained, seared animal flesh and the fish that have been bleeding and crying, they're over there. My wife doesn't believe in segregation, so sometimes I'll find caviar mixed in with my nice vegetables. But our marriage has worked because she respects my right to be a meditator and vegetarian, and I respect her right not to be.

What I've seen over the years is that it's common for one partner to be a meditator and one not. It doesn't have to be a problem if you respect the nonmeditator's right to not meditate, their right to not be as "wise" as you are—I'm being facetious—and if they can respect your right to follow this path. If both of you respect each other, then an intimate relationship has a good chance of working. If something else is off in the relationship, then it probably isn't about meditation or nonmeditation—that's just being used as a political football.

By the way, dharma students are usually more intolerant than non-meditators. It's a fact. We have this new thing that we've discovered, and it's easy to feel superior: "Look how they suffer so unnecessarily, those poor people who are not on the path." But if you closely observe the nonmeditator, you may find that he or she is actually happier than you are. That's especially true for those of you who are new, who are in the romantic phase of Buddhadharma where suddenly you're born into something fantastic. That passes.

I'll give you another example. Years ago, for the first time in my life, I moved to a residential street, and there were certain kinds of small talk that I had never been good at. I was getting to know my neighbors. They weren't big meditators, to put it mildly. The main conversation was, "Warm enough for you? Cold enough for you? Don't get too comfy—it's going to freeze up tomorrow." At first I felt like, "Can't we talk about the nature of reality?" But now I love it. I engage in conversations, and it's sincere. In one case, a neighbor and I talked about the weather for months. But then the conversation expanded to our mutual experience of being in the military. I found that this person had great depth and intelligence, and his perceptions of military life were quite thoughtful. But it took humility and learning on my part. Don't get highfalutin just because you sit quietly on a cushion each day.

When I started on this journey, I had tremendous problems with my immediate family, and it was a battleground for me. Just picture working-class immigrants; their son gets an advanced degree, becomes a professor at prestigious universities—and after ten years drops out to do this stuff. Can you imagine my poor hardworking parents who helped me all these years, and my sister and brother-in-law? They thought I literally went insane. At first I was angry and I defended myself. "Why don't you understand and support me? Can't you see that I'm high-minded? This is a noble endeavor, liberation, blah, blah, blah." Once I stopped that, I understood them: they love me, they want the best for me, they feared for my future security, and they can't grasp this.

In the honeymoon phase of this practice, you may feel so enthusiastic that you want to share your newfound wisdom with everyone around you. They may even ask you questions. There's a Zen saying: "If you meet a poet on the road, share your poetry. Otherwise, shut up."

In other words, don't teach Buddhism, just be a buddha to the best of your ability. Do not try to teach Buddhism, even if you love Buddhism. When I started, I was a nightmare to everyone.

Toward the end of my father's life, I was finally able to talk to him about this practice and he was able to listen. It took us twenty-five years. I hope you're not as dumb as I was. At least theoretically, the possibility of a more skillful interaction comes out of it not being habit energy, reactive. It may be just silence. Or you may do the same things that you have been doing, such as changing the subject. But the possibility of you being wiser and kinder and more skillful is enhanced if your words and actions come from a freshness of experience—and that comes from seeing that your reaction is not fresh. We are learning how to free ourselves from living so much of our relationships out of Pavlovian conditioning.

## The Value of Dialogue

As I learned in my family, the art of communication is central on this journey. Classical literature values self-investigation. In ancient Greece, Socrates saw dialogue as extraordinarily useful. He believed that you could find out everything important through dialogue. There are certain truths that are in us, and if we're willing to go deep enough, we can use each other to exteriorize that which is interior and not accessible. You can learn some things that you can't learn alone just by virtue of saying them to somebody else or having somebody else draw you out, meet you, and perhaps walk alongside you.

The Buddha was roughly contemporaneous with Socrates, and the dharma approach to self-understanding likewise includes dialogue. In our practice, the art of inquiry rests on the starting assumption that we don't know. Dialogue requires an intention to learn, to understand. With intention, certain energies are released that free up the mind to discover. It's liberating to realize that we don't know anything.

The essence of dialogue is total listening. For this to happen, there has to be a feeling of being at ease, relaxed and totally open. When we listen, sometimes it's only our thinking mind that listens. We hear from a cerebral point of view, we agree or disagree, challenge, find fault with; such listening is largely on the verbal level. Or we receive what someone is saying on an emotional level—"That's unfair." "I like what they're saying."—and we have a bad or good feeling about them.

But there's a deeper listening that is beyond thinking and feeling: listening with the whole being, a profound and deep state of attunement. In this approach, whoever is listening is listening to whoever is speaking but is simultaneously sensitive to the surgings that come up from within. What's required is hearing the other person's words but also registering your play of mind around their words. It's a flow, and it takes a bit of practice. It requires a balance of passive and active energy. You are alert yet receptive at the same time. At first, it may seem as if you're doing two different things at once: listening to yourself and listening to the other person. But more and more, it's a fluid movement. Eventually it's just listening.

### Listen to Your Words

In all of these examples, you can see that life is practice, practice is life. I have found that the best way to refine the ability to listen is not so much to try to listen—often that's accompanied by strain—but to see how you're not listening. Not listening means that the mind is hearing the words but part of you is somewhere else. Through seeing how you don't listen, quite naturally the quality of your listening improves.

Right speech is relationship as a practice. But right speech is not only about you saying things that are beneficial for you and others. It is also seeing the effect your words have on other people. Listen to what comes out of your mouth. When these lips start flapping and sounds get engineered into words, just what are we doing? What's happening?

Are we saying what we mean? What is our intention when we say something? What are we trying to accomplish? What do we, in fact, accomplish? Even with texting, emails, or any form of modern communication, pause to put your mind in a condition where it can best say what's right, beneficial, useful, constructive, and timely. And remember that right speech at the wrong time doesn't work. Sometimes you have to wait a few days, sometimes years (I hope not).

There are two aspects to right speech: when to speak and when to listen. Often we blurt things out or hold things back longer than we should. We don't fully absorb what others are saying because we're waiting impatiently for our turn to talk—sometimes, to say something rehearsed. Right speech is learning how to speak and when to speak, how to listen and when to listen. You're attending to the whole person. There's an energy field that's coming at you. Sometimes that person's words are not anywhere near as revealing as their facial expressions or body language.

Right speech also means hearing yourself clearly. I've given the breath awareness instructions probably a hundred million times in the past forty years. It's like being a disc jockey: "Relax, allow your body to be upright . . ." Believe it or not, ninety-nine percent of the time, I'm not bored—it's fresh for me. But every now and then it's a crashing bore: "Follow the in-breath, the out-breath . . ." When my awareness hears that flatness, that droning, that staleness, and I realize that I'm speaking from the old mind rather than as if I'm giving these instructions for the first time, the stale, rote quality falls away and my voice perks up.

As I mentioned, my wife is not a meditator. Here's one thing I learned from her about relationship. She worked in a hospital with a lot of elderly, sick Russians who were in pain and complaining. She would come home and at times she'd start to tell me about her day at work, and I would have a beautiful dharma talk to give her. But that's not what she wanted—she just wanted me to listen. It took me two or three years, but I finally learned: "Duh. You're not interested in my immense storehouse of wisdom. What you would like is for me to just be a person who cares enough to listen to you." When I told her this, she said, "Yes. That's exactly what I want." I should add that my wife is drawn to Buddhist teachings—and sometimes she actually did want a dharma angle on what was troubling her. During our marriage, I have needed to learn how to distinguish her conversational needs from mine.

What might come out of the new space that you create by attending to your own reactions in relationship? Maybe the reaction will get weaker. Maybe you will drop into silence. Maybe you say the same things that you've been saying for years but the energy is different and the other person is more able to take in what you are saying. Maybe you ask them a fresh question that never occurred to you before. It's the famous beginner's mind, the don't-know mind. It's fresh, not formulaic. And it's rejuvenating.

If you take care of yourself, then you can take care of others. Whether that assumes the shape of silence or conversation or a hug or a kiss or just looking at them in a loving way, I don't know. But you'll know.

# 7

## Working with Fear, Anger, Shame, and Other Strong Emotions

IN THE 1980S, a small group of us gathered in New York City with Jiddu Krishnamurti. We met for a few hours each day for a week. The theme was fear. We examined it, looking at it this way and that way. Those of you who have read his books or met him know he would constantly test our understanding of his teaching. Needless to say, no one understood. Everyone was wrong all the time. Despite that, we learned a lot.

The week was coming to an end and we had all worked very hard. It was a Friday, and within a half hour we were going to go our separate ways. After all this discussion about fear, what took place in the final minutes seemed like a non sequitur.

Krishnamurti placed his hands in front of him, cupping them, and kept them there. He said, "Yesterday, I took a walk along Fifth Avenue and some friends brought me to one of the top jewelers in the world. I had in my hands this extraordinary gem." He described the beauty of the gem, the lines along which it was cut, the color—he went into great detail. We were all wondering, "Has he finally gone senile?" He was in his late eighties at the time. He said, "The gem elicited my total attention. It was that beautiful. Right in the middle of the shop, I went through the gem and came to complete stillness." He mimed holding the gem, and we were all watching, rapt. Then, in an instant, he took the gem away with one hand and said, "Fear is that gem." With his other hand, he replaced the gem with fear.

Do you understand what he was saying? The energy locked up in our fears, the uncountable ways in which fear distorts our life, keeps us from doing things that we want to do and makes us do things we don't want to do—it's endless. To move through fear, even a little, releases energy that becomes something quite different.

Fear is a powerful force in every human being, maybe every creature. But this same process of transforming fear can be applied to boredom, loneliness, restlessness—all of those energies are waiting to be transformed. We call them "hindrances" or "obstacles" because they prevent us from experiencing what is said to be the true luminescence of the mind. Understanding that is half the battle.

### Yogis Are Firefighters

The vipassana yogi is a strange kind of person. We're like firefighters. I lived near a firehouse when I grew up. When I was a little kid, I would watch them. It would be quiet, the firemen would be playing cards, reading magazines. Suddenly there'd be an alarm. They'd pull on their pants and come sliding down the pole, half a sandwich in their mouth, and go right to the fire. No hesitation. That was their job. In the same way, our job is to go right to the suffering.

A number of years ago, I was at a wedding and I was seated next to a world-famous photojournalist who has won many awards and has been wounded many times. He goes right to where the danger is, where his life is at stake.

We were sitting next to each other, and I asked him what he does, although I already knew. When he told me, I said, "How do you feel when you're up close to where bullets are flying, bombs are going off, people are dying? And there you are, taking photographs of it—

brilliant ones, beautiful ones." I had seen some of these pictures; they're remarkable. I said, "Do you ever experience fear?" He said, "Of course." I said, "Well, how do you handle it?" He said, "In a certain way, it gives me energy. I bite my lip. I know that the fear is there, but the fear blends with an urge to get the picture." He was oriented toward the peace movement and wanted his photographs to show the horrors of war in ways that make the senselessness evident. I said, "Whoa, you'd never get me to do your job. I wouldn't go near it."

Then he asked me, "And what do you do?" I said, "My job is meditation. We kind of look into the mind. We have fear, too, but we just look into it." He backed off and said, "You look into fear? You'd never get me to do that job."

In my own practice, looking directly at fear was a turning point. It was a simple realization, consistent with the Buddha's teaching. This was some years ago, when I had concluded, without any doubt, that there was no escape from suffering. None. I had tried nearly all of them.

The realization that there was no escape was helpful because what I saw was the tremendous amount of energy being used to evade, avoid, deny, postpone, delay, cope with, and put up with all my fear. How much energy is dispersed by all the games we play? What if that energy, instead of being dissipated in all these escape routes, was simply turned toward the fear? What if that energy was aggregated, unified, made coherent, whatever it takes to get us to look directly at fear? At that point, our attention would be on fire.

One thing that can help generate energy and effort is understanding the enormous cost of being controlled by fear. Do you see it as a high priority in your life—to come to terms with fear? Do you see a specific, concrete instance of it, where you can't flower fully as a human being because you're afraid of something? Seeing that generates energy to face fear. Sometimes you find out that it's not so difficult after all.

Another way to help face fear, anger, or any turbulent emotion is to reflect on our spiritual heritage. If you read Buddhist texts, they talk about great yogis who have gone through the same dramatic emotions we go through. Which brings up an important point: the Buddha wasn't always enlightened. He had to get there. He had to work hard. Our approach to spiritual development in vipassana comes out of the experience of that particular human being. I think this point should be made explicit: the Buddha was not a savior. Time and time again, he said that all that he could do is point the way, but you have to do the work.

This attitude has not been monopolized by Buddhism. It belongs to all the great saints and sages who left their legacies to human society. Within the Buddhist tradition, you can read about the life of Milarepa and what he was willing to go through for freedom. He was an eleventh-century Tibetan yogi who, when he was young, used black magic to murder people. Later, he turned to Buddhism, becoming a sage. It's inspiring to read about lives like his, in whatever tradition or religion or no religion—human beings, just like us, who got fed up with being crazy, destructive, unfulfilled, and dangerous. King Ashoka in ancient India, an emperor who was responsible for the deaths of tens of thousands of people in war, became repulsed by all the destruction that he had contributed to. He became a pacific, benign, and spiritually evolved emperor/king. Maybe that's a prerequisite for all of us: a yearning for freedom.

## Inviting Trouble

Ajahn Chah, the Thai Forest master who strongly influenced my practice, vividly described a painful journey of self-awakening. During his days as a young monk, he was sometimes so discouraged, wandering alone in the forest and meditating, that he fell into total despair. He contemplated suicide many times. He talked about one particular day when it was pouring rain, and he was crying. The tears made him wet, the rain made him wet, and he just felt miserable. But he discovered something about himself: he had the capacity to sit through anything.

Self-knowledge has to do with being able to open to more and more. At times, we might even invite trouble, because we know that it's a wonderful thing to do. But we invite just enough trouble so that we can grow a bit—not so much that we're overwhelmed.

Ajahn Mun was one of the main teachers in the Thai Forest tradition. He and the yogis who practiced with him would go to the most dangerous parts of the jungle, where wild elephants, tigers, and snakes were everywhere. The reason the monks would go there was to provoke and flush out fear. They would do their walking meditation within close range of tigers so that they could hear and smell the animals. Naturally, fear came up. They would work with it through direct perception, knowing that if there was no fear, there was no problem with tigers, and if there was fear, they could be the tiger's evening meal. Now I'm not suggesting we do that. But the main idea is that they actually invited and provoked some of the emotions inside themselves that were most uncomfortable and followed them through to the end.

What does this have to do with our lives? What is the wisdom in opening up to pain? Is it even plausible that the way to get free of suffering is to face suffering?

Some people say they're afraid of being crushed by their pain. That feeling is not unfounded. Sometimes in life, you're vulnerable. You've had so much suffering, so much sorrow. Something so terrible has happened that you have to back off and find a measure of joy and peace—like pulling over to the side of the road. In that case, if you have a formal meditation practice, just do some breathing, some metta, or take a walk in nature. But ultimately the emphasis in the Four Noble Truths is that the Buddha attained full awakening by steadily observing his own mind. If you want to be free of suffering, and you know another way of getting free of it, sign me up. I haven't found it.

To start with, you might work with little pieces of dukkha throughout the day. Say you go to work and somebody who is usually friendly walks right past you, no smile. Maybe they're preoccupied with something at home, but you feel rebuffed. Become aware of it. In that moment at work is a tiny piece of suffering. Little by little, you learn how to be with your dukkha around feelings of rejection, which often go back to childhood.

Like the sense of rejection, anger also has deep roots. What I've learned over the years from people who have a lot of anger is that, in the same way, it's useful to apply mindfulness starting with smaller versions of anger—such as irritation or annoyance, which are more manageable. It could be waiting in line at a supermarket and watching someone take too long to pay their bill, and then they can't find their credit card, and you find yourself saying between clenched teeth, "Oh, come on." Start with situations that you can get a handle on and work your way up to stronger feelings.

Eventually you become aware of the cost of anger. The Buddha used vivid imagery to describe anger. He said that when you're angry, it's like you take a burning hot coal and you throw it at the person you're angry at—you hurt them but you also burn yourself. In one of the sutras, he was earthier. He said it's like throwing fecal material—you've besmirched someone else but also yourself.

As you practice with small sufferings, you develop the confidence that suffering is workable. Do you know why it's workable? Because it's observable. If you couldn't observe what's happening, you could never be free.

## A Sangha of Squirrels and Chipmunks

I had a wonderful teacher some years ago. At a certain point, he said, "It's time for you to do a solitary retreat for two months." I wasn't too happy with that, and in fact I resisted it. We had been doing group sitting and lots of chanting in the Zen tradition, and it was wonderful. He said, "No, you have to go away by yourself and sit. Do the same practice, but with no supports, no sangha, just the squirrels and the chipmunks and whatever else is there. That will be your sangha." I said, "Why?" He said, "It's time to flush out fear and loneliness. Maybe a little boredom as well." And that's exactly what happened.

Being alone for a few months, you get awfully bored. Fears that are masked in the activities of a full daily life come out. So does the loneliness that you are not in touch with, because back home there are all these lovely people around and you're having an enjoyable time with them. Suddenly it's taken away, and you drop down into a loneliness that has nothing to do with other people, whether they care for you or not, whether you love them or not. It's much deeper than that. And believe it or not, it's a rich time in practice. You're not wishing you were somewhere else or that the loneliness would go away, even though it's painful.

The mind wants to be at peace in the world. But real life is like throwing a party. We only establish friendly relationships with certain guests, the ones we invited, who responded promptly, who are well dressed and clean and polite—we only feel secure when we're around those kinds of people. We're not comfortable in a world that is full of unknowns, out of control—in other words, a party with rude guests. Often when we're down or things are not going our way, we fall into a mode of describing our situation as "I have a problem. I am defective in some way and I want to remedy it. I want to make myself a better person and fix this personal flaw." I'm not saying that perspective is worthless. But the dharma way is not studious self-improvement—it's self-observation. I've had sorrow that surfaced twenty, thirty years after the fact. Where did this come from? It came from wounds in my life that had been festering and sapping the energy I needed to really look at myself.

### The Price of Grievance

The Buddha once said that all he teaches is the practice of liberation through not clinging. When you hold on to hatred, anger, or grievance, you suffer because you're carrying that baggage, adding to the suffering that triggered your anger. Dropping that baggage depends on your ability to maintain a steady awareness without trying to get a result—just to look carefully. If you do, the grievance softens, weakens, even disappears. What comes out of that? I don't know. I do know that some people have had atrocious treatment inflicted upon them and been able to forgive. I'm not suggesting you cultivate forgiveness by play-acting forgiveness—quite the contrary. I'm saying start where you are, which is that you don't want to forgive.

Admittedly forgiveness is one of the hardest mind states to attain. You feel you should forgive somebody for hurting you. You'd be a "good" yogi if you could forgive. You could gain entry into buddha heaven if you could forgive—but you can't. That realization is as valuable as the forgiving itself. What you're interested in is not to get to some ideal place but to know the place that you actually inhabit in that moment, right here, right now. The letting go, the forgiveness, comes from seeing that you can't let go, that you're holding on. With that insight you open up, not so much letting go as letting be.

As with anger, you pay a price for holding on to grievance. It's not simply that you haven't forgiven the other person but that you haven't forgiven yourself for not forgiving them. So start by forgiving yourself. How do you do that? Again, not by trying to forgive yourself but by seeing that you don't forgive yourself.

In this practice, there is a difference between annihilation and cessation. Annihilation is when we don't like something and we want to get rid of it. Cessation involves allowing whatever is there—in this case, resistance to forgiveness—and really seeing it, allowing it to flower, letting this emotion in, because it's you. We're often quite violent to ourselves—there are certain emotions that we disapprove of and try to banish or prevent from surfacing. This path is the opposite. It's one of opening and allowing what's there to come up. You learn the price that's paid for entertaining certain mind states that make you feel righteous in the moment. You realize that not only have you damaged the other person but you've harmed yourself.

## Getting Comfortable with Discomfort

One of the most self-undermining mind states is depression. Here, I'm not talking about deep, clinical, biologically rooted depression—which may require treatment well beyond meditation—but a passing feeling of discouragement or sadness. All of us feel downhearted from time to time. Who can deny that there's sorrow in human life? The Buddha didn't hide from that fact. But he also perceived that the way to joy, fulfillment, peace is through suffering.

At an interview with a Burmese teacher, I once said, "Whenever I sit, I get peaceful and blissful and joyful. But as soon as I get up, I enter into depression." He said, "Great! That means you're ready to look. The depression didn't come from a cloud. It's something that you're now ready to face." He asked me, "How have you been facing it?" I said, "Well, I just want to quickly get the day going, not sit. I want to do active things." From the point of view of dharma, I was squandering an opportunity. Keeping busy was an escape and exit strategy, and just prolonged the buried pain.

Passing depression is not good or bad. The question is: What do you do with it? The dharma attitude is not so much attaining particular experiences—who wouldn't want to be happy?—but learning how to be awake and mindful of the experiences that you actually have. You are learning how to get comfortable with discomfort, how to not always bolt and react—to not only depression but all difficult mind states. Instead, use the breath to slow down and establish an entirely different relationship—one of friendship—with whatever turns up. Years ago, I traveled all the way to Thailand to attain more pleasant feelings. Of course, the teachers there roared with laughter. The peace that I aspired to, a peace worthy of its name, required that I get to know myself.

If depression should turn up after you've been practicing for a while—not *depression*, the word, but the energy of it—the practice would be to turn your attention to what is being called "depression." There's going to be something that is registered in the body. Usually that's the most accessible and easiest to observe. The bodily expression of depression is also more manageable. As we breathe in and breathe out, the breath accompanies us as we walk into an emotion or a bodily state that we don't like. No one wants to be depressed, but here it is now. I would call this a practice for adults, because sometimes life is boring, sometimes it's wonderful. And sometimes there's depression.

Two ways that we relate to depression are to deny it or drown in it. When we deny it, we press it down. Some people are good at that, until finally they can't do it anymore. When we drown in it, we identify with that heavy, distorting energy that has visited us. We can't see other options. If depression surfaces, just let it out and attend to it, bring full attention to it. It's an intimate observing of the energy of depression.

Mindfulness is a power. Think of it like the sun shining on a flower and the flower opening up. When mindfulness is directed to something, when its energy touches depression, fear, loneliness, or anger, there's a transformation. The energy that's been held captive in difficult mind states is released. It's free energy for you to use and live with. The practice is infinite watching. But it requires full acceptance of our mind states, allowing that energy to flower, meeting it, seeing its nature and impermanence.

Interestingly, as you learn to be mindful of difficult emotional states, you will find that awareness cannot coexist with painful mind states. There's no shame, guilt, or fear with awareness; there's no old, young, male, female, gay, straight—no identity of any sort—with awareness.

Let's take shame. Are you able to just look at shame simply as a mind state? If not, when you feel ashamed about something, the mind has a field day. The mind also loves it when you try to get rid of your shame, to put it behind you with bluster or bravado: "There's nothing to be ashamed of; I outgrew that. That situation is long over with." What the mind hates is inviting shame in: "Sit down, shame, have a cup of coffee and a muffin." It hates it when you are open and aware of shame without any motive, when you're not trying to get rid of shame, not trying to improve upon it, not trying to be heroic.

In other words, the truth in all these instances lies in the clear seeing. Clear seeing is the healing, the compassion, the insight. And that awareness is where, more and more, I encourage you to live. Just be that which knows.

In decades of teaching these ideas, I've been struck by how we humans can't seem to separate language from the energy of what the language points to. Our words condition our habit energy. *Anger, anger. Fear, fear. Loneliness, loneliness.* Once you see the difference between the raw energy of, say, loneliness and the words you use for loneliness, you may still feel lonely, but it's a bit more manageable. *Mindfulness* is also just a word, but it refers to a seeing energy. When that seeing energy touches habit energy, something new emerges.

The Buddha said that suffering was his gateway to freedom. In this strange path that he laid out for us, you come to peace by knowing its absence. When he said, "All I teach is suffering and the end of suffering," he meant that you get to the end of suffering by looking at the suffering. The main thing is to uproot our attachment to highly charged states—such as fear, anger, or shame—not to try to uproot the state itself. We can't control what's going to visit the mind, but our relationship to it makes all the difference in the world. I can sum up all of the Buddha's teaching about painful mind states in just a few sentences. It's the *Reader's Digest* Book of the Month Club version of vipassana. It's a simple contemplation whenever you find yourself suffering, whether it's mild annoyance or emotional torment: "What am I attached to here?"

# 8

Aging, Sickness, Death, and Grief

SOME YEARS AGO I was teaching a practice group on death and dying. When the class was over, I went home to relax a bit. I turned on the TV and there was an old film with Clark Gable and Carole Lombard. They were in the prime of life, lusty and vigorous. I was watching and everyone on the screen was prancing around like they were going to be there forever. Clark Gable was handsome and virile. Carole Lombard was sensual and seductive, flirtatious and funny. I knew the film. I knew the stars. I knew the bit-part players. I knew who directed it. I knew who wrote the screenplay. As I was watching, suddenly it hit me: absolutely everyone in this film was dead. Without exception, they were dead. The stars were dead. The bit players were dead. The musicians, the stunt people: dead. The people who sold the popcorn in the theaters—they were probably dead, too.

It was like an arrow through my heart. That night, for some reason, I was receptive to the poignancy of impermanence. None of us knows when our time will be up. But we will all die. No one gets out of this alive. If a person is strong enough, rather than sugarcoating it, they may be able to take the bitter medicine—that we're all subject to this strange state of affairs, that we're born and we love to be here and it's going to be taken away from us, only we don't know when or how.

Everything is not only impermanent and changing but changing in uncertain ways.

*Samvega* is a term the Buddha used for the urgency of practice when we see how fragile life is. In the Bhagavad Gita, it is said that people can live their entire lives seeing death all around and still not understand that it's about them, too. When you say to yourself, "I'm not aging; I don't feel old at all" or "I'm the same person I always was"—that is delusion, a comfy mind state that doesn't want to know about the wisdom in the Bhagavad Gita.

In a sense, there's no security. Really seeing that there's no security is the only security. Ajahn Lee, who was a master in the Thai Forest tradition, once said that if people realized how precious aging, sickness, and death are, from a spiritual point of view, they would bow down to them every day of their life. When Ajahn Chah was asked to convey the essence of right understanding, he pointed to a cup and said, "This cup is already broken." One interpretation is to value what our life is like right now. If all the political antagonisms, ethnic hatreds, racial hatreds, class hatreds, gender hatreds, and all the rest of it stopped, if we just looked at one another and understood that we're all comrades in aging, sickness, and death, could we be doing the things we're doing?

In the Thai Forest tradition, reflections on aging, sickness, and death were central. You should understand that the Thai Forest tradition is actually the Thai jungle tradition—the forests are not what we would think of as forests; you wouldn't want to picnic in some of those places, believe me. In the jungles of Thailand, fear is frequently aroused. A tiger could roam nearby at any time.

In this tradition, accomplished yogis—not beginners—were told to go out in the jungle and do walking meditation. If a tiger showed up, they were to look the tiger in the eye and realize that they and the tiger were companions in aging, sickness, and death. One of my teachers, Ajahn Maha Bua, went into a fair amount of detail on this reflection because he'd been in that very situation. When you reflect that you and the tiger are companions in aging, sickness, and death, it changes your view, not only of tigers but of those other tigers walking around dressed up as humans. It can rescue you from the ways in which the mind becomes small. If you get into entanglements, anger, and annoyances with people you work with or with your family or friends, that reflection has a way of burning right through it. If everyone in the world were doing it, I don't see how we could have wars.

Shining the light of death on life puts whatever is happening in your life into perspective. A lot of what you shine the light on doesn't stand up. Most of it is trivial, petty, not worth hurting anyone for. When I find myself falling into pettiness—someone didn't come through with something they promised, or someone is not up to snuff, or someone has an irritating quirk—if I just look at them and understand that we're comrades in aging, sickness, and death, it shifts things. Understanding that you don't have forever, and neither does anyone else, enables you to be more compassionate. These reflections soften the heart.

## *Disciples of Death*

The interest in aging, sickness, and death is an ancient one, part of all spiritual traditions and an integral part of vipassana practice. How could this topic be avoided? The urgency of spiritual life is coming to terms with this existential fact.

A friend reminded me of a chapter in the Tao Te Ching, the classic text of Taoism. Verse 76 is one of the most beautiful and concise statements about death: "Humans are born soft and flexible. In death, they become stiff and hard. Plants are born soft and pliable. When dead, they become brittle and dry. Therefore, those who are stiff and rigid become disciples of death, while those who are soft and yielding become disciples of life. The hard and stiff break, the soft and supple triumph."

The body stiffens with age. But does the mind have to stiffen along with the body? The Buddha's loud and clear answer: "Of course not."

Most of us do not have a proper education about the place of aging, sickness, and death in life. Then we wake up one day and suddenly it's starting to happen to us and the people around us, and we feel inadequate, overwhelmed, ill-equipped. Reflecting on aging, sickness, and death helps us free ourselves from an area that, in our culture, is conflicted and problematic. The Buddha's reflections are designed to get you to practice with more intensity. They light a fire under you to get on with it, to examine your life, to put your priorities in order, to see how you're living.

In Buddhism, the teachings on *maranasati*, or death awareness, are invaluable. If you intentionally take up the notion that you are subject to aging, subject to illness, subject to death, that itself can be a powerful meditation or reflection. We acknowledge that we are afraid of dying, maybe even terrified of it—and we want to be present when it happens. One of the values of practices like this is to invite what's inside us outside, to see what's there. If dharma is about anything, it's about freedom, liberation. If we're terrified of something, denying something, negating or avoiding something, we're not free.

The emphasis on confronting impermanence is informed by the Buddha's own biography. We know that Siddhartha, the man who would become known as the Buddha, was born into an aristocratic family and seemingly had everything. He was talented, intelligent, handsome, strong, competent in sports; he did well scholastically and, of course, lived in a palace. His father, the king, was told by an astrologer that his son was either going to become a world leader, such as a monarch, or a spiritual leader, in which case the son would leave home and would not carry on the lineage. Of course, the father didn't want to lose his dynasty. He arranged his son's life so that worldly joys were maximized and hardship was minimized. He tried to protect Siddhartha from seeing the suffering that could point him toward a spiritual path.

To this end, when the Buddha left the palace with his trusted charioteer, the king tried to clean up the town, get all these old, sick, and dying folks out of there and make the place beautiful so that Siddhartha's naïve delusions would not be challenged. But the *devas*—people from the heaven realms—had other ideas. Siddhartha encountered what were called the four divine messengers. First, they saw to it that an old man would pass through. The man was bent over and could hardly walk. The Buddha had never seen an old person. He had been protected, and he wanted to know who that was. He asked his charioteer, "What is that?" The charioteer said, "That's old age." "Will that happen to me?" "Yes." The Buddha was taken aback. He went through this same process when he saw a man who was sick and in pain and when he saw a corpse. He wasn't yet awakened. Then came the fourth messenger, a yogi or *samana*—somebody who had attained peace. The yogi was meditating; in contrast to the old, sick, and dead people, he was serene, content. Each one of these divine messengers delivered a powerful message to Siddhartha.

### The Drama of Stiff Knees

We are surrounded by divine messengers. The truth of impermanence and suffering are part and parcel of aging. The body grows old and breaks down. How should we observe that? Here, the Buddha's instructions are clear: when people who don't meditate feel pain, they get hit with two arrows. The first arrow is the physical pain. The second arrow is the mind, which intensifies the pain and turns it into torment.

If you have a body, you have pain. If you don't want to have bodily pain, don't get born. Say you wake up in the morning and, oh, wow: stiff knees. Go right to the stiffness. If you've been practicing a long time and you zero in on the stiffness, the power of concentration is such that you may not even have any thoughts. It's as if attention breaks the momentum of the proliferating mind. But let's assume that thoughts do come up. "Oh, my God. I'm getting older. What's going to happen to me?" Practice would be understanding that those are merely thoughts.

If you dig into the fear of aging, you will find that an enormous amount of that fear grows out of thinking. In Buddhist teaching, as we've learned, the self is just a bunch of notions, representations, and images—that's what emptiness means: we are not solid. Here, the mind makes up a notion of "I'm getting older." That can be accompanied by imaginings about what happens down the pike—a joyless life, isolation, ailments, pain, rejection, poverty. Before you know it, it's a nightmare.

The term *satipanna* is used a lot in the Thai Forest tradition. *Sati* is mindfulness. *Panna* is discernment. It's not just a vacant stare of mindfulness but rather a keen interest in investigation: "What's going on here? What is this? How did I start out with stiff knees and end up with so much drama?" In dharma, we turn everything into investigation. It's letting the fear or discouragement flower but meeting it with the mirror of mindfulness. What is this? What's happening here? You begin to see, "My mind has made up a catastrophe about the future. But all that's happening is two stiff knees."

The pain and loss of aging are inevitable. You had a certain image of yourself, and now it is shattered. Your capacities have diminished. Your ego is tarnished. You're attached to the way you used to be, when movement was smoother, but it ain't true anymore. Even strangers see you differently. In a public place, you may be singled out as elderly, and you feel wounded. But what got hurt? Who's clinging? It's always "me." Feel the energy of that hurt. Can your awareness open up to it, receive it, be intimate with it, try not to do anything to it? If so, you'll learn about yourself.

Of course, chronic pain is no joke: "Is this ever going to stop?" But that's throwing fuel on the fire. When you feel discouraged about chronic pain, that's considered a "strong object" in meditation language. You're lost in it. The mind is making up a story, turning "ache, ache" into agony. I know this from personal experience as I have aged. Sometimes it will be an hour and a half, two hours of no pain. It's like heaven. Then the pain comes back—terrible discouragement.

Awareness has no pain—that's the beauty of awareness. Please make awareness your home because you'll see that everything else is a condition that you can't count on; it comes and goes. We humans live in a conditioned realm, mind and body. Anything that arises and passes away is a condition, a small part of the brain. If you can think of consciousness as a vast field of energy, completely untouched, it's not pain or anything else—it's awareness. Instead of setting up an ideal to be pain-free, as much as we long for it, be with what is actually here in the moment. Are you feeling discouraged? If you are, there's gold in that, because it can be a dharma door into freedom—if you can stay with the discouragement and let it tell its story. All dharma practice says that the experience of aliveness is attainable, with or without a crisis. Anything that helps us be fully alive is dharma.

### A Lesson on Aging

When I was starting on this path, I received an early lesson on how to approach aging, and sometimes even transcend aging, from Sivananda Saraswati, a wonderful Indian teacher who was traveling around the United States by Greyhound bus to visit his disciples. He was eighty-six years old. I had the good fortune to travel with him for a number of months. I went wherever he went. We stayed together, and I watched how he lived. This was before the age of spiritual superstars, when lamas and Zen masters and sayadaws are flown all over the place.

Saraswati was quite amazing, fresh as a daisy, even after traveling on a Greyhound bus overnight. He was very much a contemplative. He would get up at 3:30 or sometimes 2:30 in the morning and would go right into sitting. He wouldn't even wash. He would just sit up in his bed. I had to do everything he did because that was the agreement. Sometimes he would be in that posture for hours. He would also practice physical training. At eighty-six, he could still do a headstand. He had a lot of energy. He was attentive to his diet. I wouldn't say that it was a fetish for him, but there was an attentiveness in the way he took care of his body.

At one point he told me something that has stayed with me all these years. He said that if you take reasonable care of the body, you can have a relatively painless old age. Now, he wasn't idealizing a kind of body-beautiful Hollywood hatha yoga, as if you're never going to die. He wasn't trying to present himself as a young man. He was just himself.

A lot of the aging process is out of our control. But there are ways in which we can influence our own karma. Saraswati said that if you take care of the body, eat reasonably, give the body a reasonable amount of exercise, see to it that the breath is adequate, that the water is good, that you don't have too much or too little sleep, you can have a relatively painless old age.

Why did he stress this point? He felt a relatively painless old age was valuable because, as he put it, his deepest spiritual realizations came between the ages of seventy and, at the time, eighty-six. He explained that with age, many desires fall away. Of course, he was deeply contemplative—but he felt that, independent of that or on top of that, desires naturally fall away. If the body is in reasonable health and has a reasonable amount of energy at its disposal, then the spiritual life could flourish.

### A Powerful Energy

In some ways, Saraswati was a special case. Typically fear and other emotions prevent us from even beginning to contemplate death. The first time I taught a formal program about aging, sickness, and death, I gave a talk at Cambridge Insight Meditation Center, which had just opened. A muscle-bound man, about six foot four with burly shoulders, was sitting in the dharma hall. He was so anxious that sweat was pouring down his face. In the middle of the talk, he ran out of the room. I spoke to him later in the week. He told me he didn't want to go near this topic; he wasn't ready for it. He had had a lot of depression in his life. At that point, looking at aging, sickness, and death was not a skillful thing to do.

We're playing with powerful energy here. It's not a joke to contemplate aging, sickness, and especially death, so timing is important. Before taking on death awareness, this man needed to experience more joy, to do metta (loving-kindness meditation), to practice generosity and do things for other people, to bring some happiness into his life.

The Buddha's teaching puts tremendous emphasis on self-reliance. But if a person has been seriously wounded emotionally, he or she is not ready to be self-reliant. If this is a time in your life when there's been a lot of loss and sadness, or if you're new to meditation, you probably won't be able to do death-awareness reflections. But it's useful to hear about them. Maybe some seeds will be planted and the day will come when you feel that you want to take them on. If so, I would trust that intuition.

Let's say the topic of death brings up fear: "Death is inevitable. I must die." As with other emotions, the most accessible place to practice anything that's happening in the mind is in the body. See if it's true. If you have any negative thought—it may be subtle—it will turn up in the body. Mind and body are distinguishable, but they're quite interrelated. The mind makes up a story about what's happening to the body. Usually the story is written so fast, and mind and body are so intertwined, that we can't even separate them.

Slow down the process. You will feel how the pulse changes, the heart changes, the breath changes. You feel your heart start to pound, your pulse race, fear come up. Practice would be awareness with equanimity. Equanimity means that you're not judging what's come up, you're not for or against it, you're not grasping at it or pushing it away. You're just observing the actual energy of fear in the body or mind. Think of it this way: if death has brought up fear, that means you're alive.

When you start to examine your fear of dying, what you often see is that it's not the moment of death that you're afraid of but rather the idea of your future death. The soil out of which that fear has grown is thinking. At that moment, you're not actually dying—except maybe in an existential sense. But the mind has made up a grim future that you know will come. By paying attention to the sensations in the body around fear, seeing them come and go, it becomes easy to see how much they are aroused by thoughts. Once you see that, the connection can fall away—and so will the fear.

Of course, the time will come when you actually are dying. That will be a moment just like this moment. You will be in a hospital or at home or wherever it happens. You will be breathing in a certain way. Your mind will be set a certain way. The body will feel a certain way. There will be people around or not. It will be hot or cold. It will be a real piece of life, only you will be in the process of dying.

If you take care of practice, the rest will take care of itself. The best thing you can do to have an easy death, a peaceful death, a death not full of bewilderment and torment is to practice now. You're learning how to study your mind, how to make it strong and clear and calm so that it can examine the present moment and look deeply into what's most alive for you in a certain moment. When the time comes to die, the instructions don't change; only the stage set changes.

If your practice gets to the point where there's tremendous continuity in awareness, so that you're in the timeless present, then fear of death becomes just a passing thought. Even in the moments leading up to death, there will be something fulfilling about being intimately and totally connected with the moment. It's the continuous present, or presence—no future, no past, only now. The challenge of the practice, even up to your last breath, is to live fully in this moment.

### Helping Others in Pain

As meditators, we know the importance for ourselves of staying aware as our body starts to fail. But what if you are close to someone who is seriously ill, perhaps in despair? You may likewise feel a kind of despair, a sense of separation or frustration, because nothing you do seems to help. The practice would be to work with your frustration, helplessness. It's not to figure out how you can fix the person's illness or despondency. Start right where you are, which is that you are feeling disappointment, lack of confidence or decisiveness: "What do I do now?" Maybe you feel an urge to leave or give up.

If you don't take care of that, then the mind skips over it or decides to launch into action and do something wholesome and good for the other person. But if you can take care of your feeling of frustration and helplessness, even a little bit, you have more clarity. You can see that in spite of the fact that you want to help, you're not doing so. This is important: you are learning how to live with the frustration of being helpless when someone you love is sick. Remember, you don't own life—yours or anyone else's.

You are investigating—not through anyone's theory, not even through Buddhist theory, but through your own movement. Life is teaching you. You may find that your sense of helplessness is unfounded, that in fact you are helping. Or you may find that your best intentions are backfiring and that you have gotten attached to wanting to be good, wanting to help, which is only natural. Either way, you can learn, if you're willing to move with it. There's no formula.

When someone we love grows old and changes, there's also sorrow that can't be overlooked. We compare how the person was to how they are now. This is where learning comes in. Find out if you're adding to a loved one's suffering and your own by comparing how they used to be to how they are now. See if that awareness doesn't diminish some of the sorrow for both of you.

Often we put a diagnostic label on a sick person. Society makes these labels, and the person may have taken on a label as an identity. In that sense, you're an accomplice to their pre-defined illness, treating them in a certain way. You're digging them deeper and deeper into an identity. Dissolve that label in your mind and just be with the person who is suffering.

Here's an example from my life. My father was extremely intelligent, very alert. Suddenly he developed a deep dementia, something like Alzheimer's. Unfortunately we had to put him in what was basically a nursing home. For a number of months when I visited him, I thought of him as "my father who has Alzheimer's." That label kept being used by the nurses, the doctors, the family. At a certain point I realized it was a filter. I was not seeing my dad, I was seeing "my dad, the Alzheimer's patient." Once I let go of that, I was able to make contact with him as he was, without a label. Labels come with a lot of suppositions and assumptions. How we label somebody influences even our process of perception with no diagnostic label. I could enjoy him much more—which, in turn, helped him.

My father had a good sense of humor when he had his full faculties—he always had us in stitches. He used to enjoy his own humor as he would spin out stories, and he was still enjoying that role. Here he was in a nursing home, still trying to be funny, but he made no sense. My mother, my sister, my brother-in-law, their children, my wife, myself—all of us, we just looked at each other. We were sitting there stoically, staring at him, unmoved. What he said was totally illogical, there was nothing funny about it. We attributed it to his dementia.

The practice helped me understand: "Wait a minute. I want him to be how he used to be, and he isn't." So the next time we visited and he told his nonsensical stories and laughed, I would get in it with him and roar and laugh along with him. It made him so happy—he laughed, I laughed. We had a good time, father and son.

After we left, my family ganged up on me. "Did you find anything humorous? We didn't understand a thing he said." I replied, "Well, where's the rule that I have to know what's so funny? Did you see how it made him happy to have someone laugh with him? That was better than any of the high-priced medications that he's taking."

This was a solution unique to my father. You have to find your own way of meeting the person you love on their terms. You have to find new ways to relate to them. Keep reminding yourself to be present with them, to be in the moment and cherish that. What that requires of you is a freshness and an innocence of mind. It brings you back to silence. Out of silence can come all kinds of unprecedented creativity.

I often get asked, "What can I do for someone who is dying—especially if they are not a meditator?" In fact, I get asked it more often than what I consider to be a more relevant question: "What can I do for myself when someone is dying?" Here are a few things that you can do. Sometimes you can just talk to them in a way that expresses your wisdom, your understanding. But realize that you can't give them anything you don't have. If you see your own anxiety, apprehension, frustration, or sadness, because you know what's happening to someone you love, practice with that. Some of the anxiety will weaken or even fall away and that will open up a space of clarity, calm. When you're with that person, you have a better chance of meeting them where they are and being helpful. Yours will be a response, not a reaction. You won't reflexively say the "right" things—"Don't worry" or "You'll get better" or whatever it is that you think will make the person feel good. You may even say those words, but they will land differently because it's not a mechanical reaction to illness coming from the old mind.

This lesson was brought home for me under difficult circumstances. My mother was dying. She was ninety years old, she had had a stroke, and she was in a hospital bed. She was supposed to have died within a matter of hours. We all raced to the hospital. But she lingered on for about three weeks, to the surprise of the doctors and nurses.

My mother was fighting to stay alive, and she reached a patch of real misery where each breath was exhausting. I was getting exhausted just watching her. She would work so hard to breathe. Each breath seemed to take up all of her energy, but she was hanging in there. I was holding her hand and stroking her brow. And, like a fool, I gave her a good dharma talk—"good" in quotes. I was saying, "Mom, your body has served you well for all these years, but it's now starting to run down. It's tired. There's nothing to fear. Let go." I was holding her hand, and every time I said, "Let go," her grip became tighter. Finally it was like a truck driver's grip.

It was the right thing to say, but it was wrong, totally incorrect. Obviously I was not tuned in. What was I doing, giving her that kind of teaching? I could see by the effect it was having that my words were making her more frightened. I was adding misery to her life. So I dropped all the "letting go" talk and shifted to the good old reliable metta, loving-kindness: "You've been a loving person all your life"—which was true—"and many people love you"—also true—"and you love many people. We're all here. We love you." Her hand relaxed and a little smile came over her face. Now, I didn't memorize those words from a Buddhist manual: "How to Take Care of a Dying Parent." I had to learn on the spot. I had to be able to recognize that I was doing something wrong and clear enough to do what was right for my mother, whom I loved dearly.

## The Ways of Grief

In all the scenarios of death and dying, we mostly learn on the spot; the circumstances are usually so unexpected that we can't rehearse. When I was practicing in Korea at a monastery way up in the mountains, a nun died. She was in her sixties or seventies. The custom there is that the monks are on one side of the mountain and the nuns are on the other side. They each came from their respective sides of the mountain to where the nun's body was being cremated, which was followed by chanting.

I was sitting next to a well-known Korean Zen master. He started sobbing and sobbing. I was pretty new to dharma practice—it was my second or third year—and I merely knew everything. I thought, "This is supposed to be a Zen master. People get born, they grow old, they get sick and die. What's the problem?" I felt embarrassed that he couldn't compose himself.

I had an interview with him the next day. I told him, "I thought Zen masters were supposed to be calm and at ease with whatever's happened. After all, this nun is dead. It's over with. It's the past." He roared with laughter. He said, "I don't know where you got your Zen from. It's just Buddhist teaching with a twist—a Taoist, Chinese, Japanese, Korean, or Vietnamese twist. I've known this nun for fifty years. We were good friends. I'll miss her. And so I was sobbing fully. I don't know how long it will take. But when the tears stop, then I'll be over it and move on. Do you want us to be statues?"

There's more to this story. I later studied with Ajahn Suwat, a Thai Forest teacher. I told him about watching the death cremation of the nun at the Korean monastery, that I was surprised that a Zen master there was sobbing, and that I felt foolish that I was surprised. I repeated what the Zen master had told me: that he had known the nun for many years; she was a good friend; he would miss her; he was grieving fully; and when he was done grieving, the tears would be over. I said that seemed like a good explanation to me—it sounded like what human beings do.

Still, I asked Ajahn Suwat, "What do you think?" I wasn't being mischievous, just curious. He had some hesitation because he didn't want to say anything negative. Finally he said that it sounded like the Korean monk didn't have complete wisdom, that he still had something to learn. It was as if the nun who died was *his* nun: "My nun died." There was a sense of possession and self-pity.

Then I asked Ajahn Suwat about his own teacher. He had been close to a wonderful teacher, Ajahn Funn, who had died. I said, "How was that for you?"

He told me, "Many times when I was a younger monk, I would get sad and depressed and worried about what will happen when Ajahn Funn dies. But I kept practicing with it. Years went by, and when Ajahn Funn did die, I felt deep love for him—but there wasn't an enormous amount of suffering." What he was trying to say is that when wisdom goes deep, when you understand that we all must die—and this is plausible to me—not grieving when someone dies doesn't mean you're cold—although from an outsider's point of view, it may seem that way. In grieving, equanimity can have warmth. And indifference or callousness can be a protection against strong emotions—the other side of getting lost in our feelings.

I kept drawing him out. "Do you think you repressed your grief?" He said, "No. I felt tremendous love for Ajahn Funn. I couldn't have loved him more if he had been my own father. But wisdom had developed over the years. I knew it was time for him to die. That's all."

I'm not saying that Ajahn Suwat's reaction was superior to the Korean monk's. How could I? Who knows? The practice is not trying to give you an ideal way of grieving to run after. If what turns up after someone dies is that you cry, it's not good or bad. The point is to enter into that feeling with full awareness—because that's what's happening now. If you do that, then you're not making "me" and "mine" out of your grief. You're simply allowing a natural condition to arise. Intimacy with sorrow means to throw away all the stories. One story may be the hardest to throw away: self-pity. Why did this happen to *me*? If someone were to bring up the law of uncertainty, the fact that death can come unannounced at any time, it would sound unkind, coarse, vulgar, or just insensitive.

When someone you love has died, either your practice will falter or your practice will blossom and grow by opening up to a new level of pain that perhaps you've never known. Choose the path of opening up to it, allowing it to be just what it is. Try to make the seeing unwavering, even if it's just a moment here, a moment there.

## Is There Rebirth?

The concept of rebirth is central to the Buddha's teaching. I've developed a lot of trust in the Buddha. Would the Buddha lie about it? For me, it's not either/or. Perhaps, along with the continual birth of self, there is an actual physical rebirth. After all, it makes no sense that you live and work so hard on yourself and then suddenly the body dies and that's the end of it. All your hard work on yourself—one big joke. The universe—a big joke. In Buddhism, it's thought that we learn different lessons in different lifetimes. The past lives of the Buddha—whether they're a myth, propaganda, or delusion—are interesting because they point out different qualities that were developed in previous lifetimes. To me, it's not implausible that sometimes it takes many, many lifetimes to develop patience or generosity or compassion or honesty or mindfulness.

In popular Buddhism, the kind practiced in Asian villages, people take the idea of rebirth seriously. Their aim in life is to make the best karma they can so that they have a good rebirth. There are dharma books that even detail karmic consequences—such as if you intentionally crush a mosquito, you will be reborn as an ant. I feel that's folklore, and I don't put much stock in it. But the law of karma is not ridiculous to me because the law of cause and effect seems obvious—even in your own life, you can verify it.

To be on the path is to be free. I honestly do not know if there is life after death. But let's say I never existed before, and that when I die, that's it. I would still keep up this practice because it helps me live now. Having studied various forms of the Buddha's teaching for many years, whatever I've tested has proven to be beneficial. If there is a future life, then it's whipped cream, chocolate syrup; it's icing on the cake. But if these future rewards are an illusion, you're doing something that's in your own best interest right now.

One of the Thai Forest masters I studied with, Ajahn Buddhadasa, was a wonderful human being and a great teacher. His feeling was that when the Buddha talked about life and death and being born and reborn, he wasn't talking about future lives. He was talking about this life, in which what is constantly reborn is the self. Just in the course of an ordinary day, in hundreds of thousands of moments, the "I" is born and dies. In other words, in a given moment, when we attach to something and identify with it, we're reborn as whatever that thought is—"I'm a good person, I'm a bad person, I'm an angry person"—and whenever we're aware of it, we get free of it. It's not that we're literally reborn from the womb of a mother but reborn in the sense that the mind gives birth to notions of self. Many times during the day we've relinquished self-centeredness, self-preoccupation. If we're mindful during those moments, we're free.

These are just speculations. In Buddhism, the profound emphasis is not on rebirth. It's to come to a place that was never born and doesn't die—to put it in Buddhist language, to die before you die. In Zen, they talk about the great death: the death of the ego, the death of "me" and "mine." This path leads to a deathless state, sometimes called the unborn, nirvana, the unconditioned. It's not something that we acquire. It's something that when we clear away everything that's obscuring it, we come to know what we have been all along.

### Graduation Time

Several years ago, a good friend of Cambridge Insight Meditation Center was dying. I visited her in the hospice. I walked in. I looked at her. She looked at me. We both smiled. I said, "It's graduation time." She laughed and said, "Larry, I have never felt so free." I said, "Tell me about it." She had spent a lot of time studying Christianity, even toyed with being a nun for a while. She said, "I don't feel I'm anything. I'm not a Buddhist. I'm not a Christian." I said, "That's graduation."

The art of living doesn't end just because we are going to die. The question is: How do we die? Do we die gracefully? Do we die at peace?

Ajahn Maha Bua said that at the time of death, if a person has a strong practice, it's clear that everything is dying—but not awareness. The same training that's good for life is also good for death. It's a mastery of the moment. There's no past or future, just now. It's all there's ever going to be. We'll find out, of course, on graduation day.

# 9

---

# Wise Action in a World on Fire

IN THE THERAVADA TEACHINGS, the kilesas, or afflictions of the human mind—greed, hatred, delusion, and their many offspring—are the sources of our misery. Let's assume that most everyone, if not everyone, is born with their share of greed, hatred, and delusion. How many people are on the planet? Eight billion. Multiply greed, hatred, and delusion by eight billion. Throw us all together. Just read the headlines: this is what you get.

How can you come to inner silence when there's so much outer turmoil, so much anguish, so much pain? Do we neglect the world that we live in, turn our back on what's happening, to escape into silence?

In order to be clear in the world outside, it's helpful to be able to go inside. Now, going inside can be used to escape from what's going on. Those of you who have been yogis for a while know that when you get concentrated, you leave the whole world behind. But the things that can be accomplished in silence, in meditation, also enable us to enter into action in ways that are useful and beneficial. In other words, silence is practical. It's survival. By survival, I don't mean of the physical body. I mean of a certain dignity and integrity for all of us in the face of tremendous global challenges.

Buddhism, the teachings of the Buddha, is a religion of the mind. The heart of Buddhist teaching has everything to do with the mind.

What we call terrorism came from human minds. Attempts to eradicate it, to live in a different way, what we're doing here: that also comes from the mind. The secret of both misery and happiness is in each one of our minds, not anywhere else. During times like this, it's easy to be pushed off course, to forget what we know, to not practice much, or to think we're practicing but not really doing it. I can only hint at the resources—I would say immense resources—in dharma. They're quite simple, but they have as much power as you're willing to give them. And the twenty-first century is a time when we need help.

The Buddha said that ignorance is the problem. It's not any political figure or terrorist group—those are expressions of something farther down the pike. Of course, they must be dealt with on their own terms. But the great human problem is ignorance. We don't know how to live together because we can't live with ourselves. We're in conflict. How can we expect our leaders not to be in conflict?

You may wonder why, even with a dedicated dharma practice, you may feel such unease, anger, or outrage when you look at what's happening in our country and around the world. But it's a funny thing with practice: if you're really doing it, you become more sensitive, not less. That's what being awake is: sensitive, in the sense of discerning. You begin to notice things, even if it's just a tree or an animal, anything. The sounds of a bird chirping are much more vivid. Meditation makes you dramatically more sensitive. It also makes you more vulnerable. The same discernment sees pain more readily in others if you're practicing the path of self-knowing.

There is also a strength that comes from sensitivity. In fact, the practice can't be done without a certain amount of strength. To be a yogi takes courage. It's not just the breath—in, out, in, out, nice feeling, twenty minutes is up, let's go jogging. There's more to wisdom than just calming down, as vital as that is. Yogis cry, even experienced ones. After the September 11, 2001, attacks on America, for example, someone asked me, "You've been meditating a long time. Did you cry?" I was taken aback. Of course I cried. I'm not the Buddha made of stone. This person said, "Well, I thought if you meditate, you would have equanimity." For me, seeing the firefighters did it. The first newscast showed everyone running out of the Twin Towers, and the firefighters running in. How could I not cry?

## What Conditions Produce Hatred?

September 11 was horrifying and tragic but also instructive, from a dharma point of view. On that morning I had finished my yoga session, had a nice little smile on my face; my body felt limber, breath flowing freely, lots of energy. Then I did my vipassana practice at home. The phone rang. It was a friend. "Do you know what's happened? Have you seen the news?" I thought it was good news—X got married or Y had a child. "No, I haven't." I turned on the TV and saw a plane flying into a building, and it looked like a Steven Spielberg special effects or science fiction movie. I expected Godzilla to come out or King Kong with a little lady in his hand, a Hollywood production. But it wasn't. This was actually going on. This is what happened.

After the shock of that, and emotions that I don't have to spell out, I was left with a question—I don't know if we can call it a koan, to make it sound a little more Buddhist: What is going on here? Which conditions produce such hatred? How does the human mind turn in such an extreme direction? I've been living with that.

After the 9/11 attacks—as after any incident of extreme violence close by—there was fear in the air. Those feelings are not to be trifled with, because what's being released are powerful human emotions. I know dharma works in these circumstances. But, of course, I'm in the business, so I would say that. Take the teachings and find out for yourself if this is a bunch of baloney, malarkey, or if it's something that you can use in times of trouble.

The deeper the threat when something challenges us so radically, the greater the possibility for growth on both individual and cultural levels. You have to not only recognize it but do something with it. Awareness, as always, is our best friend. Maybe to begin with, you need to pull back from the turmoil in the world. But pure practice is the opposite of pulling back. It's intimate, it's opening up, it's fully receiving your experience. It's being where there's no separation. If there's sorrow, let there be sorrow. But stay awake in the midst of the sorrow. Let that energy arise. Let it run its natural course, and sometimes it will teach you, though not necessarily in words. If you can do even a little of that, the mind gets quiet. If you're an experienced meditator, you can tap silence now and then from that clear mind, what in Zen they call "no mind."

Tending to a torn world requires a clear mind—as clear as you're able to help the mind become. Then you can return to the challenges that face you. Each one of us has different challenges. In crisis times, we face challenges with our families, at work, with our neighbors—challenges, of course, starting with ourselves. That's why I say start with yourself, always. Dharma practice is a way to better equip yourself to face your life as it is so that you will know what to do.

But this is not a solo act. The mind-centered practice of Buddhadharma doesn't exclude community. *Sangha* is a word we often hear. We take refuge. We chant, "The Buddha, the Dharma, the Sangha." In times of violence or great uncertainty, it's good that we have one another, even if it's just for a few hours a week; that we know there are people who are hurting the way we are, people who are trying to remain balanced and lucid in the midst of it. We're not different from anyone else who's suffering, except in one sense: we have a time-tested path of sanity to follow.

In other words, practice—no matter what conditions are swirling around you. Human beings are born with awareness. Awareness is with you, at least potentially, all the time, no matter what you're doing. The possibility of mustering that quality of sensitivity is our birthright. We all have it: the original nature, Buddha mind, the unconditioned. No one got shortchanged. We're born with that. It's part of our equipment.

You're always better off if your mind is clear. You're always worse off if your mind is confused. Take fear, which is one of the main emotions that surfaces in crisis. Get to know how your mind generates fear, how it fabricates fear. Even when there is something legitimately to be afraid of, the mind has a way of adding to what is factual. It has carte blanche poetic license. It makes fear into whatever it wants to. You create a nightmarish world that isn't here and may never arrive. One feeling that I've had for years, which I hope comes through in my teaching: I see most people as much stronger than they think they are. By strong, I mean inner strength, where it counts.

## The Madness of Identification

Many people draw strength from their identity. Modern life seems to rest on labels—labels about our nationality, politics, class, gender, food preferences, pastimes. There are also people who identify themselves as having no identity—who say, for example, "I'm a citizen of the world." They hold themselves out as awakened, beyond all patriotism and chauvinism. That sounds a little superior to me. It's being caught in the same trap as people who say, "I can't be a Buddhist because that's an enclosure, it's identification, blah, blah, blah." Then you create a person who's not aligned with anything—yet another group. Today, identification is madness.

After the September 11 attacks, I learned a lot about identification— by way of the American flag. Soon after the attacks, I actually had a flag hanging out of my apartment—I was shocked at myself. Here's what I learned back then, from having listened to everyone's projections: it's just a piece of cloth. One person said to me, "You can't wave the flag.

That's saying 'America, America, America!' That's not dharma." I didn't agree—I thought that opinion reflected attachment to emptiness. The issue was not whether or not you waved a flag, or whether or not you love your country. It was whether there's such a level of attachment, identification, that you set up any of those actions or opinions as a kind of fortress. Today, across all ideological lines, everyone seems to be doing that. We're doing it to each other, as individual egos and as nations.

Part of the job of vipassana meditation is to undercut labels and identification and to see with freshness. Let me put this on a bigger canvas. When you go deeper in meditation, you leave behind being, say, an "American." In the silent mind, there is no American. An American does not get enlightened—that would be idiotic, self-contradictory. Nor does a Palestinian or an Israeli, a man or a woman, an old person or a young person.

It's a subtle point of the teaching, attachment to emptiness. In Zen, they call it "the stink of emptiness." You get so pure that you think, "I'm beyond categories." Essentially you've created a dualism. The medicine for that is to understand the Heart Sutra: "Form is emptiness. Emptiness is form." You can't separate these two.

I came from a strongly Jewish background: fourteen generations of rabbis. Is that enough? That's not the deepest thing about me—it really isn't, and I know it. But it has an effect, an influence on my consciousness that I'm not at war with. It's there. There are some good things in it. There are some things that I have to watch out for because they poison my mind in certain ways.

In times of war or intense polarization, political conferences may help—I'm all for them. I'm for the United Nations, peace summits, meetings, all that. But unless the human race decides to allocate its energies in a different way, through the school system radically changing education so that what is held to be important is wisdom, compassion, and self-knowledge—for everyone, not just for people who become monks and nuns, people who have sallow complexions—it won't become a general cultural value. We have to learn how to live with each other.

We keep talking about the global economy. But we don't have a global consciousness to match the global economy. Goods circulate around the globe, but we don't have a global mind. It's an invitation for trouble. We have to start seeing that we're all in this together. It's not East versus West, Islam versus Christianity or Judaism. All that stuff is the dualism we talk about. We've all created it together. Sometimes it takes a big blow to wake up and see that we create each other.

We all have the same tribal mind. Every day, there's a new ethnic group I have never heard of before. Each one has its own pride: in its culture, dishes, dances, outfits, dignity. Endless proliferation of ethnic groups. That doesn't have to disappear—but the ferocity with which the identification is held does. How can you have a global consciousness when everyone is so provincial, so tribal?

From a Buddhist vantage point, when you work on yourself, you're doing peace work. It sounds utopian, and no doubt it is. But anytime you can become less violent, less judgmental, you have a bigger consciousness, and you understand that tribalism is superficial. It's just outer garments. We're all human. Passionate believers in any cause often feel they have a monopoly on the truth. The most dangerous things, if you read history, have been religious ideologies. When fanaticism flies under the flag of religion, get out of the way.

It's not the ethnic groups or the religions per se that are the problem. Bring it down to our level—we do it with each other, in our families, at every social level. Why can't we live together? Why can't we be at peace with each other? Because we're like warring countries: "Me." "My ego." "He said this." "You said that." It's the same dynamic. As you liberate yourself, you're contributing to all of us getting free, because it's we who make up the world.

## Am I Still a Pacifist?

In times of war, many people who have long considered themselves pacifists and advocates of nonviolence may doubt their position. If you're one of these people, you have two choices. One is to change. You're not a pacifist anymore. People change all the time. The other choice is to see this as a test of your pacifism. You're being challenged: Are you really a pacifist? I asked my first Buddhist teacher, a Korean Zen master and a wonderful human being, "If you were up close to Adolf Hitler at the beginning of World War II and, knowing where it was all headed, you had a chance to assassinate him, would you do it?" He paused and paused. He took the question seriously, to his credit. Then he said, in his broken English, "Maybe sometimes kill is okay. But I would be prepared to pay for it with karma. I wouldn't get off."

Buddhism may be the most pacific of all the world religions. The emphasis on nonviolence is quite strong. What's important is for you to work out your life and destiny and to come to terms with this. Maybe it's a struggle. Maybe you'll realize you want to stay with pacifism and that current events pushed you to the wall and you fell down, according to your deepest principles. Or maybe you'll revise your principles and say, "I was a pacifist but I'm not anymore." And then you will get comfortable with that because it's true.

Let's look at the flip side. In violent times, people who had never considered themselves pacifists may suddenly feel a need to advocate for peace and nonviolence, no matter the circumstances. They become pacifists in their own minds. Here's where self-knowing comes in: What does that label do for you? What does it do for you to find out that you have pacific urges inside yourself that you didn't know were there? Everything we do points back to the mind.

## A Place Where There's No News

One aspect of looking at the mind involves examining how we respond to the media. Right after any shocking event, many of us fixate on 24-7 news or social media. Let's say you're about to watch the news. You sit down on the couch and turn on CNN. Watch what is being shown but also watch your reactions—anxiety, anger, despair. Take it as a practice. Otherwise what happens is you get lost in good, bad, right, wrong, I like, I hate. That's far away from meditation.

Read about the five *balas* of the Buddha, the five strengths or powers: faith, energy, mindfulness, concentration, and wisdom. Essentially, what's important is to develop inner strength at a time when there's a lot of uncertainty and difficulty, when people are dying, when decisions are being made that we find repugnant, when we feel helpless to change things. We have strong reactions, some of which completely overtake us, and meditation is out the window.

The world is an unstable place. It's always been an unstable place, but right now we're acutely aware of how unstable it is. Is there any stability that we can find anywhere? There is. We can all find some good news in the media, but meditation is going to that place where there's no news. That's why we want to go there. More and more, the practice is helping us tap into that unconditioned place and live there.

In crisis times, we're all teachers, whether or not we know it. When you bring this practice into your own life, you bring more stability and sanity into your existence. See if you can help those in your family or at work who are not meditators, who don't have resources—not by just preaching dharma to them but also demonstrating it by being a bit more grounded.

Some years ago, Thich Nhat Hanh told a bunch of us how, when the boat people left Vietnam, many were lost at sea. They were on rickety little crafts. He said the boats that survived likely did so because there was at least one person who could remain calm, mindful, centered;

who was not hysterical when the vessels were hit by huge waves. If there was no one on the boat like that, the chances of getting lost at sea were greater.

Today, when the world seems to be coming apart, you may be that one person, whether or not you know it. Vipassana meditation is like special forces training, but it's inner special forces, inner SEALs, inner Marines, inner Rangers, because you have resources that people often don't have. If you can remember to come back to the moment and stay balanced with whatever awaits us, you can be beneficial to the people in your life.

### Samsara Is Not New

The world has always been unhinged—that's not new. The world is samsara. But today the stakes are higher. Let's say you're outraged about something. In that moment, are you helping the problem? If you get depressed about the state of the world—whether war or climate change or social inequities—what have you accomplished? There isn't less toxin in the world but rather one more toxic person.

Instead, go to the root of your sense of helplessness. Either do something about it or release yourself from a mental exercise that is futile. In the process, you are doing something about the problem because one of the main ways in which we all bring toxins into the world is by loading our moods on top of each other. Anyone who's met the Dalai Lama knows he's a happy man in the midst of a catastrophe. It doesn't mean he turns his back on the situation—he's completely dedicated to the political situation of the Tibetans. Put another way, you don't have to be depressed to work hard against misery or injustice. The Buddha and Jesus led revolutions that are still going on today. Their work didn't come just out of anger—it also came out of love.

Thich Nhat Hanh phrased it this way: be peace. If you want a peaceful world, start with yourself. Eliminate certain sentimentalities that are not helpful when you feel sad about what's going on. You can't help but feel sad—there's enough reason to in today's world. But if you feel sad a lot, investigate it. Sometimes we use outer events as occasions for us to be depressed about something unrelated that's bothering us inside.

## Toxic Leaders Can Set Us Free

Sometimes our sadness morphs into rage. When incendiary political figures become powerful, many dharma practitioners openly admit that they hate such people and their divisive rhetoric. But from the Buddhist point of view, what these yogis are doing is reinforcing in themselves the tendency toward hatred—and it doesn't end when somebody is voted out of office. The rage, in and of itself, is what to look at, to become aware of.

In fact, throw out the word *rage*. When you become aware, start with the body, because that's more tangible. Rather than screaming and venting, find out where your rage is located. Toxic leaders can teach you much more than the Buddha. They were sent here to help us get free—but only if you understand that and establish a new relationship to how you live.

One of the reasons people don't want to look at the First Noble Truth is that they're used to blaming others. In a troubled world like ours, it's much easier to locate the source of our suffering outside ourselves. The Buddha is saying that the dukkha of the First Noble Truth is always internal. You create suffering for yourself. So bring it back to yourself. One student kept reminding me that a certain political ideologue lies. I asked this student, "Do you ever lie?" He said, "Maybe." I said, "Guilty as charged!"

Here's why toxic figures can help you. The degree to which you live counter to the Four Noble Truths is the degree to which you are squandering energy. If your mind is clear, you can actually be a more useful person in changing what you abhor than if it's just an eye for an eye and a tooth for a tooth.

## Engaged Stillness

Is it possible to change the world? Right now, our world has lapsed into a kind of derangement. Politics, violence, climate catastrophes—the planet itself is signaling to us that something is terribly wrong. Can we be stable, calm, wise, compassionate in a crazy world? Can we make a contribution? Tiny as it may seem, we can—starting with ourselves. There's something in us that flickers. It's a flame that can't be put out by conditions, and right now the world is rife with many powerful conditions.

The human mind has taken two different approaches to address our most serious problems. In the West, the focus is usually on political negotiations or economic interventions. Legislation or new leaders will change the situation. More conferences will change it. Instead of fossil fuels, burn fuels that don't hurt the environment. All those are external modifications, which are useful. Then you have the other approach, including Buddhism, where the human mind has tended to go over thousands of years—in India, it went very deep: find out what's going on inside ourselves.

Two poles, external and internal. My understanding of the Buddha's teaching is that it's unitary—there is no inside and outside. When I say unitary, it's not to deny the importance of external modifications—clean energy, economic equity, political actors who relate to what the problems are rather than to their own egos. But we must go deeper.

We often hear about "engaged Buddhism," but in this difficult time in history, I think of our practice as engaged stillness. This phrase came about through an interaction with somebody at Cambridge Insight Meditation Center. This person didn't know the center well but found out that our teaching at the center is concerned with daily life. This person said, "Well, isn't that engaged Buddhism?" It isn't.

Engaged Buddhism is about bringing the dharma actively into the world to solve social, political, and ecological problems. The term was coined in the 1960s by Thich Nhat Hanh when war was devastating Vietnam, his homeland. He said in an interview, "When bombs begin to fall on people, you cannot stay in the meditation hall all of the time." He gave up the isolation of the monastery to tend to the victims of that war and work toward political reconciliation. In other words, he sought to apply Buddhist teachings in an activist way to reduce suffering and oppression. At the same time, he wanted to hold on to the traditional Buddhist emphasis on awareness and inner spiritual growth. He would say, "Peace always begins with yourself as an individual."

Thich Nhat Hanh was very good at being able to keep clear boundaries between dharma and politics. He felt that people should not be bound to any doctrine or ideology, perhaps because he understood that the first casualty in ideological movements is the contemplative life. In fact, that's what's unique about the Buddha's teaching: the contemplative life. If you neglect meditation—real meditation—then it's still a beneficial practice, but it's like every other popular or organized religion.

What's distinctive about the Buddha's teaching, what has been protected for all these 2,600 years, has been an approach of inner technology that is available to us. It can be used by people in any culture, any era. Those of you who practice diligently know it takes energy, time, and commitment. It's designed to free the mind of all sources of distortion.

### Drowning in Idealism

In spiritual circles, we drown in idealism. I'm not advocating cynicism. But if our idealism is strong, we tend to set up a notion as to who we want to be, and then we try to be that. For example, in the late

1960s and 1970s, I participated in the antiwar movement—we were against the Vietnam War, which had spilled over into Cambodia and elsewhere. But there was so much violence in those campus political meetings about the right way to do it, how to protest, how to succeed in changing the course of this tragedy. In retrospect, we could have been much more effective if we had taken care of our own inner war in order to help each other decide how to stop the outer war.

So no matter what your political inclination, start with yourself. When I was in the army in post–World War II Germany, I discovered that I liked crawling on the ground with my machine gun, bang-bang-bang, and getting a little medal for my marksmanship. It was like being a kid again. Then I saw what I was doing, and I was revolted. But the starting point was that I liked it.

There is a wide gap between inner and outer transformation. The Soviet Union was founded on beautiful principles that had started with Marx and gotten refined. The communist revolution was full of ideals and promises for an equal society, but there was no psychological change in it. Those beautiful principles, laws, and values were just piled on top of greed, hatred, and delusion. Unless there's some inner understanding, the kilesas pop up. It seems timeless.

In India, Mahatma Gandhi engaged in a lifetime of inner work and brought about a remarkable nonviolent revolution that kicked out the British. Yet as soon as he was assassinated, there was a bloodbath, because it was his inner strength that had held it all together—his countrymen's hearts had not changed enough. They had not done the inner work.

In college, a friend and I used to play a game. We would blindfold ourselves and open up a big history book of the world. It was a thick book, and we'd just place our finger anywhere, on any page, at any random point in history. Wherever our finger landed, there was war, pillaging, plundering, rape.

If the Buddha, not knowing what had transpired over 2,600 years, suddenly appeared and walked around and took a look at what's going on, he would be dazzled by the brilliance of science and technology. Planes that fly, cars that drive, computers where people can talk to each other from one end of the world to the other. He would be astounded. But he would also be disappointed, because otherwise nothing has changed. Human beings are just the way we were when he was becoming awakened 2,600 years ago.

Again, this is not to say don't get involved in social change. Of course you should. But the primary work is internal. We're here to change our hearts so that whatever we're doing comes from a free heart, one that is fulfilled, that has love in it. We're not cultivating love for humankind but love that is synonymous with intelligence and compassion.

In the affluent world, we're opulent in terms of the external world, but we're paupers inwardly, dead broke. There's a certain dryness, a parched quality to the heart, even with our dazzling inventions. No matter how fast travel becomes, no matter how instantaneous communication becomes, there's still an us who's doing it. Historians often explain that while laws can be rewritten—sometimes for the better— hearts take longer to change. The deepest and most thorough change, of course, would be just what dharma practitioners are doing: rooting out the ways in which we imprison ourselves.

### The Greatest Gift You Give Is You

I often get asked, "With so much that needs to be done in the world, isn't it selfish to do meditation?" My answer is no. In a profound way, the greatest gift that you can give the world is you, because you put your stamp on everything you do. Work on your limitations, the ways in which you're handicapped in relating to other humans. The world needs a few more sane, gentle, genuinely peace-loving people. If you're sitting on your cushion for two days, that seems pretty self-indulgent and selfish—and it can be. Meditation can be misused; it can be another exercise in high-class narcissism. But that's not what the practice is designed to do—quite the contrary.

In looking at the turmoil today, one thing that has helped me is reading ancient texts. The ancient mind suffered just as much as we do. Are today's conditions more complex? Absolutely. We have shrunk communications; we're all in each other's faces. Sectarianism is getting stronger and stronger—I'm this, you're that. Something dangerous is going on here.

But whatever your life is—not as an abstract, sociological, sociohistorical conclusion but from moment to moment—is your actual life. Even in times of crisis, ours is not some self-centered, self-preoccupied practice—that view ignores our interdependence. It's like the Buddha's metaphor of the acrobats. In ancient India, an acrobat climbed up a pole and instructed his assistant to climb up and stand on his shoulders. He told the assistant, "You look after my balance and I'll look after your balance." But the assistant corrected him: "No, you look after your own balance and I'll look after mine."

As you start clarifying who you are to yourself, and letting go, letting go, letting go, that's who you bring to the people in your life. You can't give them anything you don't have. If you take care of yourself, your own inner balance, you are taking care of the people in your life. If they take care of themselves, they have a better chance of taking care of you. The world is us. If you want to do good works in the world, wonderful. The world needs all the help it can get. But it should come from a place of sanity and fulfillment rather than the ego coloring what it does and backfiring because of its nature.

Of course, not all of us are meditators. In crisis times, we have to allow for individual differences. Some people have a strong reflective dimension—they're natural contemplatives. To insist that such a person be serving in soup kitchens and doing all kinds of other good work that's needed is a mistake. They can be of more benefit to the human race by going deep, because of their particular gift.

Yet even serious contemplatives interact with other people. I spent time with a number of hermits in Asia. One, who lived in a cave—he didn't even know how long—was an extraordinary gift to the human race. He wasn't doing social good on our terms. But when people would come to visit him, they discovered that what he learned by being alone and going deeply into silence gave him a clarity that was helpful to someone like me, who had come from a busy, urban life in which political wrangling dominated the airwaves.

## We Are Society

When I was a teenager, I was listening to the radio when suddenly they interrupted the show—it was *The Lone Ranger*. "We interrupt this program to announce that the Japanese have bombed Pearl Harbor. It appears that the United States is at war with Japan." My friends and I all looked at each other. Whoa.

The world is constantly changing, in uncertain and unpredictable ways. But the fact of impermanence seems amplified and speeded up today. Some people believe that with so many urgent—some may say existential—problems, this is a turning point for humanity and the planet. It brings us back to the Four Noble Truths. We all know we're suffering to some degree. How can you not be alive and not know that you are? What we don't know is that we're not helpless, that there are things we can do, that it's possible—except in the most extreme circumstances—to go beyond conditions and free ourselves and experience much more peace in our lives.

We think the problem is out there. But we are society. It's the collective energies of all of us. Some people, of course, wield bigger influence than others, people who are playing an enormous role on the world stage. But all of us are part of what is called "the world"—which means it's up to you. Some of you will become political activists, some of you will work on getting out the vote, some of you will advocate for the environment. But your mind will be clear, because it's taking care of its own afflictions—afflictions that it's imputing to others who are more visible. Times of crisis call for nonduality. Self-awareness enables us to see, to dissolve, that separation between us and them.

# 10

---

# Stories and Reflections from a Life on the Path

*Getting Rewired by the Dalai Lama*

I'd like to give you a sense of what I experienced as a powerful and wonderful use of metta, or loving-kindness. It was during an audience, an interview, with the Dalai Lama. Maybe this isn't the right way to talk about metta, which I think of as a cultivation practice—it's just who he is. I walked in and put my palms together as I assumed he would because he's the Dalai Lama. But he reached out to shake my hand, and I felt a firm, strong handshake. So I made my handshake strong. Then I felt an arm around my shoulder. Now, we didn't know each other, but I put my arm around his shoulder. Before I knew it, we were seated close to each other. A lot of touching.

On one level, we were talking. There was a conversation going on about meditation, the problems of bringing the teaching into the West, and the changes that are needed. But it was also clear that eye contact was happening—very strong eye contact. Now, as some of you know, he is an informal human being, despite having a formal role in the world. In a sense, he's the world ambassador of all of Buddhism—not officially but unofficially. There was a strong meeting of eyes—it's the only way I can put it. It was a wordless form of communication. Then there was a wordless question on my part to him: "Is this all right?" The answer—again, not in words but in his expression—was "Of course, it's just ordinary, no big deal." So the ante went up, my eyes and then his eyes. Before I knew it, there was a deep feeling of two humans just being open with each other.

What went on between the two of us was, for me, something quite interesting. A field of warmth, friendliness, and love was palpable, powerful. But outwardly we were just two strangers. I was just one of a bunch of people who were coming and going for an audience with him.

At the end of my interview, my friends were waiting for me. But I found it difficult to talk when I came out of the room. One of the Tibetans in the entourage saw that and said, "Would you like to be quiet?" I said, "I think so." He led me to an empty room and I meditated for an hour. And I had a good cry, a joyful one.

What I realized was that the Dalai Lama—I'm sure with no intention at all—rewired me, freed me of something: the residue of growing up in Brooklyn and thinking that tough guys can't be loving. That if you want to be a real man, you might have love but it has to be Humphrey Bogart–type love, where you don't show it. In fact, you put out the opposite kind of gestures and language—gruff and unfeeling. Deep down, you love, but you don't demonstrate it. And you certainly don't verbalize it. After having spent a brief time with the Dalai Lama, somehow all that seemed trivial and a waste of time and just idiotic.

What was conveyed to me—some of it in words, but most not—was how foolish we all are. We're living on this planet and we spend our time in such silly ways being stingy with our love, being careful about it, feeling violated if someone takes advantage of our love, the whole business of love. Why can't we just be warm and friendly? The Dalai Lama asked me, "Do you have a good heart?" He wasn't speaking physiologically. He meant, "Are you good-hearted? Do you have a warm heart?"

What I experienced was a human being who was comfortable, able to just be loving for no particular end and in a way that was concrete, tangible. Somehow, at the end of it, I felt slightly more mature, more appreciative of that emotional dimension, freer.

## Munindra-ji Goes to the Movies

I had an eccentric Indian teacher named Anagarika Munindra. He was one of the first teachers for us Westerners who brought vipassana to the US, and we all learned a lot from him. In the late 1970s, I had both the joy and hilarity of going with him to his first movie. When the lights in the theater turned on at the end and we walked out, he was confused. He said, "Why do people make such a fuss about this?" He hadn't had a good time at all. I said, "Well, what was happening, Munindra-ji?" He said, "I was mindful of sitting in a chair, and there was light on the screen, and people were sitting around, and images were flashing. I didn't get any satisfaction from it. What do you all see in these movies?" He was so closely following his practice that the illusion that film was designed to create didn't work. So I tried to explain movies to him.

A few months later, we went to another movie. It was *A Bridge Too Far*, a World War II film. By then, Munindra had become much more Americanized. When we came out of the movie, he was quiet—usually he was bubbly, cheerful, funny. I said, "Munindra-ji, what's happening?" He said, "All those poor people, killing one another, so much death." I said, "Munindra-ji, you have attained movie mind. Sitting in that theater, you were no longer a vipassana yogi."

## A Retreat without Retreatants

At the Cambridge Zen Center, we used to have three-day retreats once a month. One year, the retreat came up at Christmastime. I was the only person on the staff not going home for the holidays because I was Jewish. And no students had signed up for the retreat. On the evening before the retreat was to begin, I assumed that we would just cancel it. So I went to Seung Sahn, my Korean teacher, and said, "I guess no retreat this weekend." He said, "Why not?" I said, "Well, no one signed up. Everyone's going away for Christmas." He said, "Cancel? No good. You give same retreat, whether a thousand people, a hundred people, or nobody."

So I did. I wore my big gray robes. I rang bells and lit incense. I bowed to the Buddha 108 times every morning. I chanted in Korean and Chinese, forty-five minutes in the morning and forty-five minutes at night. I sat and walked according to a rather rigorous schedule. I gave a dharma talk in the evening to a dark, empty hall. I gave myself a dharma interview. I went through the same schedule as always.

The first day, I felt like a fool. I was going through all the motions, I was following all the forms, but no one was out there. It was just me, with me wondering if I had lost my mind. How could I put myself through something like this?

But at a certain point, something fell away. I saw why Seung Sahn gave me those instructions, and I'll always be grateful. I realized that the means were the ends. I realized how dependent I was on others watching me go through the rituals. In seeing all that, I was liberated from doing something for someone else or doing something in order to get something. In other words, it was just practicing. I learned that the real issue is respect for our life. The modern world is a world of quantity, where you grind out lots of products. Quality has always been the casualty. But our practice is about the quality of life. No matter where we find ourselves, no matter what the situation—cleaning a toilet, getting a Nobel Prize—in one sense, it's all the same.

## What Is Irreducibly Buddhist?

At the strong suggestion of Seung Sahn, I spent time in Japan and Korea. It was basically to strengthen my understanding of this ancient tradition. I practiced in quite a few monasteries.

But the experience backfired. I got wonderful training there and met lovely people—kind, generous. I also learned something that's obvious to me now but wasn't then: I'm not Japanese or Korean. When I started to live in Asia on a daily basis, I saw that much of what was called "Zen Buddhism" was cultural—it was not universal. It had to do with being a Japanese or Korean person.

At the time, many of us in the West were doing impersonations of Tibetans or Hindus. The Asian teachers who brought Buddhism to the United States, of course, had no choice but to be who they were. In presenting Zen, or insight meditation, or various forms of yoga or Sufism, what could they do but be themselves? In the process of teaching something that I feel is universal, they also transmitted their culture to us. And we embraced it, in many cases, without any discernment. By discernment I don't mean skepticism, but just a clear appraisal of what was happening. Living in Asia, I saw that much of what I was being trained in was Korean or Japanese values about how to eat, how to relate to women, how to raise a family—everything that a culture does for people. It became a problem for me. But it forced me to ask: Is there something irreducible? Do you get to something that has absolutely nothing to do with being Japanese or Korean or a Martian—or, in my case, someone from Brooklyn?

The answer is yes. It's exquisitely simple: the ability of each one of us to pay attention to our life as it is being lived, with a willingness to learn from that sensitivity. It has nothing to do with a particular culture. It's the practice of a human being coming to know himself or herself by paying attention, not thinking about it but being aware of thinking, not being lost in the body but feeling the body, registering all the senses— in short, becoming direct and intimate with life, moment to moment.

Meditation has no particular locus because it's essentially formless. It has nothing to do with whether or not you light incense, worship at an altar, or bow to a statue (though many practitioners do achieve genuine clarity using those ritual objects). It has nothing to do with whether you eat vegetables or meat, take your shoes off or keep your shoes on, eat tofu or don't eat tofu, shave your head or grow a beard, wear long and flowing robes or a jumpsuit. It's independent of all that—and that's where its power comes from. It's an empty mirror. Each one of us has this mirror, the capacity to see how we are actually living.

## A Walk with Krishnamurti

During the week when Jiddu Krishnamurti was at Brandeis University—this was in 1968—very few people on the campus were interested in him. So I got to take walks with him. There were still woods on the campus—it wasn't like today. The first time we took a walk, he said, "Would you mind if we just walk in silence, if we don't speak?" He said it in a very light way. But walking with someone without talking—I had never done that, and I thought it was strange. Back then, when I would walk with my friends, we would walk and talk, we would argue and debate—it was always intense. I had walked silently along the ocean by myself—but with another person, you're supposed to talk. This guy didn't want to talk. After the initial awkwardness, I realized I actually liked it.

At the time, I was very drawn to the word *meditation*. I didn't fully know what it meant. So I kept asking him, "Would you teach me meditation?" I asked him many times. He never followed up; he just kept brushing off my question.

The walks were wonderful. Sometimes a bird would chirp and Krishnamurti would stop and pause. He'd say, "Let's listen for a few minutes." Sometimes he would just stop and smile. He seemed very happy. He never made the walks into a project—"I'm going to teach you about meditation the natural way." Mostly we just walked and enjoyed walking.

Finally, on one of our last walks, Krishnamurti sat down by a tree. I did the same thing. Krishnamurti said, "Pick out anything—a plant, a flower, part of a tree. See if you could look at it for a few minutes without labeling it, naming it, or thinking about it. See if you can look at it without thoughts about its botanical name or what you've done here in the past or whether this would be a good spot for a picnic. See it without any words coloring your view of it. Just look at it with the naked eye, simply and with innocence, as if for the first time. Just look at it and pay full attention."

So I picked out a leaf and looked at it. At first my mind was busy—it didn't like doing this. I kept peeking at Krishnamurti, like, "Is this long enough? When are we going to start walking again?" Then, at a certain point, I dropped that and I just looked at the leaf—and the leaf became interesting. I saw its veins, how they radiated out. I saw its symmetry. I saw its beauty. I saw the stem and the earth around it. I felt like, "Wow, there's a whole world here." I had seen leaves hundreds of thousands of times, but I had never allowed it to be an intimate experience. I was moved to tears, which was totally unanticipated.

After about a half hour, Krishnamurti said, "Well, how was it?" I said, "It was fascinating. It was beautiful." I went on and on. I told him how much I saw and how much I learned and how I had kind of glossed over nature all my life. I told him how this time I got in close and it was very emotional. He said, "Okay. When you go back to your apartment, sit down, get quiet, close your eyes, and look at your mind that way. That's meditation." And we resumed the walk.

### The Earth Is Flat

In Korea, I and two other Americans met an illiterate monk who was considered a Zen master. One day we tried to explain to him that the world is round, not flat. He just looked at us and smiled. "How could it be round?" His worldview was medieval. We gave him a high school science lesson—that we wouldn't fall off because of gravity. We went around and around, but we couldn't get anywhere with each other.

Finally he laughed and said, "Okay, I'm just an old, illiterate peasant monk. You are all smart and educated, and you're probably right. The world is round and I can't figure that out. But knowing that the world is round, has it made you happier?"

It hadn't. We had traveled thousands of miles to learn what he knew. He was perfectly content living on his mountain.

## Styles of Practice

If you go to certain monasteries in Thailand, they talk a lot about doing walking meditation at a natural pace. Ajahn Chah, Ajahn Maha Bua, the Thai Forest school—they laugh at the Burmese style of slow walking, which many teachers have adopted in the US. The Koreans laugh at it, too. I remember being with two Korean monks when they saw some vipassana students walking very slowly—they had to fight back giggles, it was so strange to them.

In Korea, it was very different. At a monastery where I practiced, you would sit for fifty minutes and then someone would strike a wooden clapper. You would either stand up from your cushion to do walking at a natural pace or you would jump up as quickly as you could and run around the room at top speed. Then someone would hit the clapper again, and you would stop the walking or running and return to the sitting posture. You would go through the day that way. The clapper, which is two pieces of wood, doesn't make a beautiful sound; it's not like a nice Japanese bell. It's loud, intentionally jarring, to force you to let go of the exquisite, almost aesthetic peace that can come with sitting—you had to just take off and walk or run. It was an entirely different style of practice.

Or take eating. In some monasteries, one meal a day is a sign of purity, spiritual dedication. In others, it's two meals a day. If you go to Thich Nhat Hanh's monastery, it's three meals a day. Are these variations all arbitrary and irrelevant or are they highly significant? Is one meal holier, more spiritual? Three meals, not so holy? That's what is implied.

The Theravadin Buddhist monk U Pandita encourages you, as a retreat unfolds, to get down to four hours of sleep a night, maximum. You're even asked in interviews: How many hours did you sit? How many hours did you walk? How many hours did you sleep? But if you were to ask Ajahn Chah or Thich Nhat Hanh, they never give you a number. Ajahn Chah would say, "How do I know how many hours of sleep you should have? How do I know how much food you should eat? That's your job!" They're encouraging you to develop a sensitivity so that you get enough sleep or food without oversleeping or undersleeping, and without overeating or undereating, because both extremes can make the mind wacky.

Here's another variation on style: Should you keep your eyes open or closed during meditation? If you listen to Japanese teachers, the Buddha sat with his eyes half-closed, so they do, too. With Theravadin teachers, it's okay to close your eyes. Some of the Theravadin teachers will say that if your eyes are half-open, it's too stimulating and you'll be distracted.

Where's the best place to follow the breath? If you go to Maha Bua's monastery, it's the chest, the heart, because that's the seat of the mind in Buddhism. If you work with the Mahasi Sayadaw teachers, it's the abdomen. For many teachers, perhaps most, it's the nose. If you're doing anapanasati, it's the whole breath and the whole body. Which one do you want?

Some years ago, Seung Sahn was giving a talk one night and a student was confused. The student said, "I've read that in this tradition there are four stages to enlightenment. In another tradition there are eight stages to enlightenment. Another says there are twelve stages to enlightenment. Which one is right?" Seung Sahn looked at him and said, in his broken English, "How many do you want? You want four? I give you four. You want twelve? I give you twelve."

Then there's money. In some orders, monks are not allowed to touch money, or they must receive it in special ways, such as in an envelope. The Tibetans handle money comfortably, and some of the Zen teachers don't seem to feel it's a problem. But most Theravadin teachers don't handle money. Implying what? Either that money is a problem that makes for a lot of suffering, or that it's dirty and shouldn't be touched, or that it's something highly charged and complicated. Of course, it's true that money makes for a lot of suffering—that doesn't apply just to monks and nuns. Either we have too much of it or we don't have enough. Still, some of the Tibetan monks that I spent time with handled money, and they didn't seem less pure than the monks who didn't handle the money; they didn't seem purer, either. They just seemed to be pure monks who handled money and the others were pure monks who didn't handle money.

How about sex? A very big issue, relationship. In some lineages, if you're a monk or a nun, sex is not allowed. But in certain orders in Japan, Zen priests marry. Does that make them less holy?

On the path to enlightenment, attachment to views and opinions is one of the last things to go. What I'm trying to say is: go to the essence of things. If you get attached to form, you may reach the wrong conclusions about the way things are.


## A Week without Sleep

At Su Dok Sa monastery, up in the mountains in Korea, we did a three-month retreat. All you do is get up at three in the morning, bow to the Buddha 108 times, eat vegetarian meals, and do sitting and walking meditation until bedtime. There are no dharma talks, no interviews with the teacher. You just sit and walk, sit and walk. I was the only layperson there. There were two other Americans, my friends, who had become monks in the Zen tradition.

What we didn't know when we arrived in Korea was that, in this retreat, they have a tradition. On day forty-five—the midpoint of the ninety-day retreat—no sleep is allowed for one week. Should someone doze off, a monk would rap their shoulders with the "stick of compassion." When we heard this, we were ready to board the next plane out. We said, "Why didn't they tell us this before we signed up? This is barbaric. Humans shouldn't have to go through this. What does this have to do with the Buddha's teaching?" We were frightened and feeling sorry for ourselves.

The first day was torment. But we couldn't leave because we felt we were carrying the American flag, and I was also carrying the flag of laypeople, because a lot of the monks were skeptical about a layperson being there. So I put in a special request for an interview with the Zen master, who was in his late nineties. He lived in a cottage near the monastery. He was carried in on a palanquin. His body didn't work, but his face and eyes were bright as sunshine, and he looked at me and listened to all my complaints through a translator. I explained to him that it was only the first day and we were already exhausted. How could we survive a whole week?

He said, "Look, it's hard for all of us. But we've been doing this for many years. We feel tremendous value comes out of the motivation and determination. Here's the trick; it's simple. Right now, you're not allowed to sleep. It feels like a nightmare because your mind is worried about the future. It is making up all kinds of stories. There's no dharma in it." I asked him, "What should we do instead?" He said, "It's the same practice. Take each sitting one moment at a time. If you see the mind getting ahead of itself and making up what's going to happen, just come back to this sitting—or this meal, this cup of tea, this walking, whatever. Take each moment as it is, period. Give one hundred percent to that. When it's over, let it go. Then bring one hundred percent of your interest to what's next."

He was right. The problem was that, in addition to my fatigue, I was carrying around an extra burden: the *concept* of seven days without sleep. I would be able to get through the week, he said, if I put that burden down.

I'm not saying it was a piece of cake. But when I dropped what my mind made up about the possibilities of what was happening and what could happen, it just became physically arduous. From the Buddhist point of view, when you're identified with what's happening, the mind makes up a story and you can't tell the difference between an event that comes through a sense door and the mind that's making up a story almost instantaneously, based on your conditioning.

Does that mean our suffering was irrational? Some of the suffering, I felt, was quite rational. Objectively this was not good for the body. But in that tradition, the monks were willing to do it. That's how much they hankered after getting enlightened and how much they wanted to get out of this world of illusion.

Did I bring this practice back to the United States? Of course not. First of all, no one would do it. If I had a chance to do it again, I wouldn't. But the Zen master's advice has carried over into other challenges. Often a difficult situation can be managed if you know how to relate to it properly, how to take care of it, how to fully become aware of it and watch what happens with interest. During those seven days, there were times when I was hallucinating. Then it would stop. But there was a certain corner of my consciousness that knew I was hallucinating.

Whatever is happening, there's something that knows. We all have this awareness—I'll call it Awareness, with a capital *A*. The present moment should not be underestimated. Somehow we make it complex and go back to the past or imagine the future. Anything seems better than the present moment.

## Night with a Corpse

For a time, I studied with an Indian Vedanta teacher. He was getting on in age and wanted to convey whatever he knew while he still could. We went to a small village in Mexico to get away and do individual teaching, practice, training. One night, I was ready to go to sleep when he came into my little hut and said, "Larry, come on, quick. We have a great opportunity to learn something." I said, "What? Where?" He said, "There's a corpse. A dead person was washed up on the beach." The man was a laborer and had gotten drunk and drowned in the ocean. He'd been dead for about ten days. The villagers wouldn't touch him because he was from another tribe and religion. They had packed him in ice and they wondered if we, the two strangers in town, could stay with him all night and into the morning, until the priest from the man's own village came and got him.

My teacher was thrilled. But I thought, "Are you kidding me? Why would I want to stay with a corpse?" I had read about how Buddhist yogis would go to the charnel grounds to realize the fact of impermanence and the fragility of existence. It's wonderful reading, but it's different when you're actually doing it.

So we went to the corpse. It was bloated, bluish. My teacher sat on one side of the body and I sat on the other. Was there a smell? Definitely, and it got worse. My teacher had a simple method of instruction. We'd be sitting there and maybe every twenty minutes or so—there was no clock time—he would say, "How is it for you, Larry?" I'd say, "I'm nauseous. I hate this. I can't stand the smell. I want to get out of here." He said, "Become mindful of that." There was no out.

At first I was overwhelmed by the dukkha of this situation. But at a certain point, I was able to be aware of the fear, the loathing, the repulsion, the yearning to escape, to get away from this body, and the anger at my teacher for forcing me to do this, even though I'd already had lots of training in the Thai Forest tradition visualizing stages of the body's decomposition. I had gotten pretty good at it, I thought. But here was a real body decomposing, and I was not prepared.

Eventually the Four Noble Truths kicked in. I could be mindful of the fear. I could see its cause: I didn't want to face my own death. My teacher had wanted me to come to terms with the fact that I was looking at myself. The corpse was saying, without words, "You don't have forever, buddy."

My teacher told me, "This man didn't know he would die when he did. Life is precious, not just because it is life but because it is an opportunity to practice. That is the ultimate gift this man gives us." By morning I felt at ease.

## Attacking the Kilesas

Ajahn Maha Bua was an extraordinarily loving person and very funny, too. Also quite fierce. He would appear when you didn't expect him—it was part of the way he taught. He wandered around the monastery and you never knew where you would find him. Often, he turned up just when you didn't want him to be there. And he wasn't shy—he didn't have a New Age, liberal ideology. He was direct and forthright, and he always told you exactly what he saw and thought.

One day I was with the monks, and one of the monks did something wrong—he had placed a cup at the end of a table, where it could be easily knocked over. This carelessness violated the spirit of dharma, which emphasizes the importance of keeping mindfulness alive in even the most mundane activities and with the most mundane objects of our lives. (I had learned the same lesson about utmost respect for seemingly ordinary objects from a student of Sen Soshitsu XV, the now-retired Grand Master of the Urasenke tradition of the Japanese tea ceremony.)

Maha Bua laced into this person. He let him have it, in no uncertain terms. I was new—I had been there just a few days—and Maha Bua looked over and saw me. He said something in Thai to a monk, who translated it for me: "Make it clear to him that I'm not attacking this monk—I'm attacking the kilesas. It's an act of compassion, because these kilesas are harming him. And whoever gets implicated in his life, he's going to harm them as well. My anger had nothing to do with this monk as a person—he's a student of mine whom I love. It had to do with these tendencies, which have to be seen and understood and let go of."

Then there was a pause. Maha Bua added, "I'm assuming that everyone who comes to this monastery is interested in letting go of egotism and self-centeredness. If they don't want to do it, I'll do it for them as long as they stay here."

## Tom Mix at the Zendo

One of the happiest days of my life was when my father gave me a cowboy outfit with a big Tom Mix hat—Tom Mix was a famous cowboy who had a radio show. I loved my cowboy outfit, with its big hat, chaps, vest, boots with spurs, and a pair of six-shooters. I would put on that outfit and I knew who I was: I was a cowboy, and it felt great. I would walk around the house whipping out my guns. That kept me happy for about six months, until I outgrew it.

The next piece of identity was a baseball outfit. I had a professional glove that my father found in a pawn shop. I had spike shoes and a hat that read "New York Yankees" on the back. Later, it was a basketball outfit, and my mother said she'd see me from the window on my way home, bouncing an invisible basketball. Later, it was the outfit of a professor—I had found an old, weathered briefcase in London in a used-book shop. I made up a fantasy about the briefcase, that it once belonged to someone from Oxford or Cambridge.

Many years later, I was sitting in a Zen meditation hall in a monastery in Japan. We wore large, flowing robes and everyone walked around solemnly. It was formal, stylized, and beautiful—bowing and bells going off and incense wafting. Certainly, for Westerners, it seemed important and exotic. I felt like a proud man of Zen.

Then it hit me: "My God, I'm still wearing my cowboy outfit. Instead of being a cowboy, I'm this big Zen meditator." And I started laughing hysterically. My eyes were tearing up, my nose was running. I had to leave the zendo. I realized that nothing had changed. I was still identifying myself through an outfit. I had a great laugh at my own expense, and it was liberating when I realized we all do that. We look for deepest meaning in outer identities.

## An Origin Story

While leading a retreat at the New York Insight Meditation Center, I had a Sunday afternoon free before my wife and I were to take the train back to Boston. She read in the paper that there was something called the Tenement Museum, part of a tour of the Lower East Side. That's where I was born. That's where I lived until I was five. It had never occurred to me to go back there. For those of you who don't know what a tenement is, those are the buildings that immigrants inhabited. But the immigrants themselves thought of those buildings as structures where you cram as many people as possible into as little space as possible.

We went to a building that was a recreated tenement. It had clothing and books and eyeglasses—the belongings of an Italian family and a Jewish family. I was quite naïve when I went on this tour—not in the sense of innocence but in the sense of being open. Suddenly things started to come back to me about my past, and I couldn't talk for quite a while. I started to see: Did I come out of this? Did I grow up here? How could that be, considering how my life has turned out? I saw the size of what was called a bathroom, which was more like a telephone booth, with no bathtub or shower. Memories came up of living with my parents, my mother's three sisters and brother, and both of my grandparents in a space like this. I remember it being happy and full of love. But also a lot of other memories came up, too; some I don't have words for.

I saw something about my origins and sense of myself. There wasn't a lot of ego in it. I was quiet and I didn't want to talk for a while. I was moved by it. Some of it was painful, a lot of it was pleasant. But most of it was: How did I come from this? The scene conveyed to me the distance that I had traveled socially, psychologically.

I came home and told the story to a few friends. I noticed that in the telling, the story started to change a bit. It was no longer just a straight factual report. I talked about what I went through in my childhood. I saw that I was, in a way, promoting myself: Aren't I wonderful? I started in a tenement, then I was a professor, then I dropped all that, and now I'm a dharma teacher and I know how to dress and I'm a real American guy. The story picked up drama on the way. It kept changing every time I told it. I saw I could get some mileage out of it.

Now, if there were a Greek chorus, they might start singing, "Oh, don't enjoy it! Meditate your way out of this egotism!" I wasn't punishing myself for these embellishments, but I saw what my mind was doing with materials from my childhood.

We spend a tremendous amount of time in the past and in the future—we're dominated by them. What you will learn if you follow this path is that the self constantly uses the materials of the past and future to nourish itself, to build itself up. In this case, my mind used materials in the past to enhance its sense of self in the present. I didn't beat myself up over this realization. Instead, I saw how fascinating the unconscious process was. My goodness, the ego was hard at work— that's what it knows how to do.

### Lessons from a Christmas Tree

My wife and stepdaughter are from the Soviet Union. They came here as immigrants, relatively late in life. I grew up in a section of Brooklyn where pretty much everyone was Jewish; the parents were born in Russia, Poland, Ukraine, Belarus, and some in Germany. Our apartment house was almost entirely Jewish people—it was a Jewish enclave. That was our identity, our religion—not necessarily practiced but a strong cultural identity for most of us. Everyone outside of this enclave was Irish or Italian Catholic.

Each year when Christmas came around, people would say, "Did you get your Christmas tree yet?" At home, we would never have a Christmas tree. But it wasn't merely that we didn't have a Christmas tree—we passionately did not have a Christmas tree because a tree was symbolic of a Christian culture. This was a time of strong anti-Semitism, and Christmas was a Christian practice. The Jewish people who had come over from Russia and Poland carried cultural memories of feeling surrounded by enemies, protecting themselves, and identifying with being Jewish. So, no, we did not celebrate Christmas. I remember taking a walk with one of my friends in Manhattan. We passed a large insurance building. It was just before Christmas Eve and this building was lit up in the pattern of a cross. My friend looked at me, pointed to it, and said, "That's the most powerful symbol in this culture and it doesn't include us." All this was in my consciousness.

At any rate, my wife, stepdaughter, granddaughter, and I were sitting around the table, enjoying, laughing, eating good food. We have a good connection, all four of us. Two people who grew up in the Soviet Union, a granddaughter who grew up here, and myself, who grew up in Brooklyn in the culture that I've just hinted at. Suddenly my stepdaughter said, "Oh, we're going to get a Christmas tree. Should we get one for your house?" Before my wife could answer, something came out of me that was out of control: "We are *not* getting a Christmas tree for this house." It was not a mere factual statement; it was a *pronunciamento*. Anyone who would go against this, watch out. Big trouble. Everyone at the table was shocked, including myself. Whoa. Where did that come from?

Now, here is how relationship can be a fertile way of learning. When my wife and stepdaughter were growing up in the Soviet Union, Christmas trees had nothing to do with Christianity. Religion was not allowed; there were severe consequences for anyone who was overtly religious.

So in the Soviet Union, Christmas trees simply meant the beginning of a new year. For my American granddaughter, it was just a fun thing to do—to get a Christmas tree, decorate it, and put presents underneath it.

The room got quiet. But within a minute or two, I saw that my behavior came out of an old, old wound. That's one of the things that happens in meditation, so be prepared. As the mind becomes more silent and at peace with itself, certain wounds, repressed emotions, stuff that's been festering down there your entire life unexpectedly comes to the surface because you have no barriers. You're not trying to protect yourself against anything. Some of it can be painful wounds that have not been attended to or taken care of but that you've managed to live with through a kind of emotional bypass. I saw this had happened right in front of my family. I saw the combination of their stricken looks and the uncharacteristic strength of my saying "We are *not* getting a Christmas tree for this house."

In this case, relationship triggered the realization. If you're paying attention to what's going on inside you as you're paying attention to other people, you experience how the practice of relationship is self-discovery. My awareness saw an old wound. When it did, the wound lost its potency and was replaced by a peaceful, empty, nonattached mind. There was no Larry who grew up in an anti-Semitic neighborhood, who did not have a Christmas tree because that was symbolic. Suddenly I had a good laugh. I explained to them what happened in my childhood and why that wound was still present. They explained to me how in the Soviet Union, evergreen trees at the end of the year meant an entirely different thing. We educated each other.

Finally, when you look at it clearly, it's just a spruce tree. The poor tree has so much projected onto it that has nothing to do with Christmas. The spruce tree is just being a spruce tree, doing spruce tree. One culture made it a symbol of the new year coming in. Another culture made it a symbol of Christianity. My culture made it into a symbol of something alien, hostile.

What the Buddha was talking about—the real end of dukkha—is emptiness. In Buddhism, if there's no emptiness in it, it's not dharma. Emptiness is empty of what? Empty of attachment to anything as being "me" or "mine." Well, how do you do that? You can't get rid of attachment because that which is trying to get rid of it is strengthened by trying to get rid of it. The only way that I know of to loosen attachment is to see it.

The whole experience unfolded over about fifteen minutes. We resumed laughing and enjoying our food. It was only after that I reflected back and realized, "Whoa, a lot of dharma, and it's just a simple Christmas tree." The learning wasn't in the Christmas tree, it was in my mind, my heart. It enabled me to liberate myself from a wound that I didn't realize was still so raw.

### Kill Hot, Kill Cold

The following Chinese koan is based on an actual story. A monk comes to the teacher and says, "How do you live when it's very hot or when it's very cold?" The teacher screams at him, "Kill hot! Kill cold!" I was given this koan by Seung Sahn Sunim, my Korean teacher. I gave the wrong answer again and again. It's called dharma combat—you go in with your teacher, you're given a koan, you answer. I was always wrong. A bell would ring: Out!

What does it mean, "Kill hot! Kill cold!"? It means kill the concept of hot, kill the concept of cold. No one's denying that sweat is pouring down your body or that you're shivering. Those are facts. But the mind makes "hot." Before you know it, you have dukkha. The dukkha is in making hot out of a physiological response to an increase in temperature. "Kill cold" is the same thing—you're killing the concept of cold.

I finally got the koan right. One hot summer day, I came in to the interview and my teacher said to me, "How do you kill hot? How do you kill cold?" I just took out my handkerchief, wiped my brow, and left. He said, "Good. Very good." He saw that I understood not just the conceptual truth of the koan but the experiential truth. It was a sensible response to an actual condition. I wasn't making more or less out of it. What else could I do?

## 1,500 Hours

A friend called me up once and said, "Do you realize that over the years, you've given more than one thousand talks that have been recorded— more than fifteen hundred hours? And that doesn't include all the early talks that were never taped—when we would just sit down and shoot off our mouths."

You'd think that I would have burst with pride when I heard that. But instead it felt like somebody just put fifteen hundred pounds of rocks on my back. My first impulse was, "I think I'll go to sleep for ten years." I've recovered, but not completely.

You know the phrase "making a long story short"? I'm good at making a short story long. Just give me one word and I'll go on for fifteen hundred hours.

Lately I've been thinking about the fact that a lot of the questions I've heard over the years in retreats, practice groups, and interviews have to do with the wish to find inner peace. Sometimes it's put in terms of the wish to find inner freedom. If you read Buddhist books, the words typically used are *enlightenment, waking up, full awakening, discovering or rediscovering your original nature.* But a lot of it seems to be a craving for inner peace. It's a common desire of the human race.

After I recovered from the feeling of exhaustion when I heard how much blabbing I'd done over the years, I realized that, in a sense, everything I've been teaching and everything I've gone through—all the stages and phases, different techniques and methods, traveling to this monastery and that retreat center, a typical journey—boils down to this: Where can we find peace? My conclusion is: in the same place that we find sorrow. But we don't want to go to that place.

The hardest part of practice, and the hardest part of teaching, is to find ways to look at the place where the sorrow is. Do you think you can find peace outside of yourself? Isn't that what we've been doing all along? Does it work? Granted, it's intelligent, even wise, to arrange your life in a way that is fulfilling, so that, if you're fortunate, you have a certain amount of wealth, your health is cared for, your body is cared for, relationships are cared for. No one's denying that.

But what I am saying is, finally, profoundly, if you want inner peace, it's in the same place that sorrow is—sorrow in the broadest sense, whatever it is that we humans don't like. That's what wisdom is. Wisdom doesn't come just from being concentrated—not at all. Wisdom comes from facing ourselves as we are.

As a sign in a Japanese Zen monastery read: "What are you gawking at? Don't you realize this is about you?"

### Singing the Blues to Chase the Blues Away

I went to the University of Chicago, and in that neighborhood were some of the greatest blues clubs in the world. A lot of the masters, such as Muddy Waters, would come to these small clubs, and I'd go whenever I could because I love the blues. One of the many excellent musicians who played there was Buddy Guy. Someone asked him, "Why do you sing and play the blues?" He said, "I sing and play the blues to chase the blues away."

That's what the Four Noble Truths are about. We humans all know suffering; it's part of being alive. The Buddha turned that suffering into a path. He saw that the door to suffering is also the door to freedom. You have to face your own ways in which things aren't working in life. Granted, external forces can impinge upon us, favorable or unfavorable, and can stimulate suffering. But the emphasis in the Buddha's teaching is on the part we play in contributing to our suffering, adding to it, amplifying it. In the Buddhist scheme of things, ignorance is ignorance of the Four Noble Truths, the first of which is that there is suffering in life. Like the blues, the Four Noble Truths are both teachings and medicine for the troubled heart.

## Stroke of Luck

When I was eighty-three, I had a small ischemic stroke. They brought me by ambulance to the emergency room of Beth Israel Hospital. It was tremendous dukkha because my mind kept saying, "I shouldn't be having a stroke. I eat a healthy vegetarian diet. I exercise, I do yoga, deep breathing. I drink a lot of green tea. I've lived a clean life." It went on and on. Needless to say, my practice was out the window. There was an internal war going on: "How could this be? It must be some mistake." "No, it isn't. You had a stroke." "This shouldn't be happening." "But it did happen." "But it shouldn't." "But it did." Once I saw that, I thought, "Okay, time to let go of that one. Now, how can you live with some degree of fulfillment in this situation?" I needed to apply what I'd been teaching for years—but to myself. Mr. Vipassana Meditation, take a look at your own mind.

There are a lot of teachings in the Buddha's discourses that can be summed up like this: Is it possible for the mind to be healthy even though the body isn't? The Buddha's resounding answer is yes. I was uncomfortable lying there, but a large part of my suffering was caused by my resistance to the fact that this was happening to me. It's a form of clinging, attachment. When I saw the dukkha, I switched to the mindfulness channel and became aware of what I was doing. The suffering weakened and fell away.

Then I decided, "Well, since I have to lie on my back here for a week, I'll turn it into a retreat." It was Beth Israel Hospital, but for me it was a meditation center. And it was a perfect place for a retreat. Meals are taken care of; nurses come in all the time, smiling and kind. Sometimes I would just do straight-up mindfulness with breathing. Sometimes I would switch, for the fun of it, and look at the sensations in the body: pleasant, unpleasant, or neutral, as the *Satipatthana Sutra* puts it. But mostly I would just lie in bed and be aware of what was happening. I looked directly at my mind. I got to places, extended periods of time, where I felt great joy and peace.

On the second day of my hospital stay, the attending physician came into the room with a number of residents. He began asking all the basic questions, and I tried to answer all of them pleasantly. Finally, he looked at me and said, "You seem happy." I said, "Yeah, I wish I weren't here, but I'm feeling reasonably happy." Then he said, "But you do know that you've had a stroke?" I said, "Of course I do." He was trying to determine whether I was off my zonk, whether my trolley had gone off the track. He said, "What's your name? How old are you? Where do you live? Do you know where you are?" He was getting exasperated. He finally said, "Can you account for why you are so happy?"

I knew from past experiences never to mention meditation to doctors. They make up what they think is an impossibility and are quite convinced of their own judgment, even though they're literally ignorant—they don't know about this practice, but they don't know that they don't know because they're the doctor. I finally said, "Look, maybe this won't mean anything to you, Doctor, but I've been practicing vipassana meditation for many years. I know what's going on and I wish it were not so. But I know it is possible to tap into a place that is free of all this. I've been meditating and using this opportunity as a retreat, and it's brought me great joy. It's my job, if you will." It went in one ear and out the other. He walked out of the room with the residents in tow.

But shortly after that, three of the residents sneaked back into my room. They said, "We realize the attending physician felt you were losing your mind. But we know that meditation is a good thing. We have forty-five minutes before the next patient. Can you teach us how to meditate?" So there I was, lying on my back, with three residents in their white coats sitting as I droned on and gave a guided meditation about following the breath. At that moment, my wife, Galina, appeared at the door and saw what was going on. She quietly stood back, but she caught my eye and smiled. She was relieved that my brain was back to normal.

By the way, the doctor came back the next day. His questioning was more intense, because I had become even happier. It wasn't because I was insane. It was because I had access to something in us that is timeless. That may sound far away, on the other side of the moon. It isn't. It's right here.

### Weeping Willow

When I was able to take a walk, I would see a beautiful weeping willow, huge, which had come to be a friend. When I took a break, I'd sit down on a park bench and just relate to it. And I remembered a poem I hadn't thought of in many years. It's by Li Po, a great Chinese poet from the eighth century.

> The birds have vanished down the sky.
> Now the last cloud drains away.
>
> We sit together, the mountain and me,
> until only the mountain remains.*

This poem was about someone meditating with that mountain. What does that mean, "only the mountain remains"? What it means is that Li Po's notion of Li Po falls away. When that falls away, there's no

---

* Li Po, "Zazen on Ching-t'ing Mountain," trans. Sam Hamill, in *Crossing the Yellow River: Three Hundred Poems from the Chinese* (Rochester, NY: BOA Editions, 2000). Copyright © 2000 by Sam Hamill.

separation—from not only the tree but everything else. That's central in our practice.

Some of the commentaries on this poem have been rather limited. They say it's about how the beauty of nature temporarily silences thought. Yes, that can happen. But when you're a meditator, the silence can go deep, to the point where it's way beyond what the tree is. But more important, it's you, as a self-conscious being, who reinforces the sense of separation—"I am looking at this beautiful weeping willow." That falls away. You may have had moments here and there where you've had such clear seeing, and you know how the nonseparation in those moments can be profound and last for a while. It's not that the practice leads to awakening but that the practice *is* awakening. This is what Krishnamurti meant when he said, "The observer is the observed."

The means and the end are the same. It can happen spontaneously, but practice enables us to experience it more as part of our regular life, not as something sporadic or unpredictable. Cessation, the Third Noble Truth, ranges from the ordinary joys of not having a toothache or of seeing a grandchild smile to an awakening with a tree. The tree and you are together, meaning that self-consciousness is gone. You see the tree for the first time.

### The Yellow Cab

Many years ago, I had been meditating for a few hours at home and my mind was pretty still. I had to meet an old friend at a corner in Central Square in Cambridge. There was a cab stand there. I was waiting and I was very calm, very at peace. My friend was a bit late. I thought perhaps he would arrive by cab, so I kept staring at the cab stand.

Suddenly I had a vivid experience of observing a cab. I would say it was a moment of awakening. I'm not trying to romanticize it or make it an enlightenment statement or anything of that sort. I'll just make clear what happened. I looked at the cab, which was a Yellow Cab. Do you know what my big breakthrough realization was? Wow, the Yellow Cab is really yellow. That's why they call it a Yellow Cab.

The yellow was so yellow. I had never seen yellow like this before, but it was the same yellow that it had always been, the same cabs that were always lined up at that corner. So what changed? My mind just saw what was there. My seeing was deeper, in the sense of more vivid, more alive, which is to say, I was more alive. The cab didn't change. I did.

The ancients often said that Buddhist teaching was about clearing dust away from the mirror. Back then, the roads were all dusty, not tarred and paved like today; if you walked, you got dust all over yourself. That reality of daily life became a metaphor.

I'm not saying that I attained enlightenment. But to some degree, I was seeing a Yellow Cab as if for the first time. My mind was a clear mirror. It was such a joy to be alive.

# ACKNOWLEDGMENTS

*Larry Rosenberg*

This book could not have been produced without the dedicated efforts of many friends and colleagues. I am especially grateful to Nitin Patel, a longtime student of mine at Cambridge Insight Meditation Center. A brilliant biostatistician, Nitin had the vision to use artificial intelligence to transcribe all of my recorded talks from 1983 to 2023. When he first proposed this idea, I didn't have a clue what he was talking about. But while I didn't understand the technicalities of the project, I trusted his judgment. Nitin underwrote the massive transcription effort that not only made this book possible but also led to the "Ask Larry" page on the CIMC website (https://cambridgeinsight.org/ask-larry/). I am grateful to everyone on Nitin's team who worked on that exhaustive undertaking.

Madeline Drexler, my student and friend for more than two decades, read all 2.7 million transcribed words and used her journalistic skills to help weave those words into ten topic-based chapters. Madeline conducted more than a dozen interviews with me over the course of a year, helping me articulate memories from my past and thoughts about the present. She also interviewed close colleagues and students. Drawing on these in-depth conversations, she crafted the book's biographical introduction. I deeply appreciate her artistry and dedicated effort.

I thank Laura Zimmerman for reading drafts of this book and offering insightful comments. And I want to express special thanks to Jon

Kabat-Zinn, my best friend for some sixty years, for encouraging me to jump into this project, arguing that the book would create a legacy of my teachings. I also want to thank all of the students and colleagues who felt my teaching was worth sharing and who agreed to be interviewed for the introductory profile: Matthew Daniell, Joseph Goldstein, Jon Kabat-Zinn, Roshi Joan Halifax, Narayan Liebenson, Doug Phillips, and Malaika Tabors.

I owe the greatest debt of gratitude to my wife, Galina Rosenberg, who from the very outset encouraged me to take part in this project. Even when I was demoralized or exhausted, she persuaded me to keep going and supported me every step of the way. Galina has inspired me since the day we met. In our long marriage, she has taught me the real meaning of metta.

### Madeline Drexler

Book writing often sends an author into the hell realms. This book was a project from heaven. I want to express my appreciation to Nitin Patel, who conceived the idea of a volume distilling Larry Rosenberg's teachings and underwrote the effort. I am likewise grateful to Ashley Clements and Jen Zehler, the other key members of Nitin's AI-transcription and proofreading team. Ashley and Jen read several iterations of the manuscript and gave me invaluable advice and moral support.

I thank the staff at Cambridge Insight Meditation Center, including Lynn Whittemore and Madeline Klyne, who assisted in numerous ways. And I appreciate the illuminating conversations I had with Larry's friends and colleagues, who generously took time out of their busy schedules to speak with me.

My posse of friends and family kept me going through a long and intensive bout of work. Thanks to Suzanne Drexler, Cynthia Enloe, Rick Fleeter, E. J. Graff, Martha Henry, Joni Seager, Sunil Sharma, and Laura Zimmerman. E. J. and Laura—my toughest, most honest, and most trusted editors—read the manuscript and offered incisive critiques. Chris Jerome, my copyeditor extraordinaire, added polish to the final manuscript. I am indebted to Beth Frankl, the executive editor at Shambhala, who kindly took on this book and shepherded it through publication, and to Breanna Locke, a project editor at Shambhala, who gave the text meticulous attention.

Most of all, I am thankful to Larry Rosenberg, who fielded endless questions and permitted me into his life during an often difficult and uncertain period. Over the years, Larry has not only rendered Buddhadharma in his inimitable style but also introduced me to the work of Jiddu Krishnamurti, another guiding light. Both teachers changed my life.

# APPENDIX A

## *Framed Portraits in Larry Rosenberg's Meditation Room*

Larry Rosenberg has frequently expressed gratitude and paid homage to the teachers who showed him the dharma path and encouraged him along the way. Here is a list of his most important teachers, whose portraits hang in his meditation room.

The Buddha (563 B.C.E. or 480 B.C.E. – 483 B.C.E. or 400 B.C.E.)
Bodhidharma (c. 440–528 – 470–543)
Ajahn Mun (1870–1949)
Jiddu Krishnamurti (1895–1986)
Ajahn Buddhadasa (1906–1993)
Ajahn Maha Bua (1913–2011)
Anagarika Munindra (1915–2003)
Ajahn Chah (1918–1992)
Ajahn Suwat (1919–2002)
Vimala Thakar (1921–2009)
Thich Nhat Hanh (1926–2022)
Seung Sahn Sunim (1927–2004)
Dainin Katagiri Roshi (1928–1990)
His Holiness the 14th Dalai Lama (1935– )

# APPENDIX B

## *Favorite Teachings*

During a half century of teaching, Larry Rosenberg has also drawn deeply on classic Buddhist texts in the Pali canon, interpreting them in his uniquely fresh and accessible way. Here are excerpts that have shaped his thinking, enriched his practice, and spoken to thousands of students over the years.

### The Four Noble Truths

1. There is suffering;
2. There is a cause of suffering;
3. There is an end of suffering;
4. There is a path out of suffering: the Eightfold Path.

### The Eightfold Path

1. Right view
2. Right resolve
3. Right speech
4. Right action
5. Right livelihood
6. Right effort
7. Right mindfulness
8. Right concentration

### The Five Contemplations

1. I am subject to aging. Aging is unavoidable.
2. I am subject to illness. Illness is unavoidable.
3. I am subject to death. Death is unavoidable.

4. I will grow different, separate from all that is dear and appealing to me.

5. I am the owner of my actions, heir to my actions, born of my actions, related through my actions, and live dependent on my actions. Whatever I do, for good or ill, to that will I fall heir.

# APPENDIX C

## Excerpts from Larry Rosenberg's Favorite Texts in the Pali Canon

Anapanasati Sutta: *Mindfulness of Breathing*

(excerpt from *Breath by Breath*, by Larry Rosenberg)

The meditator, having gone to the forest, to the shade of a tree, or to an empty building, sits down with legs folded crosswise, body held erect, and sets mindfulness to the fore. Always mindful, the meditator breathes in; mindful, the meditator breathes out.

Kalama Sutta: *To the Kalamas*

(excerpt translated from the Pali by Thanissaro Bhikkhu © 1994)

"Kalamas, don't go by reports, by legends, by traditions, by scripture, by logical conjecture, by inference, by analogies, by agreement through pondering views, by probability, or by the thought, 'This contemplative is our teacher.' When you know for yourselves that, 'These qualities are unskillful; these qualities are blameworthy; these qualities are criticized by the wise; these qualities, when adopted & carried out, lead to harm & to suffering'—then you should abandon them....

"...When you know for yourselves that, 'These qualities are skillful; these qualities are blameless; these qualities are praised by the wise; these qualities, when adopted & carried out, lead to welfare & to happiness'—then you should enter & remain in them...."

Bāhiya Sutta: *Bāhiya*

(excerpt translated from the Pali by Thanissaro Bhikkhu © 1994)

Bāhiya said to the Blessed One, . . . "Teach me the Dhamma, O Blessed One! Teach me the Dhamma, O One-Well-Gone, that will be for my long-term welfare & bliss."

"Bāhiya, you should train yourself thus: In reference to the seen, there will be only the seen. In reference to the heard, only the heard. In reference to the sensed, only the sensed. In reference to the cognized, only the cognized. That is how you should train yourself. When for you there will be only the seen in reference to the seen, only the heard in reference to the heard, only the sensed in reference to the sensed, only the cognized in reference to the cognized, then, Bāhiya, there is no you in connection with that. When there is no you in connection with that, there is no you there. When there is no you there, you are neither here nor yonder nor between the two. This, just this, is the end of stress."

# APPENDIX D

## *Larry's Poem and Benediction*

**WHERE IS PEACE TO BE FOUND?**

Where is peace to be found?
In the same place as sorrow.
How convenient!

**END-OF-CLASS BENEDICTION**

May we continue to look into ourselves.
May we see things exactly as they are.
And may such clear, direct seeing free us.

# GLOSSARY

*anapanasati*: Mindfulness with breathing in and out.

*Anapanasati Sutta:* The Buddha's teaching on cultivating both tranquility and deep insight through full awareness of breathing.

*anatta*: Not-self. The teaching that the body, feeling, and mind states lack an enduring core and any essence or substance that could properly be regarded as a "self."

*anicca*: Impermanence, instability, flux, inconstancy.

*arahant*: A fully awakened being; a living being completely free of all attachment to anything as being "me" or "mine." One who has uprooted all kilesas and experiences no more mental suffering.

*balas*: The five powers or spiritual faculties in Buddhism: faith, vigor, mindfulness, concentration, and wisdom.

bodhisattva: In Theravada Buddhism, someone on the path of liberation. In Mahayana Buddhism, someone who vows to become enlightened in order to relieve the suffering of all sentient beings.

*brahmaviharas*: The four divine abodes, also known as the four immeasurables: loving-kindness, compassion, sympathetic joy, and equanimity.

Buddha: Literally, Awakened One; Siddhartha Gautama, a wandering ascetic and religious teacher who lived in South Asia during the sixth or fifth century B.C.E. and whose teachings form the basis of Buddhism; (usually lowercase) a person who has attained full enlightenment.

Buddhadharma: The Buddha's teachings.

Buddha-nature: The aspects of ordinary people that are, in some way, the same as a buddha, and which can be actualized and experienced through practice.

*citta*: The heart-mind, a consciousness of both thoughts and emotions.

dharma (Sanskrit; Pali: *dhamma*): Truth, natural law, duty, order, "the way things are in and of themselves." *Dharma* is also used to refer to any doctrine that teaches such things.

*dukkha*: Unsatisfactoriness, suffering, pain. Dukkha is the quality of experience that comes about when the mind is conditioned by ignorance into craving, attachment, egoism, and selfishness.

Dzogchen: A tradition and meditative practice that emphasizes a direct path to awakening by recognizing our pure, primordial nature; the pinnacle of the teachings of the Nyingma school of Tibetan Buddhism.

Eightfold Path: In Buddhism, an early formulation of the path to enlightenment, encompassing moral conduct, mental discipline, and wisdom. The last of the Four Noble Truths, it includes right view, right resolve, right speech, right action, right livelihood, right effort, right mindfulness, and right concentration.

Four Noble Truths: The foundational teachings of Buddhism that provide a framework for understanding the nature of suffering and the path to liberation. It states: There is suffering; there is a cause of suffering; there is an end of suffering; there is a path out of suffering.

hatha yoga: A system of physical exercises for the control and perfection of the body; a set of practices that aim to achieve harmony and balance in the mind, body, and spirit.

insight meditation: *Vipassana*, or seeing things as they really are.

*jhanas*: Meditative states of profound stillness and concentration.

karma (Sanskrit; Pali: *kamma*): Intentional action.

*kilesa*: A torment of mind. Craving (greed), aversion (or hatred), and delusion (or ignorance) in their various forms.

koan: A paradoxical anecdote or riddle used in Zen Buddhism to demonstrate the inadequacy of logical reasoning and to provoke enlightenment.

Mahayana: Literally, "Great Vehicle." One of the major traditions of Buddhism. Mahayana is concerned with altruistically oriented spiritual practice as embodied in the ideal of the bodhisattva. Currently the dominant form of Buddhism in China, Tibet, Japan, and Korea.

*maranasati*: Mindfulness of death.

*metta*: Loving-kindness, goodwill, friendliness, benevolence, a strong wish for the welfare and happiness of others.

*Neti Neti* (Sanskrit): Not this, not this; a method of negation or elimination when understanding the nature of reality.

nirvana (Sanskrit; Pali: *nibbana*): Liberation, the ultimate goal of Buddhist practice. Nirvana manifests fully when the fires of kilesas, attachment, and selfishness are completely and finally quenched.

Pali: The canon of texts preserved by the Theravada school and, by extension, the language in which those texts are composed.

*panna*: Wisdom, insight, discernment; correct understanding of the truth needed to quench dukkha.

samadhi: Concentration, collectedness, mental calmness, stability; the gathering together, focusing, and integration of the mental flow.

*samatha*: Serenity of mind that comes from concentration. Samatha practices lead to stillness of mind but not to insight wisdom.

samsara: The indefinitely repeated cycles of birth, misery, and death caused by karma.

*samvega*: The spiritual urgency to practice that can grow out of a heightened sense of the perishable nature of life.

sangha: The community of the Buddha's followers who practice thoroughly, directly, insightfully, and correctly. Sangha includes laywomen, laymen, nuns, and monks.

*sati*: Mindfulness.

*satipanna*: Mindfulness accompanied by discernment, common sense, insight wisdom.

*Satipatthana Sutra*: The Buddha's discourse on the four foundations of mindfulness. It covers the four subjects for deep investigation: the body, the feelings, the mind, and the true nature of these formations. The *Anapanasati Sutta* uses conscious breathing to help accomplish the same objective.

*sila*: Morality; verbal and bodily action in accordance with the dharma. The essence of sila is nonharming of others and oneself.

*sunnata*: Emptiness. All things, without exception, are empty of "self" and "belonging to self." Sunnata is an inherent quality of everything. It also refers to the mind that is free of greed, anger, and delusion.

sutra (Sanskrit; Pali: *sutta*): Discourse. The term is used in Theravada Buddhism for sermons attributed to the Buddha and certain of his disciples.

Theravada: "Teachings of the Elders." One of the major traditions of Buddhism. The only one of the early schools of Buddhism to have survived to the present day. Currently the dominant form of Buddhism in Thailand, Sri Lanka, Cambodia, and Myanmar.

*vipassana*: Insight, seeing clearly. The direct observation of mental and physical objects in their aspect of impermanence, unsatisfactoriness, and lack of an inherent, independent essence or self.

yogi: Meditator.

*zazen*: Zen meditation, usually performed in the seated position.

Zen: A Japanese school of Mahayana Buddhism emphasizing the value of meditation and intuition rather than ritual worship or study of scriptures.

*zendo*: In Zen Buddhism, a meditation hall.

# ABOUT THE AUTHORS

PHOTOGRAPH © 2025 BY MADELINE DREXLER

*Larry Rosenberg*

One of the pioneers in bringing dharma practice to the West, Larry Rosenberg is the founder and a guiding teacher at Cambridge Insight Meditation Center in Cambridge, Massachusetts. Launched in 1985, CIMC is the oldest nonresidential vipassana meditation practice and retreat center in the United States. For fifteen years, Rosenberg also served as a guiding teacher at Insight Meditation Society in Barre, Massachusetts.

Rosenberg is the author of *Breath by Breath: The Liberating Practice of Insight Meditation* (1998), *Living in the Light of Death: On the Art of Being Fully Alive* (2000), and *Three Steps to Awakening: A Practice for Bringing Mindfulness to Life* (2013), all published by Shambhala.

After having taught social psychology at leading academic institutions—including the Department of Psychiatry at Harvard Medical School, the University of Chicago, and Brandeis University—Rosenberg embarked in the early 1970s on the Buddhist path. He has studied and worked closely with many of the foundational teachers in twentieth-century Buddhism, both in the vipassana and Zen traditions, including Ajahn Buddhadasa, Ajahn Maha Bua, Thich Nhat Hanh, Seung Sahn Sunim, and Katagiri Roshi. He also worked closely with the Indian philosopher Jiddu Krishnamurti.

## Madeline Drexler

Madeline Drexler is a Boston-based journalist and the former editor of *Harvard Public Health* magazine. She has been a senior fellow at the Schuster Institute for Investigative Journalism and a Knight Science Journalism Fellow.

Drexler's books include *Emerging Epidemics: The Menace of New Infections* (2003), *A Splendid Isolation: Lessons on Happiness from the Kingdom of Bhutan* (2014), and *The People's Pandemic: How the Himalayan Kingdom of Bhutan Staged a World-Class Response to COVID-19* (2022). Her work has appeared in the *Atlantic, New York Times, Undark, Virginia Quarterly Review, Tricycle, Best American Travel Writing,* and many other publications. She has received numerous national writing awards and has been reporting from Bhutan since 2012. She began her career as a staff photographer for the Associated Press.

Drexler has been a student of Larry Rosenberg since 2000.